Ender's Game and
Philosophy

Popular Culture and Philosophy® Series Editor: George A. Reisch

For full details of all Popular Culture and Philosophy® books, visit www.opencourtbooks.com.

Popular Culture and Philosophy®

Ender's Game and Philosophy

Genocide Is Child's Play

Edited by
D.E. WITTKOWER
and LUCINDA RUSH

OPEN COURT
Chicago

Volume 80 in the series, Popular Culture and Philosophy ®, edited by George A. Reisch

To order books from Open Court, call toll-free 1-800-815-2280, or visit our website at www.opencourtbooks.com.

Open Court Publishing Company is a division of Carus Publishing Company, dba ePals Media.

ISBN: 978-0-8126-9834-3

Library of Congress Cataloging-in-Publication Data

Ender's game and philosophy : genocide is child's play / edited by D.E. Wittkower and Lucinda Rush.
        pages cm. — (Popular culture and philosophy ; VOLUME 80)
        Includes bibliographical references and index.
        ISBN 978-0-8126-9834-3 (trade paper : alk. paper) 1. Card, Orson
        Scott. Ender's game. 2. Card, Orson Scott. — Philosophy 3.
        Wiggin, Ender (Fictitious character) 4. Philosophy in literature.
        I. Wittkower, D. E., 1977- editor of compilation.
    PS3553.A655E53 2013
    813'.54—dc23
                                                    2013023124

Transmissions from the Ansible

Rules of
Engagement

01
Push 1 for Remote War

TIM BLACKMORE

The query: At Auschwitz, tell me, where was God?
And the answer: Where was man?

—WILLIAM STYRON, *Sophie's Choice*

You just got up from the cockpit wringing wet with sweat. Being a combat pilot is rough work. It's a thrill at times, but also horribly tense, and the traffic on the way home can be murder. Well, maybe not quite murder. All afternoon, your aircraft flew around even if you didn't go with it. It was dull at times, but they said you were signing up to fly the dull, dirty, and dangerous jobs.

At one point you'd forgotten to breathe, you were so focused. You watched someone get into a van, and you nearly bombed them. You remember that your daughter's piano recital was that night, so when you finish fighting in Iraq at 5:00 P.M., you leave the airbase, stop at a florist and get some roses for her. The quiet of your house is a relief after the war that day.

It doesn't seem possible to be everywhere at once, to be both there and here, at home in the United States and also daily fighting a foreign war. But that's exactly what you do: you fly a missile-armed drone aircraft. Unmanned Aerial Vehicles, or UAVs as they're called, are controlled from remote locations and can fly for a day at a time. Some can stay in the air much longer. You control the craft from the US, but it flies 7,500 miles away in Iraq, Afghanistan, and other countries. No Americans get hurt if the drone crashes or is shot down. Combat stress is more mental than physical.

Every decade the distance between enemies on the battle-field has been widening. When your grandfather or great-grandfather fought in the trenches of World War I, machine guns kept people in their burrows until they were ordered over the top. During the Cold War when a relatively few pilots could destroy most of the human population with a few hundred hydrogen bombs, people described it as a "push-button war." In Orson Scott Card's *Ender's Game*, you command a space fleet fighting intergalactic battles hundreds of light years away. You are there, and also here.

Doing Brain Damage

There are different kinds of stress in fighting. Consider the pressure on you if you were in a nuclear missile silo command center, deep underground. There would be two of you, each facing a launch station, because the military knows that it's better to have two people do a terrifying job rather than leave one alone to do it. Let's say you were ordered to launch your missile. Could you? The order would probably be given only if there were already missiles flying at the United States.

If you have a good imagination, you might think about all the television shows and movies you've seen about zombies. Yeah, the post-apocalyptic world won't be pretty. You might decide that it would be better not to launch your missile; that at least some people's children should survive. That's why the Air Force gave your bunker-buddy a gun: they have it out now and are screaming something at you about what'll happen if you don't turn your launch key. Overall, you'd rather be sailing. Or doing pretty much anything other than this.

Ender fights a war that is entirely removed from what he feels is his reality. He's as distant from battle as the people in the missile silo are. He thinks he's playing games, and he's partly right. He doesn't see a real enemy or the enemy dead. He sees only lights in a display. The drone pilot sees what the machine's radar, infrared, and daytime cameras see. She sits facing a wall of five or more screens showing maps, chat rooms, aircraft information, orders coming from command centers, and flies using a sort of gaming joystick. Because there's a one- to two-second lag between the pilot shifting the joystick and the aircraft responding 7,500 miles away, the one thing a UAV captain can't do is land or launch the machine. That must be done by someone close enough to it so that the aircraft responds immediately to a command.

In Ender's case, there's no lag. Orson Scott Card borrows some old science-fiction technology from another science-fiction writer, Ursula K. Le Guin, who invented a device called the "ansible" in her 1966 novel, *Rocannon's World*. The ansible makes instantaneous communication between people possible, no matter how many miles or even light years away they are. It's a phone that makes faster-than-light calls. Right now it's fiction, but so was sustained human flight a hundred years ago.

Part of the problem with fighting a war at such a distance is that it can be hard to feel that it's real. Hollywood rarely shows a war where your whole job is to wait, push a button, and then get out of a hole in the ground and go home. If everything passes through a series of screens, how do you know it isn't a test? If you were flying an actual plane, you'd feel sensations—the cold air, the smell of old sweat, the sun in your eyes, the sound and feel of the jet engines behind you, the feeling of gravity forcing you into your seat when you bank or throttle up. Instead, you have a mild back or headache from sitting too long at a desk.

Still, there's a sense of being immersed, as if you're living inside the world on the screens. There's also something weirdly mystical about it, like you've left your body, which is what Admiral Chamrajnagar tells Colonel Graff. He says that Ender will learn "the mysteries of the fleet," just like all those "who command by ansible know the majesty of flight among the stars." Being connected to armies light years away will let Ender perform "the graceful ghost dance through the stars, and whatever greatness there is within him will be unlocked, revealed, set forth before the universe for all to see." As amazing as it sounds, one of the nagging problems is that it involves the mass slaughter of another species.

Rib Caged

While remote combat looks as if it should involve only reason and not the physical body, that's not how we're wired. When I play chess, even against a computer, my heart rate rockets up. Watch a video gamer play—it takes the whole body. Gamers lean, lunge, turn, twist, yell and swear as they play. We get physically invested in all contests. A friend told me a story about a very calm guy, a pipe smoker, sitting in a tense meeting. As he sat staring at the table, his teeth gripping the stem of his pipe, there was a sudden snapping noise and half the pipe fell on the table. He'd bitten it in two. No matter how much we think we're calm, we're trapped in the cage of the body, the heart inside its rib prison.

If you ask someone to show you where "me" is, the thing we call the "self," the person might put a hand to their heart, or point at their head. But if your body isn't in danger when you're fighting at enormous remote distances, why would you get tense, have a fast heartbeat, get the sweats, or panic? Drone operators face the problem of bodily stress, even though they're as removed from danger as possible. Lots of people argue that video games and films make us more distant from killing, and desensitize us to violence, but drone pilots regularly suffer from PTSD, the same as soldiers on the ground.

Ender gets physically exhausted, gets ulcers, has nightmares, and is generally a wreck when he plays virtual games. Orson Scott Card shows us how easy it is to have something imaginary become real by making Ender's games thrilling. The first time I read *Ender's Game* I had to stay up all night to finish it—I had to know how each game came out.

Ender's games are real to him, and his fictional story is real to me. Partly that's because Card writes so well, but it's also because he doesn't ignore the body. He reminds us that we live in our flesh and are instinctively driven to protect it. He starts right off by slamming our heads into pain.

Blood from Stilson's nose spatters the ground. Peter chokes Ender—almost to death. Will Peter kill his little brother one day? Bonzo Madrid's body arcs upward, driven by Ender's savage desperate blow to his body. Madrid is already dead. On Earth, Peter plans for the future and pins live animals to the ground, watching them die. Card nails each act of pain, rage, or torture into our eyes.

What makes mental combat real is Card's repeated insistence that the body gets dragged into everything the mind does. The same is true for pilots flying remote aircraft or for us when we watch suspense or horror movies: how many of us stop breathing during a scene when the hero is in danger, or have to keep reminding ourselves that "it's just a movie"? There are at least two selves. One is somewhere in the brain, and the other lives in the body with all its reflexes, reactions, fears and panic attacks. Figuring out which one is the boss can be difficult.

Morals by GPS

If you kill someone, no matter how remote they seem, you've still committed murder. We are there mentally, emotionally, and physically, even if we aren't on the battlefield. Everyone is complicit in Ender's murders, including Colonel Graff, Major Anderson, the Fleet, and even Valentine, who twice persuades Ender to go back to fighting.

Valentine's moral dilemma is whether to betray her brother, or endanger the human race. The way she solves her problem is by trapping Ender in a similar one. She makes it clear to him that if he returns to battle, he will likely kill thousands if not millions of the enemy. But if he doesn't go on fighting, the human race will probably be exterminated. No matter what Ender chooses, he will be implicated in millions or billions of deaths. Only when it's much too late do we learn that the Buggers weren't planning another attack.

Hindsight is wonderful and terrible. Figuring out what to do here and now is infinitely tougher. We forget how easily we can be persuaded to go along with things that we later decide are crazy. Society—especially our family, friends, teachers, religious advisors, and people in authority—acts like a huge magnet and sets the needle of our moral compass spinning. If we're torn apart by guilt over killing others, it makes sense that we might begin to feel for the enemy.

Alienated Aliens

Some enemies seem nastier than others. Many science-fiction horror movies, like *Alien*, show the enemy as some kind of insect. Boy, do people loathe insects. Ender's great strength is that he understands his enemies no matter how they appear. That gives him the insight he needs to anticipate what they'll do next. What will make someone understand an enemy more: is it better for people to be on the ground, see each other and realize that for all their differences, there are also great commonalities between humans? Or is it better to stay back and kill with as little contact as possible? The advantage of the second way is that our soldiers are in less danger. One disadvantage is that it's easier to commit atrocities when everyone looks like an ant to you.

Ender has been set apart from the human race. He's the forbidden Third child, an outcast. In Battle School he's even more alone because he's better than the rest. He's been pushed outside not once, but twice. The wolf children who devour Ender in the Giant's Drink game show him how dangerous absolutely everyone is. No wonder Ender comes to be fascinated by and even love the Hive Queen, light years distant, on her home planet. Like him, she's an alien. She's a winner. She's hated. She's unique. She teaches him because they're alike. The more he learns from the Hive Queen, the more he sympathizes with her. Unfortunately, he also kills her.

That's Not Denial

When someone tells me off for doing something dumb, my first reflex is to say that someone else made me do it, told me to do it (and I could hardly say "No"), or that I was stressed out of my mind. The first two of these dodges put the responsibility on someone else. During the Nuremberg trials after World War II, German officers who explained that they had committed war crimes because they were just following orders were found guilty. That's why blaming someone else for "making" you do what you knew was wrong is sometimes called the "Nuremberg defense." The final excuse is that someone else somehow got inside me and did all the bad things.

All of it is denial. If we feel terrible guilt and know that we should have said no, or refused an order, then the easiest thing to do is to deny that we were ever involved. If I'm a drone pilot, and I see the missiles I fire kill a target who's just planted a roadside mine or Improvised Explosive Device (IED), I may feel sick at having killed someone, but I can reassure myself I'm protecting troops on the ground. If I fire a missile at a rebel outpost but, once the smoke has cleared, see the local villagers drag childrens' bodies out of the rubble, my conscience may ache. I could tell myself that I acted under orders, or that I worked with the best information I had, or that I didn't have any control over the situation. And anyway, the next pilot would have fired. I might be upset, but I'm a soldier and understand that this is war, after all.

The trouble usually starts when soldiers leave the war zone and try to forget what they've done. If I'm convinced, now, that there weren't any Weapons of Mass Destruction, or Saddam Hussein didn't have anything to do with 9/11 and the World Trade Center, ghosts might begin to haunt me. I have to wonder if the war made sense at all. Why did my friends die? I killed other people to keep my friends safe, but I also killed people who might have been innocent. People firing guns in the air at a wedding celebration can look an awful lot like armed soldiers going to war through the lens of a UAV camera. My explanation that I served my country and am a patriot isn't helping me with the terrible panics and flashbacks I'm having, and it certainly doesn't help the couple whose new life together was cut very short.

It's hard to look back and find wars that either have clear outcomes or Darth Vader bad guys. Soldiers everywhere struggle with what American psychiatrist Robert J. Lifton calls "surd evil." It's so senseless that even the word "absurd" doesn't do it justice. In two of his most famous books *Home From the War,* and *Death in Life: Survivors of Hiroshima,* Lifton says that when there are no good explanations for wanton torture or sadistic murders, we're confronting surd evil.

When Ender turns Dr. Device on the Buggers' home planet, he commits genocide. He could defend himself by saying that he didn't know he was fighting real battles. That's true. He could say that the military ordered him to win in any way possible. That's also true. If Ender tried to use the Nuremberg defense, we'd allow it because Ender is a kid, and we don't expect kids to know better, yet.

Robert Lifton has connected what we understand as surd evil and killing at a distance. The United States has perfected killing by remote control. People who operate lethal injection machines used in prisons don't know who administers a killing dose to an inmate. Their ignorance is supposed to prevent them from feeling guilty. The more distant we are from killing, the more that death can seem pointlessly brutal. It can leave what Lifton calls a "death imprint" on the survivor. The death imprint is a sense that the dead are more real and present than the living. The burden of survival is one of the things driving the military's suicide rate to its current record highs. There are times when grief about pointless death is too much to bear.

Human Guidance

In *Ender's Game,* people in power see and record everything all the time. Drone warfare is also about seeing. At the beginning of the wars in Iraq and Afghanistan there were a few dozen drones in the air. Now there are nearly ten thousand. They hang high out of sight, but produce truckloads of information every hour, enough to cause the Central Intelligence Agency to move thousands of workers into drone image analysis. Drones now fly along the Mexican-American and Canadian-American borders. In the next ten years probably between a third to a half of all flights will be made by drones instead of jets with human pilots. We're living in a world of remote control.

Ender's Game suggests that remote war has terrible effects on us, just like all wars, because we live in a moral universe from which there is no escape. Card warns us that if we remove ourselves from killing or try to deny we're part of it, things only get worse. We may have already lost our way because our moral GPS doesn't work anymore. Ender finds redemption when he discovers the queen the Buggers left for him.

Ender learns that everything we do will be remembered by someone. If we've done something we're sorry about, we have to find a way to connect with those who were once our enemies and become the people who speak the truth about their deaths. That's the idea of the Speaker for the Dead. But only a human being can Speak for the Dead. No machine, no drone, can do the job. It can't be done by remote.

02
What Would Saint Thomas Aquinas Do?

JENNIFER SWANSON

In *Ender's Game*, Ender Wiggin is faced with an enemy who wants him dead—Bonzo Madrid. In *Ender's Shadow*, Bean is faced with the same thing in Achilles. The two boys deal with their similar situations in very different ways. Ender waits for Bonzo to make the first move and then acts to defend himself. He kills Bonzo in the fight, but this was not his intention—he simply wanted to deter Bonzo from ever attacking him again.

Bean, on the other hand, moves against Achilles almost immediately after Achilles's arrival at Battle School. Bean ultimately does not kill Achilles, but he makes it clear that without a confession, he will leave him to certain death, suspended in the air ducts. While Bean's goal is to save his own life, his plan is to kill Achilles if he will not confess to his murders.

What, if anything, is the moral difference between Ender's and Bean's actions? Does it matter that Bonzo ends up dead while Achilles does not? Or is it the intentions of the boys that matter?

But I Didn't Mean for That to Happen!

Thomas Aquinas was a thirteenth-century Catholic priest who is considered to be the Church's greatest theologian and philosopher. One way that Aquinas's work still influences current philosophy is with the *principle of double effect*, which originates in his discussion of homicidal self-defense in his *Summa Theologica*. This principle is concerned with evaluating the moral permissibility of an action that will lead to a foreseen yet unintended effect that we usually think of as wrong. It is most commonly used today in the moral debate over euthanasia.

If a terminally ill patient is in a terrible amount of pain, sometimes the physician will administer an extremely high dose of painkillers. While the doctor's intention is to alleviate the patient's pain, he also knows that his action will result in the death of the patient. According to the principle of double effect, this is a permissible action even if we believe that doctors are morally obliged to never act to end a life. This is because the patient's death is merely a side effect of the attempt to relieve his pain, and not the intended result of the doctor's action.

Why Didn't He just Leave Me Alone?

Ender meets Bonzo ("Not bahn-zoe. Bone-so. The name's Spanish") Madrid shortly after he arrives at Battle School. Bonzo is the commander of Salamander Army, which is where Ender has been assigned. He insults Ender because of his small size and tells him that he is not allowed to practice with the others or take part in their battles.

When Ender begins practicing with some of the students from his launch group instead, Bonzo attempts to stop him until Ender reminds him that no one can give orders regarding free play time. Furthermore, the more Ender practices, the more his trade value is enhanced—and trading him is exactly what Bonzo wants to do.

Bonzo is forced to rescind his order, but Ender continues to obey him regarding participation in battles until the day that Salamander is facing certain defeat by Leopard Army. Ender disables three opponents and the battle ends in a draw.

While most of the other students assume that this was Bonzo's strategy, the members of Salamander Army know better. Bonzo becomes even more filled with hatred towards Ender. That very day, he trades Ender to Rat Army. Before Ender can leave, however, Bonzo punches him and berates him for disobeying orders.

When Ender gets promoted to Commander of Dragon Army, he turns a group of underage, undersized, and inexperienced boys into the best army in the school. When they face

Salamander Army—Bonzo's army—Dragon wins in less than a minute, despite Bonzo having a twenty-minute time advantage. Ender realizes that the situation has only succeeded in adding fuel to the fire—turning Bonzo's already boiling rage murderous.

Things come to a head when Bonzo and some of the other boys corner Ender while he's taking a shower, and Ender convinces Bonzo to face him alone. Ender knows that he must win quickly or not at all.

When Bonzo goes for the attack, Ender succeeds in getting him off balance and manages to position himself with his back to Bonzo. Ender then lunges upward, driving his head into Bonzo's face. As Ender turns to see blood pouring from Bonzo's nose, he knows that he has won the fight and he can just walk away. But it's not that simple—Bonzo will come for him again. The fight must be finished now, and for good. Ender kicks Bonzo in the chest with both feet and then maneuvers under him in order to deliver a final blow to his crotch.

When Bonzo finally collapses to the ground, Ender knows he has done something terrible. He returns to his room with his friend Dink, where he begins to cry. "I didn't want to hurt him!" he cries. "Why didn't he just leave me alone!"

Those in charge don't confirm the death, saying merely that Bonzo has been graduated and sent home, but eventually Ender realizes the truth. Although it was in self-defense, even though his own life was at stake, Ender feels terrible about what happened. He has killed another student, another boy.

Aquinas, Meet Ender Wiggin

What would Aquinas say about Ender's actions? Well, according to the doctrine of double effect, Ender has done nothing morally wrong. Bonzo presents an immediate threat to Ender's life in the moment, meaning that Ender is acting in self-defense. As long as Ender is defending himself, his actions are permissible.

Furthermore, Ender is aware that Bonzo will try again to kill him, and he wants to send a message that will prevent that. He does *not* want to kill Bonzo, nor does he intentionally try. He simply wants to prevent future confrontations. Bonzo's death is merely a side-effect of Ender's attempt to save his own life both in the moment and going forward. This being the case, the application of Aquinas's principle of double effect does not make it appear as though Ender has done anything wrong.

From the Streets to the Air Ducts

In *Ender's Shadow*, Bean faces a similar situation. Growing up in poverty on the streets of Rotterdam, children form groups, known as "crews." Bean tells Poke, his crew boss, that what she needs is a bully to protect her crew. He says, "You give food to bullies every day. Give that to *one* bully and get him to keep the others away from you." But there's just one question—what to do if once the bully is bought, he won't hold up his end of the bargain? "If he won't," says Bean, "you kill him."

Rather than choosing someone "big and dumb, brutal but controllable" as Bean prefers, Poke chooses a smaller boy, smart, with a deformed leg, one who calls himself Achilles. ("The name is not pronounced uh-KILL-eez, it's pronounced ah-SHEEL. French.") The children successfully overpower him, but Achilles outsmarts them all, seizing leadership of the crew even while lying helpless on the ground. Bean alone sees the danger, telling Poke, "Kill him. If you don't kill him now, he's going to kill *you*." But then it's too late. Achilles takes over the crew, but he never forgets Bean's exhortation to Poke. And Bean knows it. Fortunately, he leaves for Battle School shortly afterwards, becoming a member of Ender's Dragon Army.

When Bean is promoted to Commander of Rabbit Army and meets his soldiers for the first time, there is a new Launchy in the army. In the back of the barracks, "several inches taller than Bean remembered, with legs of even length now, both of them straight," stands the new boy. "Ho, Achilles," says Bean.

Bean knows that a confrontation is inevitable, and that Achilles still wants to see him dead. He knows that he must remove Achilles from the school one way or another in order to save his own life. But he's half Achilles's size—he has no chance at defeating him the way Ender defeated Bonzo. He will have to find a different way.

One night soon after, Bean calls Achilles to his room and tells him that they're going into the air duct system together. That's how Ender won all those battles, he says—they spied on the other commanders and the teachers through the air ducts. Achilles is thrilled. This is his opportunity to get Bean alone.

Unfortunately for Achilles, he soon finds himself suspended in midair by a deadline. He can't climb the line, nor can he reach any walls. He is at Bean's mercy. When he points out that Bean isn't a killer, Bean tells him, "But the hot dry air of the shaft will do it for me. You'll dehydrate in a day. Your mouth's already a little dry, isn't it? And then you'll just keep hanging here, mummifying."

Bean demands a confession—for the murder of Poke, for everything he's done. He tells Achilles he has a choice—to "dry out on the line, or let the teachers know just how crazy you are." Achilles confesses to the seven murders he's committed and is removed from Battle School.

Aquinas, Now Meet Bean

What would Aquinas say about Bean's actions? While it's true that Bean does not actually kill Achilles, it's clear that he would have had no problem leaving him to die if Achilles had not met his conditions. Achilles avoids this by confessing, but Bean could not have been certain that this was going to be the outcome. He was fully prepared to bring about Achilles's death.

Bean's behavior is different from Ender's in that while Ender actually does kill Bonzo, that isn't his goal. All he wants is to scare Bonzo so much that he will never attack Ender again. While it may have been unrealistic, he continued to hold out hope that they could continue to coexist at Battle School. Bean, on the other hand, knows that there is no chance that he and Achilles can stay there together, and his ultimate goal is to make sure that Achilles is gone—no matter what it takes. Even if it means Achilles has to die.

The problem is that when Bean implements his plan, when he invites Achilles into the air ducts, he's in no immediate danger. Therefore Bean's actions cannot be interpreted as self-defense. He intends to kill Achilles if that's what the situation requires, and Achilles's death would have been no accident. It would have been murder, and Aquinas would never have condoned it.

Does this mean that Ender is in the moral clear? While it seems that Aquinas would say yes, based upon the principle of double effect, perhaps we should take another look.

Is Ender's Battle with Bonzo Just?

Aquinas was a guy with varied interests—after all, not all three thousand pages of the *Summa Theologica* are about the doctrine of double effect. He also discusses something that we call *just war theory*—the set of criteria that any violent conflict must meet in order to be considered just. While he's not considered to be the originator of just war theory, the *Summa Theologica* contains a still-influential attempt to lay out these criteria. His three conditions are as follows:

1. **A just war must be waged for a good and just purpose, rather than in an attempt to gain something for oneself or to demonstrate power**

2. **A just war can only be waged by a proper authority, such as the state**

3. **Even during periods of violence, peace must be a central goal**

Since the thirteenth century, just war theory has been expanded to contain many more conditions, but the question is the same—how can we know when war is morally justifiable? Today, just war theory is considered to have three main components, each with its own set of rules:

A. ***Jus ad bellum*, which addresses the right to go to war**

B. ***Jus in bello*, which addresses acceptable conduct within war**

C. ***Jus post bellum*, which addresses issues of justice once the war has ended**

One of the rules of *jus in bello* is the *proportionality condition*, which states that soldiers may only act with the amount of force that is proportional to the end they seek. To act with greater force than is necessary is morally impermissible. The use of weapons of mass destruction, for example, is generally seen as a violation of the proportionality condition because their use is disproportionate to legitimate military goals.

What can just war theory tell us about the permissibility of Ender's actions with regard to Bonzo? Ender himself admits to Bean that he acted with excessive force: "I knocked him out standing up. It was like he was dead, standing there. And I kept hurting him." It seems now that Ender may not be as morally justified as he initially appeared.

In fact, this isn't the first time that Ender has encountered this situation. Before leaving for Battle School, he faces down the school bully, Stilson, and handles it the same way he does his fight with Bonzo. Knowing that if he doesn't decisively come out on top, he'll be facing a pack of boys tomorrow, Ender continues to kick Stilson even after knocking him to the ground. He knows that he must "win this now, and for all time." But he isn't unaffected by what he's done—once left alone, he cries, just like he will later do after the fight with Bonzo.

Ender knows that he has used much more force than what was necessary to defeat Stilson. He admits as much when Colonel Graff visits him at home the next day. Upon being prompted by Graff to explain his behavior, he says, "Knocking him down won the first fight. I wanted to win all the next ones, too. So they'd leave me alone." This seems to indicate Ender's awareness of the disproportionality of his response to Stilson even as he attempts to justify it. Does the fact that he uses the same justification after his fight with Bonzo mean that he believes it is valid? Maybe, but the fact that he is so upset seems to call this into question.

If Ender's Behavior Is Bad, Why Does It Seem So Good?

If Ender's killing of Bonzo is morally unacceptable by the tenets of just war theory, why does Card present it as justified? To answer that, we must look at Colonel Graff's reason for refusing to interfere in the situation even though he knows Ender's life is in danger. After all, they're depending on Ender to save the world from the Bugger invasion!

When General Pace tells Graff that it is "unconscionable" to not have military police standing by to intervene when Bonzo inevitably attacks Ender, Graff points out that once Ender is commanding the forces in a real battle, there will be no military police there to back him up. Ender must be forced to stand on his own. As Graff puts it, "Ender Wiggin must believe that no matter what happens, no adult will ever, ever step in to help him in any way." He then says, "If he does not believe that, then he will never reach the peak of his abilities." When Pace rather astutely points out that neither will he reach that peak if he is dead or permanently crippled, Graff simply says, "He won't be."

Ender's method of dealing with Bonzo proves to Colonel Graff that not only does Ender have the battle skills to beat the Buggers, he has the mental fortitude as well. He is capable of being the commander that they need. The very attributes that drive him to continue to fight Bonzo until Bonzo's dead are the ones that will enable him to hold up mentally in war. The fact that he's able to recognize that he needs to stop Bonzo once and for all that day in the bathroom is part of what demonstrates that he can be the commander they need.

None of this, however, would necessarily be enough to justify Ender's behavior. For one thing, the war against the Buggers itself might not have been just. The Buggers did not initially realize that humans were intelligent beings, and once they saw this, they did not attack again. The war was thus completely unnecessary. However, even if we assume that it *was* a just war, and that General Graff was right about how Ender's actions helped prepare him to win it, none of that may be enough to justify those actions.

After all, sometimes it's true that our bad qualities can lead to good results. Ender goes on to defeat the Buggers and save the world, and part of the reason that he's able to do so is because of his immense mental strength that drives him to do whatever must be done. But just because they can be used to bring about good results doesn't mean that those bad qualities aren't still bad. In the end, Ender can be considered a hero for saving the world, but he is a flawed hero nonetheless—one whose flaws were necessary for his victory.

03
Winning Without Honor

Shawn McKinney

If I was on Earth during the Third Invasion and only knew what most humans then knew, I would be terrified of the Buggers and I would want to live. I would want to live so badly that I would support fighting back against the Buggers, and I would even want to live so badly that I would accept, in my mind and my heart, the death of innocent Bugger civilians and even children.

But I also know that being scared doesn't make something bad into something good, and just because I would do something doesn't mean that it is right to do that thing. And, no matter how badly I want to live, there are still some things more important than being alive.

Would you sacrifice an innocent person to stay alive? What about the love of your life? What about a child? What about a school full? I believe that most of us can agree that our life is not more important, even to us, than the lives of dozens of innocent children. If that's true, then shouldn't we feel the same way about alien children? If I won't trade the lives of twenty innocent human children for my own, how could I justify trading twenty innocent alien children for my own? Here's how: if those twenty innocent alien children are being kept in the same house as the super evil alien leader who will kill twenty million human children if he is not stopped, and if the only way to stop him is to destroy the entire house.

That is the kind of nightmare math Colonel (later Commander) Graff, Mazer Rackham, and the rest of the International Fleet (I.F.) command had to compute. They weren't comparing their lives to alien children, they had to decide how many alien children Valentine was worth, and Peter, and every other human. How many alien innocent lives are all human lives together worth? The Buggers' previous attacks created a threat to the existence of the entire human race.

Buggers versus humans, one race versus one race; this seems like more straightforward, simple math. But, it can't be this simple, can it? Well, no, it really isn't. The most important problem is that the Bugger civilians didn't attack humanity, so they don't deserve to die. Innocents are innocents regardless of race or nationality. If we were just killing the people trying to kill us, nobody would lose any sleep over war and Mazer could have told Ender the truth about leading the Third Invasion.

Killing innocents, and in this case killing all of the innocents, means that we need to really, really think before we act. Is there any way we can possibly justify killing all of their babies just to keep ourselves alive?

For centuries, philosophers, leaders, and lawmakers have looked at the doctrine of just war theory to guide them in deciding what is and isn't justified in war. In World War II the US was justified in going to war in defense of others, but Japan and Germany, as aggressors, were not. Unfortunately for I.F. Command, most interpretations of JWT forbid starting wars, using weapons of mass destruction, and committing genocide. But, if we look deeper into the unique conditions of the Third Invasion I think we can make a reasonable case that starting an invasion and ultimately using a weapon of mass destruction to commit xenocide was justifiable.

The Enemy Outnumbered Him a Thousand to One

If Jet Li and I were walking down the street and he decided to beat me up, there isn't much I could do to stop him. I'm not a Kung Fu master; I haven't even been in a fight in my adult life. Just like Ender couldn't beat Bonzo and his friends in the shower. At least, Ender or I couldn't win these fights fairly. Is there some reason why anyone should let someone beat them up just because they're stronger? No, of course not. All the more so if Jet Li is planning to beat me to death like Bonzo seemed to want to do to Ender. Self-defense would be meaningless if you couldn't defend yourself against a more powerful opponent.

An essential tenet of just war theory is that a state must be able to defend itself. This notion traces back to a precursor and component of just war theory called the Doctrine of the Double Effect.[1] DDE provides criteria for determining when it is morally acceptable to do an ostensibly good thing that also has a bad consequence. DDE comes from the medieval Catholic philosopher, St. Thomas Aquinas, who sought to understand how a person could defend themselves from attack without sinning, even if they killed the attacker in the course of defending themselves. Just war theory also inherited a requirement from the Doctrine of Double Effect that requires discriminating between military and civilian targets in war. Weapons of Mass Destruction violate the discrimination requirement because they unavoidably and indiscriminately kill civilians in large numbers. Dr. Device is a perfect example of the indiscriminate nature of Weapons of Mass Destruction. What happens when self-defense is only possible through indiscriminate violence?

If the fight is with an overwhelmingly powerful opponent, then extreme measures have to be taken to have a chance at successfully defending yourself. If extreme measures, or even fighting 'dirty', can't be used, then we're back to doing away with self-defense every time our attacker is a lot tougher than we are. This is what Ender realized after he killed Bonzo; "the only power that matters" is "the power to kill and destroy, because if you can't kill then you are always subject to those who can, and nothing and no one will save you." If you aren't willing to do whatever it takes to win, then you will lose to someone who will.

The Bugger military always outnumbered the human military. The Buggers had colonized numerous planets and therefore possessed far superior resources. They were more scientifically advanced. This makes the Buggers like Jet Li or Bonzo; Ender and I can't win unless we cheat. In this case, cheating means using Dr. Device, attacking the Bugger home world, and killing everything and everyone on that world.

---

[1] Jennifer Swanson has a different take on just war theory and the Doctrine of Double Effect in the previous chapter.

The I.F. can use Dr. Device, or any other weapon of mass destruction, because if they don't, they can't beat the Buggers. If they can't beat the Buggers, then humanity can't defend itself. So far so good: humanity can cheat to win, we can win without honor: we can use Dr. Device.

So I Killed All Their Children, All of Everything

"They decided that when they attacked us."

Okay, we're in a creepy place: I'm not comfortable slaughtering innocent children, even if they are aliens. Yes, of course, such a sentiment is a good sign we're sane and decent, but the Buggers attacked us. That fact is really important. The Buggers came to humanity and tried to set up a new colony where we already were. When we sent a ship full of people to see what was going on, they killed every last human being on that ship. It isn't just that the Buggers outnumber us and have more military power. It isn't just that we can't stop them without cheating. All they have done is kill humans: every single human being they ever came across they killed. As far as any human being knew, they would keep killing every single human being until there weren't any more to come across.

Unless they are actually trying to exterminate the entire human race, right now, then it's not okay to kill all of them first. Committing genocide is usually seen as a violation of the Just War Theory requirement that military force be proportionate to legitimate goals (annihilating a city of millions to save the lives of thousands of soldiers is unjustified) and that inherently evil methods (for example, genocide, ethnic cleansing, mass rape) are never justified.

If the Buggers just wanted to replace our Government with their own, or simply wanted to make humanity a vassal race that paid them taxes, I don't know if it would be okay to kill the entire race of Buggers. On the other hand, imagine there's an extremist with a remote detonator in an apartment building full of a hundred other, innocent people. He's about to detonate a bomb in a school that will kill a thousand innocent people. It is proportionate, if necessary, to blow up the building the extremist is in and kill one hundred innocent people in order to save one thousand innocent people. If you take this scenario to a logical, if impractical, extreme, it is proportionate to kill all of a certain kind of innocent people in order to defend all of another kind of innocent people.

This is the sort of thinking Mazer and Graff had to engage in. Ender didn't have it bad. Ender was a kid and he was duped and he deserves a clean conscience. Making the decision, choosing, wanting to murder a billion innocent babies, that's what Mazer and Graff had to do. No matter how bad Ender thought his childhood was, he could still say "I didn't want to kill them all. I didn't want to kill anybody! I'm not a killer!" He didn't have to make the adult decision. He didn't have to choose who would live and who would die. Having to want that and prepare for that and sacrifice for that and live with that for the rest of your life—that's having it bad.

Ender started to grow up a little bit after meeting Valentine on the lake before Command School. He decided then that Valentine's life was worth more than another life, that "he would do anything to keep alive." When Bonzo was trying to kill Ender in the shower, Ender was justified in killing Bonzo. Even if Ender had to kill Bonzo's cronies, he would have been justified. It would have been different if Bonzo was just trying to embarrass Ender or just beat Ender up, but he was in the act of trying to kill when Ender got him first. Ender didn't do anything that wasn't already being done to him; he just did it a little bit sooner than the other guy. As long as the Buggers were trying to kill every human, the I.F. was justified in doing what was necessary to protect humanity.

We Are the Third Invasion. We're Attacking Them

No one's really justified in complaining about a fair fight. Certainly, whoever starts the fight shouldn't be complaining if they lose. Everyone can agree on this, but this isn't really what the I.F. did. The I.F. attacked the Buggers before they could attack humanity again. Just War Theory requires that a state go to war only if it's fighting for a 'just cause.' The only universally accepted just cause is self-defense. How can staring a fight, throwing the first punch, possibly be self-defense? At least the I.F. believed, and reasonably so, that the Buggers were coming back to finish humanity off. But if you are starting a fight, even with a past enemy, can you really say you're acting in self-defense? If not, then killing all those Bugger babies with Dr. Device doesn't seem justifiable.

I see two ways to categorize an attack: a pre-emptive strike or just an attack. In other words, either the Buggers really were going to kill a bunch of humans again (even all humans), in which case using Dr. Device on their home world was a pre-emptive strike, or hostilities between our two races were at an end and we simply attacked them out of the blue. There isn't any decent justification for an unprovoked attack and justification for pre-emptive strikes is tricky.

If you hear that someone is planning to beat you up, it makes perfect sense to keep your eyes out for that person, maybe even actively avoid them. But it would be insane to sneak into their house the night before and kill their entire family. Ender doesn't cripple every kid in Battle School that gives him a dirty look. He doesn't pick fights with the other kids. He doesn't neutralize every potential future threat. He isn't Peter.

Somewhere between those extremes is the line and we need to make sure the I.F. hasn't crossed it. Peter seems to be at war with everyone from the earliest age, so he never cares about other people as equals or even deserving of decent treatment. Ender demonstrates this amazing empathy for every living thing he thinks about. Ender wouldn't make a pre-emptive strike. Even if the only way to win and save his life was to kill a future opponent and its family, Ender might not. He didn't even mean to kill Bonzo. This is part of the reason why the I.F. doesn't tell him that is exactly what he is doing until after the fact.

Try to imagine this in the context of self-defense. What would it take to justify killing an entire family before one of them attacks you? First, you would need extraordinary evidence that he was coming for you. Second, he would have to be attacking you so soon that you didn't have any other effective options. Next, he can't just be coming to kill you, but coming to kill your entire family, or worse. Finally, killing his entire family must be the only way to protect your family. Even trying to imagine an example veers between ridiculous and horrific and leads me to wonder if there is a decent example in the context of self-defense, or if war is uniquely ridiculous and horrible at the same time.

It would be ideal if the I.F. could ask the Buggers if the two races were still at war, or even talk to the Buggers about it. Without that option, the reality of the situation is that, by any reasonable estimation, the war is still going strong. This matters because it transforms a pre-emptive strike into merely one battle amongst a history of them.

A pre-emptive strike justified as self-defense always entails a prediction: a prediction that the victim of your strike will attack you if they aren't stopped first. Sometimes this prediction is very reasonable and can be made with a high degree of accuracy. But, even the best predictions can't be made with one-hundred-percent accuracy. All predictions are made by assuming that the future will resemble the past in relevant ways.

The sun has come up every other morning, so it will continue to come up in the future. Unfortunately, astrophysicists have claimed that this isn't true because in billions of years the sun will get so big it incinerates the earth and after that will shrink and extinguish. On the other hand, science-fiction authors have claimed that humans could figure out a way to tame and reignite the sun billions of years before this happens, so even the astrophysicists could be proven wrong. . . . The point is that the very best predictions can be wrong, and anything less than certainty is less than what we want to base a decision to kill an entire race on.

If the Other Fellow Can't Tell You His Story, You Can Never Be Sure He Isn't Trying to Kill You

Even if all of these other conditions are met, it still isn't okay to use Dr. Device to exterminate the entire Bugger race. Remember, killing Bugger babies and Bugger farmers is bad. Even if the Bugger army attacked us first, even if we are hopelessly outclassed by their military might, and even if they are actively trying to exterminate the human race, we still don't want to kill their babies. Ender never even wanted to kill Peter, or Bonzo. The Buggers never targeted civilians. Killing is bad, and it would be worse to kill all those innocents in order to stop their army, if we could have talked them out of it. Or, heck, even bribed them, blackmailed them, conned, cajoled, you name it and it probably would have been better than xenocide.

"Maybe they gave up and they're planning to leave us alone." "Maybe. You've seen the videos. Would you bet the human race on the chance of them giving up and leaving us alone?" Gambling with the lives of two entire races is all we're left with if we can't communicate. This is the situation the I.F. was in, the Buggers didn't even have language, they only had telepathy. If the I.F. could've only talked to them somehow, then xenocide wouldn't have been necessary. As Graff said, "They don't have language at all. We used every means we could think of to communicate with them, but they don't even have the machinery to know we're signaling. And maybe they've been trying to think to us, and they can't understand why we don't respond." And Ender replies, "So the whole war is because we can't talk to each other."

Communication is the most important thing in the universe: talking is the only way to avoid fighting. If you can't communicate, you will fight. Thankfully, on Earth we can communicate with each other, even though we sometimes choose not to. If we don't speak with the living, all we can do is speak for the dead.

04
Is Ender Wiggin a Cheater Cheater Bugger Eater?

JOAN GRASSBAUGH FORRY

Any decent person who knows what warfare is can never go into battle with a whole heart. But you didn't know. We made sure you didn't know. You were reckless and brilliant and young. It's what you were born for.

—MAZER RACKHAM to Ender Wiggin

The most haunting passages of *Ender's Game* are the ones where Ender discovers that he has not been playing a game at all, but has been engaged in real warfare. Ender makes this terrifying discovery when he's brought to a control room where he will command his fleet in a battle simulation that he is told is his "final examination in Command School."

He's told that the observers in the room, who were not present in previous simulations, are there to evaluate his performance. Ender surveys what he believes is a battle simulation, noting that the major challenge is that the battle will take place surrounding a planet inhabited by Buggers. The ships in Ender's fleet are armed with weapons called Molecular Disruption Devices or "Little Doctors."

Ender asks if he is permitted to use these weapons against the planet itself. Mazer Rackham, his teacher and legendary war hero, vaguely cautions against doing so. He tells Ender, "You decide whether it would be wise to adopt a strategy that would invite reprisals."

Exhausted from years of grueling training, isolation, and manipulation, Ender rails against his teachers, thinking to himself, "Forget it, Mazer. I don't care if I pass your test, I don't care if I follow your rules. If you can cheat, so can I. I won't let you beat me unfairly—I'll beat you unfairly first." Ender believes that if he breaks the rule against using the Little Doctors against the planet, he will fail his examination and will not continue on to become a commander. "I'll never have to play a game again. And that is victory," he reasons.

The battle ensues and Ender deploys the Little Doctors, using them to destroy the Buggers' planet. After his penultimate "victory," Ender is confused by the celebration of the commanders who had been observing him.

> Men in uniform were hugging each other, laughing, shouting; others were weeping; some knelt or lay prostrate. . . . Ender didn't understand. It seemed all wrong. They were supposed to be angry.

Ender soon learns that not only was he engaged in real warfare against the Buggers and not a simulation, but also that his commanders and teachers expected him to break the rule and use the Little Doctors against the planet.

Mazer Rackham, legendary commander and Ender's teacher, explains:

> There were no games, the battles were real, and the only enemy you fought was the buggers. You won every battle, and today you finally fought them at their home world, where the queen was, all the queens from all their colonies, they all were there and you destroyed them completely. They'll never attack us again. You did it. You.

Ender's commanders and teachers made him believe he was playing a game, that the game had clear rules and that he would be penalized for cheating. However, Ender learns that it was expected that he would break the rules, that he would cheat, and that cheating was consistent with winning.

Ender's progression from Earth to Battle School to Command School is rife with instances where Ender breaks the rules of the games constructed for him. Contemporary sport is another arena where rule-breaking and cheating are important issues. The parallels between contemporary sport and *Ender's Game* are most apparent in considering how Ender's achievements through creative strategy might constitute *normative cheating*—or, as D. Stanley Eitzen, a prominent sport sociologist, defines the idea, "acts to achieve an unfair advantage that are accepted as part of the game."[1] In sport, gaining a competitive edge over your opponent by using methods that are not explicitly outlawed or manipulating the rules of the game to work in one's favor is commonly simply referred to as 'strategy'. Normative cheating takes strategy a step further. Players gain a competitive edge over their opponent by breaking rules. However, such forms of cheating are accepted and commonly justified as being 'part of the game'.

Thinking about Games

Philosophers of sport think about games in two main ways.

The first way is called *formalism*. Formalism refers to the idea that games are defined entirely by their rules. The game of basketball, for instance, is defined by certain facts about the game.

Basketball is played on a rectangular court, throwing the ball through a hoop scores points, and the team with the most points at the end of the allotted time wins. Rules *prescribe* how to play the game. In basketball, shooting the ball into the hoop from some distances earns a team two points, while making a basket from other distances earns a team three points. But rules also *prohibit* actions, and lay out consequences and penalties for when prohibited acts occur.

The rules of basketball prohibit players from pushing members of the opposing team. If one player pushes a player on the opposing team, a foul is called and a penalty is issued against the pushy player and her team. Depending upon the circumstances, the pushed player's team may be awarded possession of the ball. Or, the pushed player may have a chance to earn points by means of free throws. This is one example of how rules both prescribe and prohibit in the formal construction of games.

The second way to think about games is *conventionalism*. Conventionalism is the view that games are not only their formal rules, but are also defined by surrounding norms and cultures. Games include a range of practices that are accepted as

---

[1] D. Stanley Eitzen, "Ethical Dilemmas in American Sport: The Dark Side of Competition," *Vital Speeches of the Day* (January 1996).

matter of convention or custom. Convention may permit some actions, even if these actions are against the formal rules. In basketball, when a game is close near the end, the losing team may intentionally foul a member of the opposing team to stop the clock. Stopping the clock, even if to allow the opposing team an opportunity to score points via free throws, may enable the losing team more opportunities to score as they regain possession of the ball. It's a matter of convention that the losing team will intentionally foul to stop the clock in a 'foul-for-profit' strategy. However, intentionally fouling is explicitly against the rules of basketball.

Fouling is usually treated as a matter of accident. The pushy player did not intend to harm her opponent by pushing. Rather, the pushing was an accident. Intentional fouls, because they are the result of an intentional act, are met with a stiffer penalty. But when players intentionally foul at the end of a game to stop the clock, these fouls are treated the same as those regarded as a matter of accident. Convention dictates that these intentional fouls be treated as a matter of strategy. After all, these fouls usually do not injure the opposing players. And, if referees *did* start to treat these fouls as truly intentional or flagrant fouls, outrage would follow from players and fans!

Conventionalism accounts for important cultural features that influence how games are played. Conventionalism also attributes agency to players, coaches, and referees in shaping how games are played. But conventionalism complicates our view of what is morally acceptable in the context of game-playing. The fact that some practices are a matter of convention may be used as a justification for morally questionable practices.

Trash-talking is typically accepted as part of the game of basketball. Some justify trash-talking as a strategy. Players try to gain a competitive advantage by getting inside opposing players' heads, throwing off their mental focus. Even though trash-talking is allowed by the rules and is accepted as a matter of convention, it is not clear that trash-talking is morally justifiable. Trash-talk often consists of trading insults, and the more degrading the insult, the more effective the trash-talk is at throwing an opponent off his game. Are trash-talking players cultivating good character? Are they respecting their opponents? Are they respecting the game itself? Perhaps not.

The games Ender plays in Battle School are no different from game-playing in sports in these respects. Ender struggles with the tensions between formalism and conventionalism. Ender exercises creativity in interpreting the rules and conventions of the games and battle simulations. We know from the beginning that his commanders intentionally cultivated his creativity through orchestrated isolation and manipulation. Nevertheless, Ender participates in shaping the games themselves and the conventions surrounding them.

Cheating and Deception

Cheating occurs when players attempt to gain an unfair competitive advantage by breaking the rules of the game. But cheating is not just breaking rules. Basketball players who break rules by repeatedly committing fouls are not cheating. They are just bad at playing the game of basketball. Cheating also includes the intent to deceive. Cheaters attempt to make it appear as if they are following the rules when they actually are not. Basketball players who play rough when the referee is not looking, and commit actions that would be considered fouling, may be said to be cheating. These players are attempting to gain an unfair advantage by deceiving the referee into believing they are playing within the rules of the game when they are not.

But not all actions that include the intent to deceive are cheating. In many sports, players are consistently engaged in attempts to deceive their opponents. Football players fake throws and handoffs, basketball players fake shots, and baseball players lead off in attempting to steal bases. Successes in sport depend upon players' abilities to deceive their opponents! Teams can even employ trick plays to deceive opponents and gain a competitive advantage.

Youth basketball teams occasionally use "The Barking Dog" play to inbound the ball and score. The player taking the ball out slaps the ball and one player from his team drops to his knees and barks like a dog, distracting the other team's players so that the ball may be inbounded under the basket for an easy two points. While all of these actions involve the intent to deceive, they are not cheating. The players have not broken any rules, and are not attempting to deceive players or referees into thinking they are following the rules when, in fact, they are not. This kind of deception is readily available for opponents to use, and thus, fair.

Ender uses this kind of strategy in the battleroom when he uses the guns that freeze opponents, rendering them immobile, against his own soldiers. Ender instructs his soldiers to freeze a boy and use him as a shield. Even though Ender's army begins at a disadvantage by having one or more frozen soldiers, the boys who act as shields allow his soldiers to maneuver more freely around the obstacles and among opposing soldiers. This strategy had not been used before and bewildered Ender's opponents. The commanders seem to regard this creative use of strategy as cheating, punishing Ender and his army with increasingly difficult challenges. Ender's army has to battle more than once during a day, on short notice, and against more than one army at a time.

In the context of these difficult challenges, Ender feels justi-fied in introducing techniques that might qualify as cheating. Bean brings a thin, nearly invisible line of rope into the battle-room, which allows the soldiers to change directions as they move around the star obstacles. In the battle against the Griffin and Tiger armies, Ender puts his soldiers into a formation, some-thing he had never done before. This confuses and distracts his opponents. The strange formation allows Ender's Dragon Army to perform the victory ritual and open the battleroom door, which technically ended the battle and constituted a victory.

Angry that Ender seems to have cheated, Major Anderson loudly claims that the rules would be revised in light of Ender's "little maneuver." Ender indignantly claims that he beat Major Anderson and the other teachers who manipulated the para-meters of the game. Anderson claims that Ender's battle is not with his teachers, only with his competitors, and Ender expresses frustration with his situation, acknowledging its inherent unfairness when he shouts, "How about a little equal-ity?" Ender is then reprimanded for his insubordination, and he tells Bean, "I don't care about their game anymore. . . . I'm not going to play it anymore."

Expected Cheating

Normative cheating—defined, again, as "acts to achieve an unfair advantage that are accepted as part of the game"— combines rule-breaking, the intent to deceive, and the problems of conventionalism. The acts are unfair because they involve rule-breaking. The competitive advantage is not available to all players, only to those who would risk breaking the rules. However, this claim to unfairness is often countered by the fact that cheating acts are rampant in sport.

Is it still cheating if everyone cheats? Because cheating acts are rampant, condemnation of acts of normative cheating is difficult. Claims that actions are wrong because they break the rules ring hollow when declared in a culture where such acts have been normalized and are expected.

For example, the use of prohibited substances or methods in sport, or doping, is an example of normative cheating. Governing bodies of sport detail rules that prohibit performance-enhancing substances and training methods. Doping is against the rules, but many stakeholders in sport—athletes, coaches, and fans alike—claim that doping is a logical response to meet the increasing demands and pressures of sport. Doping may be against the rules, but what other choice do athletes have when their teammates and opponents are doping? In this case, avoiding cheating is an act of rebellion.

In another example of normative cheating, American football players may be coached on how to hold or use illegal techniques without getting caught. Such practices are defended as just being a part of the game. In 2009, University of Florida linebacker Brandon Spikes was caught gouging the eyes of University of Georgia running back Washaun Ealey when the two were stuck at the bottom of a pile of players. Video shows Spikes jamming his fingers through Ealey's facemask into Ealey's eyes. Similarly, in 2012, Michigan State University offensive lineman Jack Allen gouged the eyes of Ohio State defensive lineman Jonathan Hankins when the two players were on the ground. We cannot know whether the gougers were coached on how to gouge their opponents' eyes, but the response to each incident reveals why these are cases of normative cheating.

After each of these incidents came to light, some commentators noted that these sorts of things happened at the bottom of piles all the time. They implied that the wrongness was not in the eye-gouging itself but in the fact that these players did so when they were exposed on camera. In other words, what's

regretful about the eye-gouging isn't that one player deliberately caused harm to another when he was helpless to defend
himself, but that the gouger was caught. It's expected that
players will do anything to gain a competitive advantage,
including endangering the eyesight of their opponents. Those
who think otherwise are outsiders who misunderstand the culture of intercollegiate football.

Other commentators rightly claimed that such actions are
wrong and can't be tolerated. The gougers broke rules. Their
conduct was not only unsportsmanlike, but it was also harmful.
In the case of Allen and Hankins, the Big Ten conference determined that Allen did not violate the conference's policy on
sportsmanlike conduct. Though video clearly shows Allen's
hand reaching into Hankins' facemask, and Ohio State coaches
were concerned enough about the incident to bring it to the
attention of the governing body, the incident was dismissed as
just being part of the game, a heat-of-the-moment act that is
common in fierce competition.

Ender's actions in Battle School are regarded with similar
ambivalence. Though he is reprimanded, he is clearly *expected*
to use questionable strategies to respond to the escalating challenges devised to defeat him and his army. It's not clear that his
strategies are against the rules in a context where the teachers
and commanders regularly change the rules, reinterpret them
to serve their own interests, and fail to make them explicit.

Cheating in Ender's Game

How do these reflections on sport help us broaden our understanding of the dilemma Ender faces in destroying the Bugger
planet? Ender learns that he was expected to cheat, a seemingly textbook case of normative cheating. The games that are
constructed for Ender by the commanders suffer from similar
assumptions, inconsistencies, and ambiguities in custom and
convention as in the sport examples we've been looking at. But
did Ender *really* cheat?

Ender interpreted Mazer Rackham's caution against using
the Little Doctors on the Bugger planet as a rule. Ender chose
to break that rule, and in choosing to do so, he believed he was
cheating. But the rule was not explicitly stated, it was a matter
of assumed convention—one should not employ tactics that

would invite retaliation. Even if we grant that Ender did indeed break a rule, he did not do so with the intent to deceive. Instead, Ender cheated with the intent that he would be caught! He hoped that his blatant rule-breaking would cause the commanders to reprimand him, fail him, and send him home.

However, Ender's actions *did* help him gain a competitive advantage against the Buggers that, ultimately, *was* unfair to his opponents, the Buggers. But Ender's act of cheating is not directed at the Buggers, it's directed at the commanders. Ender sees his commanders as his opponents, shifting the parameters of the game. Not only is Ender playing against the Buggers, but he is also playing a sort of game against the commanders. He's like a quarterback who disagrees with his coaches' play-calling and runs a different play instead. It's not clear whether Ender is indeed cheating. He could just be disobeying his commanders. Such acts have their consequences, but they are not against the rules of the game.

The problem with Ender's dilemma in the final battle is that he was expected to break the rules that the commanders set out for him. Whether we think Ender cheated or not, the ominous aspect is the culture and conventions surrounding his final battle. It's a culture in which Ender has been manipulated, a culture in which the rules are unclear, and a culture in which questionable actions are regarded as just part of the game. That's what makes *Ender's Game* a case of normative cheating.

Is Ender even playing a game at all? In the final battle, it's revealed that he is not playing a game at all, but that he has been involved in real warfare against the Buggers. It could be that Ender was playing a game against his commanders, but it was profoundly unfair. The equivocation between game-playing and warfare can be seen as the central injustice that the commanders commit against Ender. He's manipulated into believing that he's just playing a game, when he is actually engaged in warfare.

This equivocation is present in sport culture as well. People regard sport as a metaphor for war, and stakeholders in sport perpetuate this metaphor through language. Sports fields are referred to as battlegrounds, players are called warriors, and coaches commonly refer to meeting rooms as command centers or war rooms. Warfare is a context in which rules do not apply, and if players regard sport as warfare, questionable behavior is easily justifiable.

But, the claim that players are just playing a game may just as easily contribute to questionable behavior such as cheating. If players are just playing a game, they might not see their actions as serious, even if those actions involve potentially serious harm to others (such as in the eye-gouging incidents).

It's easy to regard the commanders' manipulation of Ender as wrong. They compromised his ability to make decisions freely. They took his childhood from him and deprived him of an open future in which he was free to choose his fate. They created a culture in which harm to others was regarded ambiguously. That's what gave me nightmares after I read—and re-read—*Ender's Game*.

Perhaps the parallels between *Ender's Game* and contemporary sport should prompt us to question whether the norms of sport are just as troubling and insidious.

Minds and Bodies

05

Where Does Ender's Consciousness End?

Yochai Ataria

In the battle room Ender becomes a super-warrior. This is not because of any physical prowess—Ender is much smaller and weaker than all those around him. Ender's advantage lies instead in his ability to alter his state of consciousness, that is, to adapt himself to the changing conditions of his surroundings. Ender understands how to operate in the absence of gravity; he understands that when there is no gravity he must change the way he acts, thinks and speaks:

> "From now on, you forget about gravity before you go through that door. The old gravity is gone, erased. Understand me? Whatever your gravity is when you get to the door, remember—the enemy's gate is down."

The other children fighting in the training room cannot understand this; inside the room they go on thinking and acting as they would outside, where the rules of gravity apply. They are not flexible enough to adapt their consciousness to the changes in their surroundings: they are stuck on the "worldly," normal, setting. Dink is one example of this narrow-mindedness:

> He had seen what Ender was doing, but he had not understood the orientation that it implied. It soon became clear to Ender that even though Dink was very, very good, his persistence in holding onto the corridor gravity orientation instead of thinking of the enemy gate as downward was limiting his thinking.

Without the force of gravity we must think and act differently. The state of consciousness must undergo change. To a certain extent, in order to operate successfully in a room without gravity it is necessary to "change" the body.

Then-college student Emily Calandrelli during a reduced-gravity flight.

Source: NASA, "Already a Star, Calandrelli Tells Students to Aim High." http://www.nasa.gov/audience/foreducators/already-a-star.html

It is because these children are unable to relinquish the established concepts and beliefs upon which their lives are based that many of them can't adapt to their new environment: "because of their insistence on a gravity that didn't exist, the boys became awkward when the maneuver was underway, as if vertigo seized them." Ender, on the other hand, functions naturally under the new conditions and also teaches the others how to do so. This makes him a super-warrior in the battle room and eventually enables him to defeat the Buggers.

The Sense of Self and the Body

Any transfer from the surroundings to which we are accustomed, and according to which our body has developed, into a foreign environment to which our body is not suited turns our concept of the world totally upside down. This is certainly the

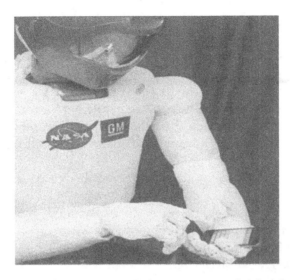

A NASA robot—Robonaut—tweets by remote control. A headset that allows the controller to see "through" Robonaut's cameras, aids the human "pilot." In this situattion the sense of self passes from the controller's body to the robot.

Source: NASA, "What Is Robonaut?"
http://www.nasa.gov/audience/forstudents/k4/stories/what-is-robonaut-k4.html

case when moving from the world governed by the force of gravity to a zero-gravity environment. We become disorientated and our body, with which we are so familiar, becomes a stranger to us.

Although the external appearance of our body remains the same, the difference in physics (lack of gravity) forces us to live as though we are no longer the same creatures. Since the self is embodied, or grounded within the world, through the body, if the physical world changes, then so does the self. If we want to survive, we must learn to live in this unfamiliar new body; and we must change our way of thought accordingly. In order to carry out simple activities, for example going from one place to another, we must change our way of thinking and acting and, like babies, learn to do everything from the beginning. This is Ender's natural talent.

In a way, a dramatic change in the world around us is equivalent to exchanging the body for another—some kind of avatar. The appearance of the body may remain the same, but owing to the radical change in the surrounding conditions, it is in fact a new body in a new world. This may seem strange, yet it happens to us all the time: for example when we are playing a particularly successful game on a Playstation we feel our sense of self being transferred to the character that we are playing. NASA has used this ability in order to create a remote-control operated robot, although the result isn't really a remote-control operation but rather a transfer of the sense of self from person to robot.

The possibility of shifting into a new body raises the following question: to whom does this body really belong? This isn't a simple question. For instance, an experiment known as The Rubber Hand Illusion creates confusion between our hand and a rubber hand, making us feel that the rubber hand is part of our body. The subject's hand is placed on a table, but out of sight, and an obviously fake rubber hand is placed in sight on the table, just in front of the subject. Then the fingers of the subject's hidden real hand are brushed simultaneously with the fingers of the rubber hand, in view of the subject. There's no deception here—the rubber hand is obviously false and the subject knows what's being done—but nonetheless, subjects report that they begin to experience this rubber hand as if it were theirs. When asked to close their eyes and use their other hand to point to their real hand, subjects even point to the wrong one! There are excellent videos of the experiment on YouTube.[1]

This experiment demonstrates that the body does not belong to us (our sense of ownership) in the way that we would like to think it does. Rather we can mislead our consciousness with simple and transparent manipulations.

What Are the Boundaries of the Self?

Oscar Pistorius is a South African sprinter with a double below-knee amputation who has competed in short sprints at the world championship level and the Olympics. Springy prosthetic limbs are attached the stumps of his legs when he runs, and he surely experiences his contact point with "the world"

---

[1] And see Matthew Botvinick and Jonathan Cohen, "Rubber Hands 'Feel' Touch that Eyes See," *Nature* 391 (1998), p. 756.

Does the body end where the prothesis begins? Or rather does it (the body) end where the ground begins? What is the difference between the biological leg and the prothesis? Although these are difficult questions, it seems that a perfect prothesis can become a part of the subject.

Oscar Pistorius at the 2012 London Paralympics. Author: Chris Easton.

Source:http://commons.wikimedia.org/wiki/File:Oscar_Pistorious_2012.jpg

where his blades meet the ground—if he experienced the boundary between himself and the world outside of himself at the meeting point between his upper legs and his prostheses, it's hard to imagine how he could run at all—much less how he could run so well.

Where does the world begin and where does the body end—where is the boundary between the two? Consider a prosthetic hand attached to a stump that's holding a fork: both the fork and the prosthesis are biologically not part of the body. We control both of them with a projected sense of agency, but while the fork does not "belong" to us, the prosthesis does, and we only feel a sense of ownership towards the prosthesis, not the fork.

This distinction becomes yet more blurred when we think about a blind woman perceiving the world through a cane which, technically, is a tool in the same way as a fork (and not in the same way as a prosthesis). And yet the cane is part of the blind person; that is, the blind woman perceives the world through the cane. In this case it is true that the cane is merely a tool, yet in the same way the body is also merely a tool or a medium enabling us to perceive the world. Thus a blind person is in-the-world through her cane: her consciousness incorporates the cane.

Ender and the Queen

In the battles against the Buggers, Ender controls a fleet of space ships through a computer. Mazer Rackham, the much-admired commander who directed the fleet's forces in the second invasion and defeated the Buggers, teaches Ender that the only way to beat the Buggers is through total control of the fleet. He must maneuver his fleet as he does his own body, at least as well as the queen of the Buggers controls her troops: "You will have to be better with a fleet than you are with your body or no one will be safe with you in command. Lesson learned?"

Ender must find a way to establish close contact with his fleet of spaceships, he must make them an integral part of himself. Yet the link between him and the ships under his command can't be the same as that between the queen of the Buggers and her fleet: The queen is the mind of one organic body, one organism, whose limbs are scattered throughout space in sophisticated battle ships. In other words the queen is "a brain in a vat" directly connected to all of its ships. None of the individual ships has intelligence or will, only the queen:

> "Every ship acts like part of a single organism. It responds the way your body responds during combat, different parts automatically, thoughtlessly doing everything they're supposed to do. They aren't having a mental conversation between people with different thought processes. All their thoughts are present, together, at once. A single person, and each bugger is like a hand or a foot."

By contrast, the human space fleet is made up of individuals each with his or her own self-consciousness and free thought. The fleet is not one body controlled by one brain.

In order to defeat the queen, Ender must have the same control over his fleet as she has over hers, even though it can never be part of his organism as it is hers, in the same way that a prosthesis, as successful as it may be, can never be part of the organic body. A successful prosthesis can become *transparent* or *embodied*—it can become part of the sense of self—but never part of the organism. This is exactly the connection that Ender must create with his fleet, yet without any direct physical contact. In order to achieve this goal Ender must internalize the concept that one's body is only a medium that enables one to be in the world. Notice however, even though the body is merely a tool, the self is not disconnected from this tool, and that's because my body is the tool I am: I *am* my body.

The Secret of Ender's Victory

In order to defeat the Buggers Ender must understand how the queen thinks and how she acts. He must find a way to extend his consciousness in order to incorporate the whole fleet into it.

We have seen how Ender became a super-warrior in the zero-gravity training room by successfully changing his state of consciousness upon entering. His consciousness and body both altered, while his actions in the zero gravity space, in which those from the normal world are not valid, adapted themselves to the different reality.

The way to make a total change in consciousness, enabling a person to think like the other—to become the other—is through identification. Indeed, in order really to think like the other, we must be able to be present in the other's body. This is Ender's talent. His ability to change his state of consciousness, to alter the body, enables him to make the space fleet into his own body and to begin thinking and acting like the queen.

As Ender is told, "We had to have a commander with so much empathy that he would think like the Buggers." In order to think like the Buggers, Ender must fully adopt their zero point, must understand how it feels to be a Bugger, or more accurately, how it feels to be the queen. To this end Ender must be able to see the world from the queen's point of view, namely, to feel the boundaries of the queen. Ender's boundaries must be replaced by those of the queen, and his body must cease to be the tool that Ender is, becoming instead a human-machine hybrid version of the queen's organism.

If we think about it, we too have this ability—in fact, without it we would not be able to survive in the modern world. A change in the boundaries of the sense of consciousness and the sense of self is not foreign to us. For example, when driving a

car we really "feel" the boundaries of the car (even emotionally), as though the car were part of our body; we are able to
pass between two obstacles with the car, and we do this just as
well as we walk down a crowded street without bumping into
people around us.

By contrast, when driving a remote-controlled car we do
not feel its exact boundaries and we are likely to have acci-
dents—remote-controlled cars do not become part of who we
are, but rather our sense of self remains in the body. For
Ender, remote control is not enough. In order to exert full control over the fleet he must identify with the tool that he is
commanding and control it in the same way that race drivers
control their vehicles: the boundaries of the self must stop
being those of the organic body and become the boundaries of
the car.

In the case of a connection that is not immediate, such as
that of driving a car, the problem is acute. Ender understands
this and therefore asks Rackham, "But how do I control the
ships?" Rackham replies that "you must learn their strengths
and limitations; you must make them into a whole."

In order to succeed in controlling the fleet of ships Ender
must find a way to extend the boundaries of his consciousness
outside of his brain and his body, he must take his thoughts
directly out of his head and into the world. This is possible
when we understand that cognitive activity is not rooted in any
one location, it can happen both inside and outside of our
selves.[2] Cognitive processes are not restricted to one's brain but
rather occur within the world.

For example, my father works without a calendar and therefore, when he arranges a meeting, he recreates in his head the
schedule that is in front of him and remembers when he is free.
This is cognitive activity within the head. If he were to use
some kind of calendar, my father would perform the same
action exactly but this time with the help of the external world,
the cognitive activity thus taking place in the world. In one
case he "opens his calendar" in his head, and in the other in the
external world. If this example is not convincing enough, let's
think about a man that has totally lost his memory. In this case

---

[2] Andy Clark and David Chalmers, "The Extended Mind," *Analysis* 58:1
(1998), pp. 7–19.

the external calendar completely replaces the cognitive activity that previously took place inside his head.

As part of his cognitive process, Ender's consciousness extends past the giant screens out into the world. He does not simply watch the ships. Rather, his consciousness extends to them and incorporates them: his cognitive activity takes place in the world. The fleet of space ships becomes part of his cognitive activity; he projects a strong sense of ownership onto the fleet of space ships and in this way the ships become part of Ender. Of course, the process of adaptation and identification does not take place at once. He must work and train just as we practice in order to learn to drive a car. And indeed, we see that at first Ender still has difficulties in controlling the ships: "they always won despite their mistakes, their miscommunications."

As the battles continue and his experience increases, Ender's level of confidence grows:

> The better Ender knew them, the faster he could deploy them, the better he could use them. . . . The trust was complete, the working of the fleet quick and responsive. We look like a bugger fleet.

As trust grows so does the sense of ownership. In other words, the sense of ownership is a precondition for the sense of trusting our body.

Over time Ender's cognitive abilities grow stronger, the boundaries of his cognition alter—the boundaries become more flexible. At his peak, all the team becomes part of Ender's cognitive processes: "Part of what I am is her [Petra]." The fleet is his body and he is deep in a new state of consciousness within which, as a result of identification, the memory of each one of the commands becomes his memory but not as some kind of brain-in-a-vat: "And just as he remembered that game, apparently Bean remembered it, too, for his voice came over the headset, saying, 'Remember, the enemy's gate is down'."

Our consciousness, just like Ender's, is not trapped within our body or our mind. Our consciousness can leave the boundaries of the body and go out into the world. In daily life this finds expression, among other things, in the ability to use tools, for example the blind woman's cane becomes part of her. Our physical borders are not our absolute boundaries.

As technology advances, the limitations of the body decrease, and at the same time the gap between the boundaries of the actual body (organism) and the boundaries of the mind grows. In this way the sense of ownership extends in a fundamental way and accordingly the cognitive processes become less restricted to the organism's close environment and instead take place at a distance—exactly as in Ender's case.

06
Hive-Queens and Harms

PAUL NEIMAN AND DANIEL DRUVENGA

Telepathically controlled robot arms. That's effectively what the Buggers are to a hive-queen. Think bees or ants, but with sentience—self-aware consciousness—existing only in the queen. Suppose you want to pick up an object. As soon as you make this decision, your body responds immediately to your thought. In the same way, a queen only needs to *think* to effect an instantaneous response from the Buggers.

"They aren't having a mental conversation between people with different thought processes," Mazer Rackham explains to Ender.

"You don't need to have a conversation with your hand about whether it wants to pick up a book, and a hive-queen doesn't need to discuss with a bugger where to pilot a space ship. She just thinks it, and the bugger does it."

When a hive-queen dies, the Buggers she controls cease to operate. All of their biological functions continue, but without the will of the hive-queen, they become unresponsive, inert. This is what Ender discovers from the videos of the second invasion. After Mazer destroys the hive-queen's ship, the other Bugger ships are left uncontrolled. "They did not fire on him. They did not change course. Two of them crashed into each other and exploded—a needless collision that either pilot could have avoided. Neither made the slightest movement." Deprived of the connection with their former controller, the Buggers become incapable of responding to any stimuli, even to save their own lives.

What this shows us is that the Buggers have no mind of their own. They're only the telepathically-controlled robot arms of the hive-queen. For a queen, losing a few Buggers is like you clipping your fingernails. Nothing of value has been lost, and you can always grow new ones. Killing a hive-queen, on the other hand, is something quite different. As Mazer points out, "Only queen-killing, really, is murder."

Queens have their own thoughts, desires, and dreams, and are much more like human beings. While killing Buggers may be morally insignificant, killing a hive-queen is murder, and attempting to kill a whole species of hive-queens is xenocide, the attempted extermination of an entire alien species.

Xenocide and Murder

What intuitively seems to make xenocide so morally awful is the sheer size of the crime. An entire species wiped out of existence. When Ender kills Bonzo Madrid, the moral harm is limited to the death of a single individual. With Bonzo's friends cowed by the force of the attack, Ender is able to escape without harming anyone else. But suppose he had. Suppose that instead of taking out his frustrations later that day in a harmless mock battle against Tiger and Griffin Army, Ender had gone on a killing rampage throughout the Battle School. The size of the crime would have grown with the number of bodies he left in his wake.

How does Ender's capacity to kill one human being, or two or twenty, compare to xenocide? Ender's record is only slightly morally worse than Mazer's. In the second invasion, Mazer only kills one sentient being, the hive-queen controlling the Bugger fleet. Before Ender ever encounters the Buggers in battle, he has already killed two sentient beings—Bonzo and Stilson. Given that one hive-queen can control an entire fleet of Bugger ships, it's likely that there are relatively few hive-queens. Quantitatively, xenocide of the Buggers is only slightly worse than what Ender has already done. If xenocide is morally distinct from mass-murder, it must be due to some additional harm that is committed, not against any individual, but against the community of hive-queens.

A Bugger Community

A sense of community can be an important part of one's identity, whether you're human or hive-queen. Think about the instant connection you feel when you meet a person from your hometown, or who went to your high school. Even if you've never met this person before, you have a shared background with shared meanings that can form the basis of your interaction.

Words like "Tremper" or "The Spot" have a particular meaning for you if you're from Kenosha, Wisconsin, but are meaningless if you're not. The loss of this community would harm you by damaging this aspect of your identity. On an individual level, it's like getting old and watching all of your family and friends die around you. Suddenly there is no one to reminisce with about old times. You become isolated from the experiences that you feel are so important to you—that shaped who you are and how you think of yourself. Sure, you can talk about these things with other people, but if they weren't there, they won't share the same feelings about them as you do. What's significant to you may sound trivial to those who are not a part of the same community, who don't share the experiences and meanings.

Any sense of community that the Buggers shared could only have existed between hive-queens. The connection between a hive-queen and her Buggers cannot form the basis of a community. The Buggers are merely telepathically controlled robot arms. It would be like trying to carry on a conversation with your hand. While it's certainly a useful appendage, it just doesn't have a lot to say. But the hive-queens can and do communicate with one another. The basis of the hive-queen community is harmony, queens who "loved and helped each other instead of battling." These hive-queens share a common history and vision, and draw the meaning and purpose of their lives from it.

But is community really an important part of hive-queen identity? Human beings belong to a community to fulfill their physical and psychological needs. Neither children nor adults can flourish without others to care for and about them. A single hive-queen, with all of her Bugger appendages, is more than capable of fulfilling her physical needs. And even though all human beings belong to a community of some sort, that doesn't mean they make it part of their identity. There are always some people who try to escape from the communities they find themselves in, be it their family, a social group they've grown up with, or geographical location. Since hive-queens do not need a community to survive, as humans do, then why assume that they find the same value and meaning in community as humans?

Despite the hive-queens' ability to communicate instantaneously over vast distances, Ender finds them all together on their home planet. As Graff and Bean inform the other children after the final battle, "All life activity has ceased on all other planets. They must have gathered their queens back on their home planet." There is no strategic reason for the hive-queens to have done this. Given their experience with Mazer in the second invasion, they know that humans are willing to kill hive-queens. So why put the entire species at risk by gathering all of the hive-queens on one planet that could be destroyed? As Graff reports, these hive-queens have returned from other planets from which they could have controlled their fleets of Bugger ships. Why return home in the face of such danger?

It seems that the only possibility is that the hive-queens came together, just as human beings do in dark and perilous times, for the comfort and companionship of community. In the wake of natural disasters or mass shootings, people turn to one another and to their community. Sometimes this is just to meet physical demands. When your house is destroyed by a hurricane, it's helpful to have a community to find you a new place to stay and to help you rebuild. But experiencing and overcoming the disaster together strengthens the bonds people have to one another, to the community itself, to the sense of home. With their ability to instantly communicate across the stars, the hive-queens could easily have co-ordinated the defense of the home planet without being physically present together. But shared experiences are a significant part of belonging to, and identifying with, a community. Talking to someone on the phone, or even by video, just isn't the same as being there with them. Not for human beings, and, apparently, not for hive-queens.

The way the hive-queens retreat from their colonies and come together to protect their home planet shows that it means more to them than simply a point of origin. The hive-queens' willingness to face the danger posed by the human invaders, is an example of how their community is based on love and helping one another. While hive-queens no doubt believed that their planet was well-protected, they were wary enough of Ender's skill to have secured the hive-queen cocoon on the colony Ender himself would eventually establish. Nevertheless, the hive-queens gathered and remained at their home planet for the final battle. This demonstrates the value the hive-queens place on their community.

When Ender commits xenocide, he destroys not only a number of individual hive-queens, but also the communal identity that the hive-queens shared. Even if, quantitatively, Ender's xenocide and his acts of murder at the battle school had been identical, his crime against the Buggers would still be morally worse because of the extra harm of the destruction of the Bugger community. The families of Stilson and Bonzo will certainly grieve the loss of their children. But, supported by other family members as well as the other communities they belong to, it will not disrupt their identities to the same extent as the xenocide of the Buggers. The lone survivor of Ender's xenocide is permanently cut off from communication with all members of her former community.

Incomplete Xenocide

The survivor of Ender's xenocide has lost more than the lives of her fellow hive-queens. She has lost the community that formed her identity and gave her life meaning. But for this harm to exist, someone must exist to experience it. This suggests a somewhat morbid implication: would Ender have done less harm had his xenocide not left any survivors?

Quantitatively, it is morally worse to kill five hive-queens than to kill four. On this level, stopping short of complete xenocide is always preferable. While the surviving hive-queen may never recreate the community she has lost, she at least has the opportunity to create a new community, with new meanings, history, and identity. Human survivors of genocides, such as the Holocaust, may add the experience to their understanding of themselves. Part of what it means to belong to the Jewish community includes having an understanding of how the Holocaust has shaped Jewish identity and history.

The surviving hive-queen is capable of reproducing her entire species, and this allows for the possibility of a new hive-queen community to arise. By stopping short of complete extermination of the Buggers, Ender's xenocide avoids the harm of an additional murder and leaves open the possibility of a future community of hive-queens.

Hive-Queens and Humans

Because the hive-queens cannot communicate in any meaningful way with the Buggers they control, this relationship cannot form the basis of any community. But just as you cannot have a conversation with your hand, neither could you have a conversation with a hive-queen. When Ender finds the cocoon, he realizes, "they can only talk to me, and through me."

The inability to communicate in meaningful ways makes it impossible for humans and Buggers to belong to the same community. But this is not to say that it would be impossible for the Buggers and humans to live in peace, or even to work together. Once they knew each other as intelligent beings, it would be possible for them to assist each other in meeting needs for survival, or even advanced technology. But without Ender, or some other mediator, these interactions could never go beyond merely functional assistance. Buggers and humans could work together on a project—say, building a spaceship with Bugger technology but suited for human use—but they could not *share* the experience in any way more than how a human being and a dog can share the experience of going on walks together.

Humans might justly complain that they have been robbed of the opportunity to know and interact with past cultures that have been destroyed through genocide. That one can never get to know how the Aztec people would have developed over time, how their culture could have enriched one's own, is a loss for humans living today. Suppose Aztec culture had been preserved and developed by members of the Aztec community instead of being violently destroyed. But even then, some form of communication between the Aztec community and outsiders would be necessary for the culture to add any value to the outsiders' lives. This is something that humans and Buggers can never do without the use of a mediator such as Ender.

The sources of harm from xenocide are in the number of deaths of sentient individuals, the destruction of their community, and the loss that other sentient beings experience as a result of no longer being able to interact with this community. Although both hive-queens and humans can feel the impact of the first two sources of harm, because the Buggers and humans cannot communicate without a mediator such as Ender, this last harm cannot be experienced. While far from blameless, the incomplete xenocide produced less harm than if it had been completed, from the perspectives of both humans and the surviving hive-queen.

07
Humanity beyond Humanity

JORDAN PASCOE

When the Buggers first attacked humans in the First
Invasion, it was accidental—a scouting mission gone wrong.
When the Buggers returned in the Second Invasion to colonize
the Earth, the human race tried everything they could think of
to forestall a war: "we used every means we could think of to
communicate with them," Colonel Graff tells Ender on the ship
headed to Eros, "but they don't even have the machinery to
know we're signaling. And maybe they've been trying to think
to us, and they can't understand why we don't respond."

"So the whole war is because we can't talk to each other,"
Ender concludes. He's right: the problem isn't that the Buggers
aren't sentient, rational beings, but that their mode of communication is so alien to humans that we had no way to *know* that
they were rational and sentient, and we had no way to communicate a possible peaceful solution. And so Ender becomes
the Xenocide, blasting the Buggers into oblivion.

As we learn in *Speaker for the Dead,* the sequel to *Ender's
Game,* Ender's sister Valentine would give this problem a
name. Writing as the historian Demosthenes, she distinguishes
between *framling,* "the stranger we recognize as human, but
from another world," *raman,* "the stranger we recognize as
human, but of another species," and *varelse,* "the true alien"
with whom no conversation is possible.[1]

---

[1] EDITORS' NOTE. These terms are Scandinavian-derived. The plural of *raman*
is *ramen,* though the term 'raman' (like 'human') can be an adjective as well
as a singular noun.

From the perspective of the people who lived during the First and Second Invasions of the Bugger wars, the Buggers are *varelse*: no conversation is possible, and so there is no way to know their intentions or goals. There can't be moral obligation to *varelse*, any more than there can be moral obligations to animals: we can try to do no harm, we can try to leave them alone, but when conflict arises, and conversation is impossible, self-defense is the only option left us. And so, the logic goes, Ender's xenocide is justified, since no one could possibly have known that the Buggers were truly *raman*, and therefore deserving of respect.

Ramen and Rational Beings

But Ender doesn't see it this way. For him, the Buggers are *raman*, and though he discovered too late that they were trying to communicate with him, he carries the burden of guilt for the human race for failing in its obligation to respect those who are *raman*: those who are rational, thinking beings, with their own ends, and thus part of the moral community.

Valentine's notion of the moral community owes much to the eighteenth-century German philosopher Immanuel Kant, who famously argued that morality consists in respecting rational beings as ends in themselves. Kant, like Valentine, would not see an important moral distinction between those who are human (*framling*) and those who are *raman*—all those who are rational beings are deserving of respect.

Kant tells us that "human beings, and in general every rational being, does exist as an end in himself." Beings that are "ends in themselves" must be treated as ends, Kant says, and never merely as a means to our own ends. Which is really a fancy philosophical way of saying that we musn't use people for our own purposes, but should respect them as persons with their own ends, projects, and goals. Beings who are ends in themselves can make their own choices, and we have the obligation to respect their right to do so.

So for Kant, human beings are "ends in themselves" not simply because they're human, but because they are one sort of rational being. This distinction suggests that Kant is defending an account of the moral community that is not limited by a biological distinction between humans and non-humans, but between those with a certain set of capacities (namely, rationality) and those without. This may seem like a redundant distinction, but for those concerned with the outer edges of the moral community—those thinking about the obligations owed to fetuses, for example, or animals—the shift from a species-based definition of the moral community to a capacities-based distinction can make all the difference.

Kant wasn't really thinking about fetuses or animals when he developed this distinction—he was trying to explain why persons are uniquely deserving of respect, and the capacity he settled on was *having a rational nature*. And he, like Valentine, was more than willing to consider the possibility that alien beings might fulfill this criteria. Kant was both a philosopher and an anthropologist, and in his work on anthropology, he considers the possibility of rational life on other planets—or, in his words, "*non-terrestrial* rational beings."

Kant, like Ender, thought that these non-terrestrial rational beings—or *ramen*—might be able to teach us a great deal about ourselves. Kant says of the human race, "we shall not be able to name its character because we have no knowledge of *non-terrestrial* rational beings that would enable us to indicate their characteristic property and so to characterize this terrestrial being among rational beings in general." In this remarkable passage from his 1798 *Anthropology from a Pragmatic Point of View*, Kant suggests just what Ender discovers: that the true moral nature of humanity is exposed when human beings are confronted by alien others. Only when we can compare our own nature to that of another breed of rational beings can we fully characterize our own capacities and natures.

Ramen and Race

The practice of comparing ourselves to alien others isn't always as humanistic as Ender (or Kant) might hope. Kant wasn't only concerned with comparing human beings to "non-terrestrial" others: he was also, infamously, the philosopher who first defined "race" as it is still understood. By defining the differences between the human races, and speculating on how these differences arose, Kant thought we might become more informed about our own: only when the "American" race was held up to the "European" race could their particular characteristics be recognized.

By exploring racial characteristics side by side, Kant hoped to better understand the human race as a whole. For this reason, he defends the study of the human races as an important element of the brand-new field of anthropology: the study of man, he suggests, must involve a comparative examination of human difference. It ought to come as no surprise, therefore, that he suspected that even a comprehensive study of the human races could not tell the whole story: we would need another, alien race to compare ourselves to in order to fully understand ourselves.

Ender himself suggests as much, when he publishes, in the years after the Bugger wars, *The Hive Queen and the Hegemon*. By telling the story of Peter Wiggin, Earth's Hegemon, in tandem with the story of the Hive Queen, Ender reveals the common humanity (so to speak) in both. But Ender, unlike Kant, is writing as a Speaker for the Dead: he is concerned *only* with the shared humanity of humans and Buggers. If Ender had approached this comparison from a different perspective—say, like Kant, he had been writing a scientific account of the difference between humans and alien others—he might have come to rather different conclusions.

Anthropology, Xenology, and the Trouble with Talking Trees

Two thousand years after the first Bugger invasion, the human race is rocked, once again, by the discovery of intelligent alien life when colonizers on Lusitania meet the Pequeninos, an intelligent alien race that look strikingly like pigs (hence their nickname, the "piggies"). Starways Congress, the governing body of all human worlds, decrees that the piggies are not to be disturbed. They are, however, to be studied: the discovery of the Pequeninos leads to the development of a whole new science: *xenology*, or the study of rational, alien races.

Xenology is a curious science. It assumes both that its objects of study are alien, and that they are rational. This is to say that it studies those who are unlike us (alien) and those who are very like us (rational). And it raises a difficult question: does studying alien others get in the way of respecting alien others?

History suggests a partial answer to this question: xenology isn't the first field to be born from a confrontation with alien others. Anthropology, which emerged at the end of the eighteenth century, was similarly motivated by an encounter with alien others. Kant was one of the earliest anthropologists, writing at a time when European colonialism had begun to circle the globe.

Speaker for the Dead tells the story of the early xenologists on Lusitania, who are able to study the Pequeninos directly, and their findings travel by ansible throughout the colonies, fueling the new academic discipline of xenology. It is such a new field that many of the methods and rules are unclear. Starways Congress dictates a doctrine of "minimal intervention," meaning that xenologers are to study the piggies, but should try to share as little as possible about human development, science, and ideas.

Libo, Lusitania's second xenologist, was both a scientist and a humanist: he felt both bound to study the piggies without interfering in their beliefs and practices, and to respect them as members of the moral community. His beliefs lead to a series of "questionable activities"—he and the xenologists who follow him share human literature, agriculture, and technology with the piggies in order to improve their quality of life.

But even in this breach of the Congressional rules, the xenologers assume human achievement as the standard by which all others must be judged, without considering the possibility that the piggies might have things to teach them.

As Ender tells Lusitanian xenologists Miro and Ouanda, they are so focused on learning *about* the piggies that they have not begun to learn *from* them. When the Pequeninos tell the xenologers they talk to trees Miro and Ouanda "play along," but never really imagine that the trees can talk. This, Miro argues, is "standard anthropological practice." When the piggies kill Libo, eviscerating and dissecting him for reasons the humans cannot understand, Miro and Ouanda puzzle over their motives, but do not hold them accountable. In doing so, they treat the piggies like glorified children who are not responsible for their actions. The piggies may be *raman*, but they are not yet equals.

Like Libo, Kant was both a philosopher and a founder of the field of anthropology, and his findings in these two fields are instructively, and similarly, conflicted. As a philosopher, he thought that all members of the human race had dignity and were deserving of respect—but as an anthropologist, he was primarily concerned with *classifying* non-European races, arguing that the European race had developed beyond the other races.

Kant's writings on race betray a condescension similar to Miro and Ouanda's "playing along with" the piggies—non-European races are interesting objects of study, but they need the aid and intervention of Europeans to help them develop their capacities, which lag behind those of Europeans. Likewise, the Lusitanian xenologers (and the Congressional rules to which they are bound) assume that the Pequeninos lag behind the human race, and that by sharing human culture and technology they might speed their development.

Kant's anthropological writings pose serious problems for his moral philosophy, and raise questions about whether he truly thought *all* human beings were truly deserving of equal dignity and respect. The Lusitanian xenologers, each of them self-identified humanists, face a similar dilemma: their xeno-logical practice, which positions the Pequeninos as *objects* of study, threatens to undermine their humanistic recognition of the piggies as *ramen*, creatures with dignity and rationality equal to that of humans.

Only Ender, who is unhampered by xenological constraints, and who has spent the last two thousand years mentally con-versing with the last Hive Queen, seems able to respect the Pequeninos as equals. This may be because Ender, unlike Miro, Ouanda, and, for that matter, Kant, isn't interested in studying the Pequeninos: he comes to them as a Speaker for the Dead, one whose task is to engage and understand, rather than to study and to *know*.

But Ender comes to the piggies not only as Andrew Wiggin, Speaker for the Dead. He is also Ender the Xenocide, and he knows that the human race has not always been *raman*. When they sent the fleet to the Bugger homeland, and destroyed an entire race of sentient beings, humanity acted as *varelse*—as an alien race who killed without first trying to respect and understand others. The Buggers have forgiven him for this, but he has not forgiven himself, and he knows that the human race is *raman* only if it succeeds in respecting the dignity and autonomy of other alien races.

A Community of *Ramen*

Ender's sense of responsibility for the xenocide of the Buggers drives his commitment to building an equal and respectful relationship with the piggies. But this isn't all he's after: he's also trying to find a home for the Hive Queen on the Pequeninos' world, and to find a way for humans, piggies, and Buggers to live together on Lusitania in a community of *ramen*.

Though the human race has come a long way towards respecting alien species as rational beings in the two thousand years since the Buggers' first attack, there is reason to suspect that they would be resistant to Ender's plan. Until Ender instigates a treaty that binds humans, piggies, and Buggers alike, no one had attempted to enter into agreements *with* the piggies. Piggies are not recognized as equals capable of entering into political contracts, but as an infant race to be studied and protected.

And the piggies are, let's admit, an easier sell than the Buggers. They're mammal-like and they've learned human language and expressions. Other than the whole eviscerating-and-dissecting-people problem, they're an appealing and non-threatening alien race. The Buggers, on the other hand, are the stuff of nightmares, and no matter how badly the human race feels about the xenocide, they are unlikely to embrace the Buggers as neighbors and equals.

This resistance to truly accepting the Buggers as *raman* isn't just aesthetic—it's not just that they look (eeuw) like gigantic insects. The original problem remains: the Buggers, unlike humans and piggies, don't communicate through speech. They communicate instantaneously by sending images directly into the minds of others—just as the hive-queens communicate with their workers. This makes the Buggers seem more alien than the piggies, and this instantaneous communication is precisely what made the Buggers such a formidable foe in the Bugger wars: an entire fleet, acting on one thought, like one giant, extended being.

Kant's Hive Mind

Kant imagined a race of rational beings who could, like the Buggers, communicate instantaneously. If such a race were to exist, who could not "think in any other way but aloud," he argued, it would be difficult to see how they could live peaceably together—unless they were all angels. This is because the sort of instantaneous communication the Buggers use dissolves

the distinction between intentions and actions. If I know everything you are thinking *as you are thinking it*, then I know what
you intend or desire to do, even if you choose not to act on it. If
you have a desire to hit me, it makes no difference whether you
manage to hold yourself back—you are accountable for your
desires, just as you are for your actions.

This capacity for instantaneous communication shapes the
moral life of the Buggers. In *The Hive Queen and the Hegemon*,
Ender recounts how, in order to expand the Bugger race and
colonize new worlds, the Hive Queen had to give birth to other
hive queens who could live peaceably with her—and this
meant killing many hive queens along the way. The hive
queens who survived were those whose thoughts revealed a
desire to live peaceably with others.

If the Buggers' instantaneous communication makes them
into something like Kant's angels—incapable of deception or
destructive intentions—what does this suggest about the
human race? Kant suggests that, if the human race were to
compare themselves to a species capable of instant communication, we would discover that our defining characteristic is the
capacity to deceive: we are beings who like to explore the
thoughts of others, he said, but to withhold our own thoughts.
This isn't necessarily a form of lying, but it is a kind of dissim-
ulation, and it explains why human beings find communication
with the Buggers so unsettling: when a hive queen communi-
cates with them, mind-to-mind, it feels like a kind of invasion,
and it forces them to reveal themselves in ways they rarely
must in human communication.

We said, at the beginning, that the distinction between
raman and *varelse* turned on the capacity to communicate.
Ramen are rational alien beings with whom we can communicate and reason, while *varelse* are alien beings with whom no
communication is possible. The xenocide of the Buggers was
justified if the Buggers were *varelse*; when *The Hive Queen and
the Hegemon* revealed them as *raman*, Ender's victory became
the human race's greatest crime.

But given the radical differences between human and
Bugger communication, we might state the problem differently: are human beings, from the perspective of the Buggers,
raman or *varelse*? For creatures who communicate totally, intimately, and instantaneously, might the human tendency to

communicate only some things some of the time, to dissimulate and to lie, mean that we cannot be known and understood? In order to live peaceably with humans, the Buggers must learn a new and terrifying skill: to trust those who should not be trusted.

If human beings are to be *raman*, they must do what Ender does—and what Kant suggests—and ask what their encounters with the Pequeninos and the Buggers has taught them about themselves. They must, in a sense, become xenologers of the human race.

But xenology isn't enough. As the cases of Libo and Kant suggest, our ability to respect others as equal, rational beings, is often undermined by our desire to study and categorize them, and to treat them simply as objects of inquiry. As xenologists and anthropologists, we can learn about others, but we are unlikely to learn *from* them. We ought, instead, to learn from Ender, for whom piggies and Buggers aren't just *ramen*— they are, in a stronger sense, *persons*, or equal members of a shared moral community.

08
The Enemy's Gate Is Down!

JEREMY HEUSLEIN

Of all the quotable lines woven throughout *Ender's Game*, the most quotable is: "The enemy's gate is down." What makes this phrase so remarkable and quotable is its power and focus. This phrase is the centerpiece of Ender's strategy, which revolutionizes Battle Room tactics. In his final Battle School battle, it is the only motivating goal.

It also is spoken by Bean in the final battle of the Formic Wars, when Ender is again outgunned and at the end of his proverbial rope. On both occasions, it proves stimulating, revolutionary, and paradigm-shifting. We can begin to understand why this is so through the lens of phenomenology—the study of how we experience what we experience.

"I am climbing up the floor," Ender thinks when confronted with the sight of carpet on the wall in his launch shuttle. In entering the shuttle and already reorienting his perception against the impression of gravity, Ender has already begun to consciously restructure how he situates himself in his world. To give the scene its full context: Ender sees the carpet on the wall and we're told:

> . . . that was where the disorientation began. The moment he thought of the wall as a floor, he began to feel like he was walking on a wall. He got to the ladder, and noticed that the vertical surface behind it was also carpeted. I am climbing up the floor. Hand over hand, step by step.

This experience foreshadows the reorientation that Ender enacts in the Battle Room, since it is precisely the same movement that occurs: the disregarding of an old structure of perception (the gravity of the hallway) and a realignment (the enemy's gate is down) based on the shared element of the body.

The Genius of Reorientation

There is a threshold that Ender and other Battle School students cross, the oddity of which Petra points out to Ender, where gravity snaps: the space between the corridor and the Battle Room. In the Battle Room, gravity is manipulated to discard the gravity of the corridor and enable the zero-g Battle Room environment, but between these two places there is a chasm. It is a chasm of perception. Ender does not realize this in his first trip to the Battle Room, but he quickly discovers the ability to center his perception differently, from an orientation based on his falling body.

> For a sickening moment he tried to retain his old up-and-down orientation, his body attempting to right itself, searching for the gravity that wasn't there. Then he forced himself to change his view. He was hurtling toward a wall. That was down. And at once he had control of himself. He wasn't flying, he was falling. This was a dive. He could choose how he would hit the surface.

In this moment, the old habit of his body-consciousness (one weighed down by gravity) asserts itself as Ender's perception, but through a redefined body-consciousness, and Ender orients into a dive, falling downwards. This orientation and perception of the world enables more possibilities for Ender's body, for example, he can choose how he hits the wall. It takes habit and practice in order to perfect his movements in the battle Room, as he adjusts to the new world and reconstructs an orientation around his "falling" body. It is not until his first battle that Ender fully articulates the famous phrase and structures the whole Battle Room world with the novel orientation, since he has never seen a pitched battle before.

> Abruptly he felt himself reorient, as he had in the shuttle. What had been down was now up, and now sideways. In nullo, there was no reason to stay oriented the way he had been in the corridor. It was impossible to tell, looking at the perfectly square doors, which way

had been up. And it didn't matter. For now Ender had the orientation that made sense. The enemy's gate was down. The object of the game was to fall toward the enemy's home.

This is how Ender begins his own re-education. While in Salamander, Ender does not gain much experience utilizing his re-oriented perception of the Battle Room, but upon being transferred to Rat especially for Dink, his real education begins. Not only does he practice his re-oriented position, but other toon members do as well. Ender gains further insight, as do we, to the imbedded nature of the old orientation when other soldiers question why they have to attack on their backs. Ender internally notes that Dink

had seen what Ender was doing, but he had not understood the orientation that it implied. It soon became clear to Ender that even though Dink was very, very good, his persistence in holding onto the corridor gravity orientation instead of thinking of the enemy gate as downward was limiting his thinking.

Retraining the Body

This reveals another phenomenological truth: the perception of the world placing the enemy's gate as down is not a mere *mental* shift. While it takes a conscious intention, it is also that, in getting into the habit of placing one's body in that direction—with your feet towards the door—the body retrains the mind. Both conscious intention and bodily placement are required. But this is hard to maintain, as the old orientation returns whenever they leave the Battle Room. Ender admonishes Dragon Army on their first day so as to cement the understanding:

From now on, you forget about gravity before you go through that door. The old gravity is gone, erased. Understand me? Whatever your gravity is when you get to the door, remember—the enemy's gate is down.

The body and its orientation as a habitualized manner of being in the world must be retrained. In doing so, many possibilities open up, and, frankly, Dragon mops the floor with the other armies. Ender and Dragon army has its own sign of victory, when the enemy soldiers reorient to their perspective and their gate becomes down. Even in his last battle at Battle School, where Ender is emotionally broken down, it's the acknowledgment of this reorientation, this change of the world into a new one, that sparks his strategy—a different way to win the game—and leads to victory. This occurs again, at the final battle of the Formic War.

Ender's re-orientation of the Battle Room not only is a bodily re-orientation, but one of conscious intention. It enables new possibilities and it opens new doors towards the goal, which in the case of the game is victory. A final point to consider here is that the re-orientation of his body which enabled new worlds of possibilities lingers in Ender's consciousness, in his bodily habits, which are irrevocably linked to his intentions and abilities.

Consciousness inhabits the body. This is to say that consciousness has habits that are linked to the body, as we have seen in the old perspective of corridor gravity still at play in the Battle Room. But consciousness does not merely play in the perceptual level; it extends into abstract thinking, but such thinking always occurs in the body. Consciousness *inhabits* the body.

Consider for example the final battle in the Formic war. In the final battle when Ender and his jeesh are attacking the Formics' homeworld, Ender (although with humanity) outnumbered a thousand to one is reminded of the bodily shift, which impacts the habits of abstracting consciousness. Bean, instead of taking control of the simulation, whispers the re-orienting, world-possiblizing phrase: "Remember, the enemy's gate is down." In *Ender's Shadow*, we learn that Bean does not know why his comment sparked Ender into action, whether it gave him any ideas or not, but through a phenomenological understanding of the meaning of that phrase, we understand that the remark activated a habit of Ender's consciousness. He disregarded what the world looked like (the rules of the game) and played by a different set of rules.

Ender specifically acknowledges this when he remembers Mazer's warning about using the MD Device against planets. In both the final battles, Ender

> had won by ignoring the enemy, ignoring his own losses; he had moved against the enemy's gate. . . . And the enemy's gate was down.

The world needed to be changed, the orientation shifted. This was not merely a mental exercise, but one of the body. The habits, the disciplines, and the strategies that enable Ender to win were corporeal.

Bodies and Worlds

This focus on the body was anticipated by the insights of two great phenomenologists, Edmund Husserl and Maurice Merleau-Ponty. Both of them argue that the body is the body is the center, the zero-point, of orientation. The body is the center of possible actions, and from it consciousness structures the world and how we perceive it and act in it.

Husserl makes the world a correlate of consciousness, but he aligns this world always with an actual consciousness, that is, an embodied consciousness, a consciousness in its world. The term he uses for this bodily experience is the German word *Leib*, which means a living, perceiving, active body. A corpse is not a *Leib*; it does not have a world. It is the *Leib* that serves as the zero-point of orientation. In some ways, *Leib* can be said to exist outside of the space that it enables—this means that the living-body formats the constitution of space: its layout, its foreground, and its background. Space appears as an arena of possible actions, revealed through the potentialities of the body.

Every kind of consciousness—perception-consciousness, phantasy-consciousness, memory-consciousness, and others— relates back to the body. The body still serves as the zero-point of orientation. At the highest level of abstraction and ideation, transcendental consciousness (the formatting consciousness that formats the world) has its body, a transcendental body but a living body, a *Leib*, nonetheless. This is how we can understand the structure of Ender's experience before the Battle Room, in the Battle Room, and beyond. His world is constructed by a consciousness that has at its center a body, whose perceptions enable possibilities.

Merleau-Ponty, inspired by Husserl's reflections on the body, took the analysis a bit further. It is the living-body, as the zero-point of orientation, that can act. The perceptions of the living-body enable the possibilities of action. We are in the world to accomplish tasks, goals, and games, but perception enables all these possibilities. Merleau-Ponty also says that our bodies, our perceptions, and hence our possibilities, are not divorced from our histories. Our bodies are *living* bodies, unfolding in their own histories.

Our bodies exist in time as well as in space. In short, we form habits. Our habits, phenomenologically understood, are not mere mental dispositions, but they constitute the body-consciousness's field of possibilities. We can see these ideas in play in Ender's experience of the Battle Room.

The Creative Answer

The scenes from *Ender's Game* reveal that perception and orientation in the world are habits that make certain things possible and others impossible. One of the elements of Ender's genius is the creative and corporeal re-imagining of that world, for example, Graff climbing down the ceiling. It also reveals that our manner of perceiving the world is neither strictly empirical (due to the senses) nor intellectual (due to consciousness); we perceive from a nexus of conscious intention and sensuous experience.

Our bodies help create the world around us. Perhaps this is one of the reasons why the Formics found it so difficult to communicate with us: the body-consciousness of the two species was so drastically different; we and the Buggers lived in different worlds because of our different bodies.

The Formics do not merely have a hive mind, but they have a hive body, as the queen directs the drones like fingers and toes. The consciousness that we as human beings consist of is fundamentally in the world in a different way—our bodies are singular, unitary, isolated moments. Perhaps, it was also Ender's flexible body-consciousness that permitted the link between the Formics and Ender, upon which Jane (another type of body) is born, as we learn in *Speaker for the Dead*.

Ender's Game inspires us again, as it reminds us to keep a flexible body and mind. It invites us to dream new worlds and to change this one. It may be hard to break one habit, to exchange one set of possibilities for another one, but the creative answer is out there: the enemy's gate is down.

Who
Is Ender?

09
Ender-Shiva, Lord of the Dance

JOSHUA HALL

> Soon enough Ender Wiggin will . . . dance the graceful ghost dance through the stars . . .
>
> —Admiral Chamrajnagar, *Ender's Game*

Believe it or not, it's no exaggeration to say that *Ender's Game* has been the most transformative book of my life. In fact, when I first read it, at the age of fifteen, it almost single-handedly initiated a crisis of faith in me that ended up lasting for eight long years.

The reason that *Ender's Game* was able to do this is that it's full of important philosophical ideas (a fact attested to by the very existence of this volume and its many chapters). It should come as no surprise to fellow science-fiction fans—and fans of *Ender's Game* in particular—that science fiction is full to bursting with philosophical ideas. But the skeptical reader need not fear; in this case, at least, you don't have to take my word for it. Orson Scott Card's 1991 edition of *Ender's Game* mentions his Master's degree in literature, and that all "the layers of meaning are there to be decoded, if you like to play the game of literary criticism."

So if you think you might have found a hidden layer of meaning in *Ender's Game*, it's a lot less likely that you're just crazy, and a lot more likely that there really is some hidden meaning there—and maybe even one that Card himself consciously put there to be found! One such hidden layer, intentional or not, is the series of unexpected connections with the Hindu tradition.

An Ancient Hindu "Battle Room"

What we call "Hinduism" is widely considered one of the most important philosophical and religious traditions of Asia, and is the original source of such important ideas as *karma* and *reincarnation*. Its most famous scripture, called *The Bhagavad Gita* (or just the *Gita*), is an excerpt from one of Hinduism's two central epic poems. Literally translated from Sanskrit into English as the "Song of God," the *Gita* can be usefully understood as a kind of Hindu New Testament, since it comments on and updates what could be thought of as the Hindu Old Testament, a group of sacred theoretical and practical writings known as the *Vedas*.

The setting for the *Gita* is a war for succession between two sets of cousins, the righteous Pandavas and the treacherous Kauravas. And the central conflict is that the hero, Arjuna, filled with doubt about engaging in this familial civil war, seeks out the (ultimately shocking) advice of his personal chariot-driver Krishna, who turns out to be a divine incarnation of the god Vishnu. The gist of Krishna's divine advice is that every person on Earth possesses an immortal soul, has lived an almost infinite number of past lives, will live an almost infinite number of future lives, and must therefore merely carry out their sacred duty without regard for causing or experiencing death.

In Arjuna's case, since he belongs to the warrior caste, this sacred duty amounts to waging a just war against his family, realizing that killing them really only amounts to bringing about their next reincarnations (as opposed to destroying them forever). In other words, the apparent life-and-death battle that is about to begin at the end of the *Gita* is actually better understood as a kind of *Ender's Game*–style battle room, because the whole thing is ultimately a staged exercise, used for (spiritual) training, from which the soldiers' souls emerge unscathed. The similarities between *Ender's Game* and Hinduism in the *Gita* don't end there, however.

The Divine Wiggins Trinity

The three primary gods of the Hindu pantheon—Brahman, the creator-ruler, Vishnu, the savior, and Shiva, the destroyer and restorer—have a surprising amount in common with the three Wiggins siblings in *Ender's Game*. Although the issue of gods in Hinduism is quite complicated, the most important thing to note here is that, in one way, every sentient being together makes up both God and the cosmos—but we humans don't yet know that we're God (at least not for as long as we're living uneducated earthly lives).

With the help of the sacred teachings of Hinduism, however, we slowly begin to figure it out. When this happens, at the moment of death, we become free from the cycle of births, deaths, and rebirths (called *samsara*), and thus reunite (or re-identify) with God (an experience called *moksha*). Now, whenever each soul (or *atman*) achieves liberation in this way, the cosmos literally gets just a little bit smaller. Eventually, every single *atman* eventually achieves this realization and freedom, at which point the entire cosmos winks out of existence, leaving only God behind—alone, and perfectly conscious of himself. But things don't end there, with the destruction of the world.

Every time the world ends—because this entire meta-cycle (or *kalpa*), according to Hinduism, has happened, and will happen, an infinite number of times—God, as it were, eventually begins to fall back asleep, to dream the dream that we call the world. Essentially, this means that God again splits himself into the seemingly-separate souls, us, who find ourselves bound all over again in the cycle of reincarnation, in Shiva's dance of re-creation.

In *Ender's Game*, similarly, the three siblings, Peter, Valentine, and Ender Wiggin, are obviously the three most important characters, and one can already see a connection between them and the three central Hindu gods in the Wiggins' names. First, "Peter" means "rock," which is connected to the fact that Jesus allegedly chose Peter to be the first Pope (that is, the rock-like foundation of the Catholic Church). And by the end of the novel Peter Wiggin has become the "Hegemon," or supreme ruler, of Earth. Second, the most famous historical figure named "Valentine" is of course the saint who inspired Valentine's Day, an important symbol of love in Western culture. And Valentine Wiggin is the most likable and loving of the three siblings, doing her utmost throughout the novel to save both Ender and Peter. And third (pun intended), "Ender," the nickname that Andrew Wiggin adopts, could be understood as a synonym for "finisher." And Ender eventually finishes off both the war and (almost) the entire "Bugger" species.

Good Old Videogame-Style Detachment

A second important similarity between *Ender's Game* and Hinduism in the *Gita* is that ethically right action according to both of them involves nothing more than the detached fulfillment of one's duty. In the Sanskrit language of the *Gita*, the phrase for such detached action is *karma yoga*, which one translator, Barbara Stoler-Miller, translates as "disciplined action." Disciplined action, she explains, is any action performed, not impulsively or with calculating self-interest, but rather as a form of worshipful service to God. In fact, detached action is so important that the *Gita* even attributes it to God himself.

In *Ender's Game*, similarly, what allows Ender to be so successful in the near-genocide is that he coldly and cerebrally carries out the battle "simulation" as ordered by his superiors. It is also crucial in *Ender's Game*, as in the *Gita*, that this detached attitude not be natural, nor pursued and enjoyed for its own sake or its consequences, because the result of this is, in *Ender's Game*, Peter's sociopathic viciousness, and, in the *Gita*, the demonic type of human being.

The World-Soul's Hive-Mind

The last important similarity I'll discuss between *Ender's Game* and Hinduism in the *Gita* involves the aliens' "hive mind" and the Hindu concept of the "world soul." The Hindu concept flows naturally from the idea of pantheism, because if God is (in some sense) everything, or at least every*one*, then ultimately all thinking is really just God's own thinking—even though that thinking is scattered across billions of different human brains. Therefore, each of us is actually plugged into one giant divine mind, even though we don't experience things that way.

In the thirteenth chapter of the *Gita*, Krishna explains this idea with the analogy of a military general coming to know a field of battle. God, he explains, is the "field-knower in all fields," experiencing the world from the perspective of each human being, and knowing the world through the sum total of each human being's seemingly-separate knowledge.[1]

---

[1] *The Bhagavad-Gita: The Song of God* (Signet, 2002), p. 100.

So What?

Even if I'm right that there are meaningful similarities between *Ender's Game* and Hinduism in the *Gita*, why is it worth thinking about these similarities, much less reading about them?

One interesting aspect of these connections is their function as a subtle form of foreshadowing. If you know anything about Hinduism before you read *Ender's Game* for the first time, then you might know that parts of Hinduism are deeply counterintuitive and troubling to our commonsense way of looking at the world. And if you were to pick up on these connections that I have suggested, you might even guess that, although Ender is the protagonist of the novel, he may not turn out to be a perfect hero. Remember, as one example of this foreshadowing, that the Hindu god to which Ender is connected is the same one that callously destroys the entire cosmos, and on a regular basis!

Even more fascinating, though, is that this connection frames *Ender's Game* as in part a criticism of Hinduism and, by extension, Western stereotypes of Asian politics and political philosophy. To see this, all we'll need to do is to quickly go back over each of the three important similarities from before—but this time, with an eye to the critical dimension hidden in each of those similarities.

Pathological Deities

It's clear as early as *Ender's Game*'s first chapter that Ender comes from a screwed-up family. First, there is his older brother Peter's abusive behavior toward Valentine and himself. Peter, at first among his siblings, and then later in his political activities, is a true tyrant. And in light of the connection I have shown between Peter and Brahman, one result of this connection seems to be that there is something similarly tyrannical about this Hindu supreme God. For one thing, Brahman, at least in some respects, literally incorporates the entire world into himself, and with apparent disregard for the tremendous suffering of those he rules. Similarly, Peter compares himself, in Chapter 2, to a puppeteer, and Card also describes Peter, in Chapter 9, as perfectly controlled and perfectly self-interested.

Second on the "screwed-up" charts, Valentine, although a loving and supportive sister, is ultimately only able to slightly lessen the horror of Peter's behavior, and even ends up getting caught up in—and becoming partially responsible for—some of the worst political things that Peter does. In fact, Card describes Valentine, in chapter nine, as not only being a master manipulator, but also as someone who enjoys being manipulative.

As a result of this connection, then, the salvation offered by her Hindu counterpart, Vishnu (aka Krishna), would ultimately be empty, a merely apparent delivery from one type of bondage (to Peter-Brahman) to another. In other words, just like Vishnu's salvation still takes place with Brahman understood as the entirety of the cosmos, so Valentine's attempts at saving Ender and the world from Peter arguably fail to free anyone from the clutches of Peter as Earth's Hegemon.

And finally, in regard to screwed-up-ness, in Chapter 10 Ender self-consciously repeats, on other kids (such as Bean) in the military school, the exact same manipulations of which he has been the victim. Similarly, in the final chapter, Card describes Ender as being most exhilarated by the possibility that the battle "simulator" possesses for control. But what's even worse is that Ender even finds himself wondering, in chapter eleven, whether his own manipulations are even managing to undermine the manipulations of those above him. One result of this connection, then, would be that whenever Shiva dances a new cosmos into existence, his dance is always ultimately choreographed by Brahman, and all for the sake of Brahman's hegemonic control—which, as it turns out, is exactly what Hinduism tells us is the case!

Unethical Indifference

That Ender pursues an ethics of detachment becomes clearer and clearer as *Ender's Game* progresses, as when, for example, in the seventh chapter, Card describes Ender's anger as "cold, and therefore useful." More disturbingly, near the end of *Ender's Game*, Ender goes forward with what he believes to be his final battle simulation even though he believes his intended course of action will disqualify him from becoming supreme commander—and thereby leaving the human species without its only hope. At this point, I would argue, the game has truly become Ender's entire world.

But the most obvious objection to Ender's ethical attitude of detachment is his near-xenocide of the alien species. His method there, as throughout *Ender's Game*, is to accept the inevitability of the game, and then play it as well as he can—his only passion being breaking as many rules and undermining as many of the gamers' plans as possible. You can already see this in the first chapter, where Ender consciously violates the etiquette of school-fighting by kicking the bully when the bully's down (which is, as it turns out, exactly what the officers watching him wanted him to do, namely, to be ruthless in pursuing his self-interested objective).

The deepest problem with Ender's method, though—and this is certainly true in the real world—is that the "powers that be" are perfectly comfortable with their pawn trying to fight them. In fact, having the energy to fight them is actually required to be a good pawn in the first place. Since Hinduism, along with many other aspects of classical Asian thought, affirms this same ethics of detachment, the implication seems to be that it (and they) too can have potentially disastrous political results.

Yellow Bugger Hordes

The final implied criticism of Hinduism and Asian political philosophy that I will discuss is the one that flows from the similarities between the aliens' "hive mind" and the concept of a "world-soul" in Hinduism. From the very beginning of *Ender's Game*, Ender shows a troubling openness to such group-think, as Card describes him as being "too willing to submerge his will in that of another, unless that other is an enemy."

As Ender matures in the school, however, he becomes more and more committed instead to a kind of defiant individualism, with his primary innovation as a commander being his decision to break his team down into smaller, self-directed groups. But this individualism remains deeply indebted to the very communism it opposes. For one thing, Card describes Ender's fleet, because of their formations and movements, as resembling an alien fleet. And for another, Ender's primary weapon in the war against the aliens, "Dr. Device," like all of the cutting-edge human technology of the time, was originally ripped off from the aliens' own technology.

Given this communistic aspect of the alien species, it is not surprising that the main earthbound enemy in *Ender's Game*, originally published during the height of the Cold War in 1977, is the communist USSR. Additionally, one of the most disturbing things about the aliens to the humans in *Ender's Game* is the queen-worker structure of their society, and the concept of "worker" has always been of key importance in communism. Finally on this point, the most menacing thing of all about the aliens is that they appear as a homogenous horde, with a hive-mind like those found in ants and bees, and this is the same racist stereotype that continues to influence many Westerners' perception of Asian peoples, especially the racial group that makes up the communist nation of China. In this last respect, it seems likely that Card is echoing—although in a subtle, and perhaps also critical way—Robert A. Heinlein's famous novel *Starship Troopers*, whose "Bug" species is more explicitly linked to Communism and China.

A Political Warning

The way that the humans in *Ender's Game* deal with the aliens after the aliens' near-xenocide is troubling in several specific ways. First, Ender only leaves Earth to learn more about the aliens, like a Eurocentric anthropologist preparing for a dig among "the natives" (as discussed in another chapter of this book). Second, Card puts an implied justification of the near-xenocide in the mouth of the queen herself—namely that, since the aliens were the initial aggressors against the humans (based on an underestimation of humans' capacities), the queen feels no resentment at the attempted xenocide.

This sounds alarmingly similar to the kind of stories that people in the Western world have historically used to justify European imperialism and colonialism in Africa, Asia, and the Americas. In other words, the only thing that appears to lessen Ender's crime in *Ender's Game*, and the only thing that prevents Ender from being presented as a complete monster, is that the beings he destroyed are presented as nothing more than slaves bound to their hive-mind. Unfortunately, finally, this is something which many people in our world still attribute to Asian nations today. And it is past time that we— inspired by *Ender's Game*—overcame this prejudice.

Card's own perspective in *Ender's Game* on the Asian tradition of Hinduism seems decidedly ambivalent. This is clearest in the person of Ender himself. As the protagonist (and perhaps hero?) of the novel, Ender is strikingly similar to the Hindu god Shiva—often known as "Lord of the Dance"—who is both the great destroyer and the great restorer of the cosmos. And although *Ender's Game* as a novel ends with an emphasis on the former, destructive, aspect, it is only the first of (at present count) twelve novels, in the next several of which it is the restorative aspect of Shiva that predominates.

So *Ender's Game* constitutes just the first few steps of Ender's Shiva dance, and therefore, in the novel as well as our own world, hope still springs eternal.

10
How Queer Is Ender?

Nicolas Michaud and Jessica Watkins

"**F**uror Over Orson Scott Card's Anti-gay Views Drives 'Superman' Illustrator to Leave Comic," reads a recent headline on *Entertainment Weekly*'s website.

Artist Chris Sprouse stepped down as the illustrator working with Card. The author of *Ender's Game* is not shy about his anti-gay-marriage stance, and because of that many people protest his work. Card, who serves on the board of the National Organization of Marriage (a group that works to advocate against gay marriage) does not just believe gay marriage is wrong, but that homosexuality itself is an immoral danger to society and the soul.

As virulent as Card's anti-homosexuality stance is, it seems there's a good chance that we can find anti-gay messages in *Ender's Game*! It's not a stretch, as the main bad guys are the "Buggers," which is a term often used for gay men. But we think there may be more beneath the surface of the story. Interestingly, we've found that *Ender's Game* may actually be very sympathetic to forbidden male love . . .

There are many who argue that Orson Scott Card is in fact homophobic, and whether he is or not, we can say that he certainly is a proponent of heteronormativity—the idea and tendency towards treating heterosexuality as normal and homosexuality as odd, wrong, or queer. In Kate Bonin's "Gay Sex and Death in the Science Fiction of Orson Scott Card," Card is quoted as having said: "Gay rights is a collective delusion that's being attempted."

It's *queerness* that is our focus here, because calling someone "queer" has its roots in calling someone "weird," making him or her an outsider or "Other." The term has been used derogatorily against gays, but recently over the last couple of decades the term is now also used to describe a philosophical movement called "Queer Theory." And it helps us understand how books like *Ender's Game* create gender, sexual, and identity categories *that don't exist biologically.* In fact, if the queer theorists are right, then it seems as a society *we* create our own "Buggers"—scapegoats; people we can treat like insects—to help us establish our place on the "inside," solidifying our traditions, roles, and hierarchies.

Identifying the Enemy

Imagine that a father and son are on a ship that is attacked by a horde of Buggers. Both men are horribly injured. Luckily, Ender is not far from the scene and, in another bout of heroic violence, makes quick work of the Buggers and rescues the hapless victims. Finally, after a tragically long time, Ender gets them to a hospital. They are both rolled into the emergency room at once. The doctor walks into the room, looks down, and pronounces the father dead. Looking at the boy, however, the doctor says, "I cannot operate on him; he's my son."

How is this possible? . . . Think on it for a moment.

Do you find the answer comes to you easily? The doctor is the boy's mother. Most people struggle with the answer. We've heard many interesting answers ranging from, "Was the doctor Jesus?" to "Was the doctor the father's clone?" But by far the rarest answer is, "The doctor is the boy's mom." Why? Well, the answer is one that has motivated a great deal of feminist and queer theoretical thought. Queer theory actually has its beginnings in feminism—not just the political feminism that tells us that women are equal to men, but in the feminist insight that our society, language, and norms all work to repress women. That's why the doctor riddle is one many people find impossible to solve.

Haven't you ever noticed that, when it comes to many professions, the *respected* ones are imagined as male? What do you imagine when you imagine a doctor? How about a *nurse?* Who do we think of when we think of a pilot? How about a *flight attendant*? Professor? *Teacher*? Notice that over and over again in the highest level professions we imagine men, but the lowly ones . . . women. What about a Major, or Admiral? When you think of the military, does a woman come to mind in *any* rank? We bet that we could have changed our riddle some so that its focus was an Admiral, rather than a doctor, and it would have the same result. . . .

Almost all of the terms we use to describe something positive have a masculine connotation and all of the weak and negative terms have a feminine connotation. "He runs like a girl," and "He throws like a girl," are examples of the fact that it's part of our linguistic and social psychology to believe women are inferior. And our language helps maintain that Otherness. Our female author has even been told (and not just by men), "Don't be such a girl"—which is not just impossible but really, *really* offensive—and it is not accidental that there is no feminine equivalent of "manning up" to something. So the short story is that our society has a deep disrespect for women, and it isn't their intellectual or physical inferiority that results in only *one* girl attending Battle School, but the fact that society purposefully keeps them down.

This Othering has led many thinkers to consider the ways we identify a person or a group of persons as others. Gay men, for example, are treated very much as Others in our society. Consider how often gay men, especially, are in danger of violence and abuse. Generally, we applaud masculinity as the best characteristic a person can have. Much in the way that Rose the Nose (commander of Rat Army) waggles a massive virtual penis in front of the boys, our society seems to say, "Be in awe of this, but don't like it! If you do, then you are *queer.*" What we begin to realize is that if we have a deep disrespect for women in our society—as evidenced by our language—then part of the reason we have such deep disrespect of homosexuality, especially on the part of men, is *because they are "choosing" to be feminine.* In other words, we treat them as people who must *want* to be abused because they could be on the "inside"—men who are proud of their masculinity—but instead choose to be outsiders. They disgrace the awesomeness of being a man by choosing to indulge in the lesser, the Other, the feminine.

Many of our rules and beliefs about homosexuality have their start in rules warning men that it is bad to be feminine.

It is not uncommon for ancient texts to admonish men for reducing themselves to "womanliness" while praising the virtues of being a man. We often read those texts as making statements about homosexuality, but the idea "homosexuality" is new, while hatred for the feminine is very old. In fact, one verse from the Bible's book of Leviticus (18:22 "Do not lie with a man as one lies with a woman; that is detestable") is often used by opponents of gay marriage to indicate that homosexuality is sinful, but, historically, it is more likely a condemnation of men willingly taking on a subservient—*women's*—role.

When we consider the historical context, we realize that ancient cultures differentiated between the "right" way for a man to have sex with a man and the "right" way for him to have sex with a woman. Sex between two men was common and respected in ancient Greece, but this sex usually occurred while both men were standing, facing one another *as equals*. This differed greatly from the subservient, bent-over position women (who could not be citizens) were expected to take during sex. So, the admonition is against men who willingly play the *role* of the lesser (the woman), rather than against sharing their bodies or their love with other men.[1]

Being a Bugger

What is important to realize, from a queer theory perspective, is that *man* and *woman*, and *heterosexual* and *homosexual* are not clear biological categories. We are of course taught that boys have penises and girls don't. (In other words, the boys have something special that the Other, the girls, lack.) We're also taught that there is a clear line between straight and gay. This is especially true for men. We have some acceptance for bisexual women, but any man who claims attraction to men is immediately, and permanently, placed in the category, "gay."

Firstly, let's look at why queer theorists think those distinctions make no sense. Well, obviously there are more "sexes" than male and female. There are, of course, hermaphrodites, for instance. And do you really want to say "having a penis" or "having testicles" makes someone a man? Are all men who have

---

[1] Richard Sennett, *Flesh and Stone: The Body and the City in Western Civilization* (Norton, 1994), p. 41.

had their penises or testicles removed no longer men, even if it was in some sort of military accident? What about men who have been castrated due to cancer or illness?

We might argue what makes male-female is having either XY or XX chromosomes. But there are people who have XXY or XXX chromosomes. There are even cases in which someone *has a penis* and looks like what most of us would consider a "man" but has *no Y chromosome!* So how the heck are we supposed to divide the sexes into just two when there are so many different phenotypes (people who have one penis, a vagina, or two penises, or a penis and a vagina and so on) or different genotypes (people who have XX, or XY, or XXX, or XXY, or XYY)!?

Secondly, can we really be sure that there are just "straight" and "gay"? Sure, there are bisexuals, but even the whole idea that there are "homosexuals" is a relatively new one. During ancient times, there was no real idea of homosexuality. People were attracted to different people. It was not unusual for a man to engage in a same-sex relationship in his youth and then go on to marry a woman and have children later on. Even during the middle ages there was no clear concept of sexuality as we view it now. The distinction was mostly between "sin" and "not sin." Sodomy (also, interestingly, called *buggery*) was pretty much any sexual action that was sinful, which was not specific to homosexual relationships.

Although laws against sodomy (those sexual practices deemed to be deviant, often including sex between two men) became common by the middle ages, laws against *being* gay really don't become common practice until the nineteenth century, as is the case with the Labouchere Amendment of 1885, which made it possible to prosecute a man for homosexuality even if sodomy could not be proven by making a vaguely defined idea of "gross indecency" illegal. As a result, the amendment made it, by default, grossly indecent to be homosexual, regardless of sodomy. Famously, this act was used to prosecute Oscar Wilde (author of *A Picture of Dorian Gray* and *The Importance of Being Earnest* whose "love that dare not speak its name" can be found in many theorists' interpretations of *A Picture of Dorian Gray*).

If queer theorists and current scientific theories are correct, we all exist not as heterosexual or homosexual, but on a *spectrum* from preferring same-sex sexuality to opposite-sex sexuality.

(Queer theorists would even complain about categorizing people as being "same" sex or "opposite" sex, but for the sake of concise communication, we'll stick with those terms). Some people are biologically predisposed to being interested in the same sex and some the opposite sex, but there would also be many people in between—not just bisexual people, but people who *mostly* prefer men or *mostly* prefer women. In our society, we're terrified to think that many of us are born somewhere on the middle of this spectrum, because we've been taught to hate and fear same-sex relationships, so we cannot even *think* about it!

Books like *Ender's Game* are part of what defines our gender roles for us. Philosophers like Eve Kosofsky Sedgwick help us understand how literature and language help define and express gender and sexual roles. We read *Ender's Game* and learn that most women don't belong in Battle School. They should be empathetic, like Valentine and to a lesser degree like Petra, and love us and support us in our violent (even genocidal) rages. And we learn that even if we like to look at male bodies, that we gotta be strong, deal with it, and be men! Kate Bonin, in her essay "Gay Sex and Death in the Science Fiction of Orson Scott Card," makes it clear that such self-control is essential: "Though gay sex is figured as intensely appealing, it is a resolutely forbidden fruit. Characters who 'give in' to homosexual impulses are punished."[2] *Ender's Game* teaches us to suppress our own bisexual or homosexual feelings and biology.

How Gay Is Ender?

Sedgwick points out in her book *Between Men* how almost impossible it is for men to have any kind of bonding with, or desire for bonding with, other men in our society. We have very little allowance for any kind of male relationship that doesn't involve a woman. She describes the "homo*social*" desire as meaning the desire for men to have relationships, of any kind, with other men. And a homosocial environment is one that is exclusively or largely exclusive to males (and often hostile to homosexuality). With only one exception in the form of Petra, the entire Battle School experience is homosocial. Boys live together, shower

---

[2] Kate Bonin, "Gay Sex and Death in the Science Fiction of Orson Scott Card," *New York Review of Science Fiction* 15:4 (2002), p. 21.

together, sleep together, and plan and execute battles together.

Consider the Battle School. Analyzing it through language, subtext, and imagery, we see a great deal of homosocial, as well as potentially homosexual, implications. James Campbell, in his article "Kill the Bugger: *Ender's Game* and the Question of Heteronormativity," comments thus on the boys' characters and stations:

> They are libidinal animals in a highly structured homosocial environ-
> ment. Reading the novel for sexuality, then, is not merely a matter of
> discovering (or imposing) some wink-wink-nudge-nudge allegory on
> the text, but rather eliciting the patterns of desire that emanate from
> its characters as sexual agents. (*Science Fiction Studies* 36:3, 2009,
> p. 494)

Remember Rose the Nose's first interaction with Ender? On Rose's lap sits his computer display of a larger-than-life phallus, while he has forbidden Ender the use of his computer outright. Sure, this may be a simple childish tease, but it is also a sexualized symbolic display of dominance.

The power struggles between the boys often take on sexual meaning, imagery, and language. Computer desks again feature in a later power struggle when Ender learns how to hack the computer of Bernard, another boy who threatened Ender, to send everyone messages saying, "COVER YOUR BUTT. BERNARD IS WATCHING" and later, after Bernard's cronies attack Ender, "I LOVE YOUR BUTT. LET ME KISS IT." These accusations of homosexual attraction embarrass and degrade Bernard. Even the official battles themselves—the primary focus of education at the Battle School—are homosexual in nature: they are battles between male participants, in which one side "wins" by penetrating the corridor protected by the other team.

Sedgwick would likely point out how very sexual the imagery is here and notice that it is males who are engaging in that sexuality with each other. Someone might argue that these battles are not truly homosexual because the thing the boys are competing to penetrate is the entrance to a corridor, and so it seems they are fighting over a *feminine* symbol rather than a masculine one. At best, though, this means the battle fought by all male participants is a macho war over who gets to possess a woman's body!

Male-male attraction is as significant a theme as male-male violence in the book. When Ender meets his first commander, he was overwhelmed by his appearance: "A boy stood there, tall and slender, with beautiful black eyes and slender hips that hinted at refinement. I would follow such beauty anywhere, said something inside Ender." There is no way to describe this passage without having to account for an *attraction*. Something in Ender wants to follow Bonzo. Card makes no attempt to shelter us from males finding other males beautiful.

It doesn't take long, however, for violence to emerge out of that homosocial relationship. Bonzo threatens that he will "have" Ender's "ass someday." Later, Bonzo and several friends approach Ender to attack him in the shower. The pages of descriptions of the scene paint a picture that is more than vaguely homoerotic: Bonzo strips naked to fight naked one-on-one with Ender in a hot, steamy, slippery battle that is finalized when Ender connects "hard and sure" with Bonzo's groin. Sedgwick would see here the fact that in *Ender's Game*, homoerotic interactions almost always result in punishment. These sexual encounters—or even the suggestion of such—are "punished" by demoting, degrading, or killing the transgressors.

Not all homoamorous (love or affection between same-sex persons) relationships in the book are characterized by violence in *Ender's Game*. Many are characterized by forbiddenness, regret, or dissatisfaction. Alai, Ender's first friend at Battle School, sends him in to his first battle with a kiss, which Ender guessed was "somehow forbidden." The kiss was accompanied by the word "Salaam," which is Arabic for peace and which is commonly used with brief kisses between men sharing the greeting, so the kiss may have meant nothing sexual at all. It is interesting, then, how Western readers— indeed, perhaps even our Western characters, like Ender himself—may immediately assume that it does mean something sexual! In fact, among queer theorists, there is some controversy over whether queer theory itself assumes a common Western, white cultural backdrop. Either way, what we do see is affection between men that is *forbidden*—they want to be close—emotionally or physically—but *can't*!

In what seems like it must be a purposeful move, Card creates a Greek-style mentorship between Ender and Mazer Rackham, Earth's hero of the previous Bugger war. Greek mentorships usually involved an older man and a young man who engaged in a learning relationship that often also involved sexuality. For his training, Ender and Mazer *share a bedroom* while they work together to learn to think the way the Buggers think. Keep in mind that "Bugger" has been used, for a long time, as derogatory slang for a man who engages in sexual deviance. And this is on the asteroid *Eros*, named for the Greek god of love! *A man and a boy are sharing a bedroom on Eros so they can learn how to think like Buggers.* We don't have to read deeply into this to see that something very homosocial, if not homosexual, is happening.

When Ender gets transferred from the Battle School, his close friendship with Bean—a promising child who serves as one of Ender's toon leaders—is interrupted, and readers are provided a window to Bean's secret heart, which is tender and full of a possibly forbidden love for Ender. Because Ender's news was delivered just before lights out, Bean must undress in the dark and crawl into bed. He begins to sob, then turns to self-inflicted pain to control his agony. Bean first "tried to put a name on the feeling that put a lump in his throat and made him sob silently," for "once he named the feeling, he could control it." We are left with the question, 'What is the feeling?' because Bean falls asleep before our narrator gives us a clue.

In these relationships, it seems as if Card paints a beautiful and tragic tale of lust and love between men. Card details those relationships according to a clear pattern: male acknowledgement of, and even love of, male beauty is acceptable—though never rewarded—as long as males do not take the step toward sexualizing that beauty. When they do, they are punished by humiliation, degradation, violence, and even death.

Tainted Love

So. *Ender's Game* is rife with male sexuality, and it normalizes for us the idea that men are beautiful and that other men may love them from a distance, but any notion or expression of sexuality toward them should not exist. We end up back were we started. What is treated with the deepest loathing? Not the male body or deep (even forbidden) love between men. What seems to be truly judged and warned against is the feminization of any of these males; the sexual act in which one male supposedly feminizes himself by engaging with another sexually or by expressing his love outwardly (unlike Bean, who, in manly fashion, stifles and hides his love of Ender).

What if it is actually the feminine that *Ender's Game* is the most "phobic" about? There certainly is evidence in *Ender's Game* that women are not thought of particularly highly. We have only two developed female characters—a soldier in the Battle School, and a sister who later philosophizes (in *Children of the Mind*) that women are simple creatures who cannot really love men fully.

So from a queer theoretical perspective, *Ender's Game* may not suffer from a violent fear of male bodies or male love, but instead from a fear of those things which we deem to be female. Perhaps *Ender's Game*, and the Enderverse in general, aren't so much homophobic as they are sexist . . . expressing the yearning and suffering of a deep unrequited love between men, which can never really be eased by the inferior love of women.

11
Is Ender a Mormon?

JAMES HOLT

Well, no not really; unless you count the fact that his mother was brought up a Mormon. However, the Enderverse might be. Orson Scott Card *is* a Mormon (or to use the full title, a member of the Church of Jesus Christ of Latter-day Saints) and as such it may be unsurprising to find Mormon beliefs and values suffusing many aspects of the Ender Saga.

As all literature is grounded in the experiences and beliefs of the author, storytelling sometimes lays bare the soul to the whole world. Though Card suggests otherwise where his religion is concerned: "Any analogies to Mormon ideas in the Ender books are entirely unconscious and unintended. When I do such things deliberately—as a sort of wink to those who get the joke—it's very obvious and needs no confirmation from me."[1]

I think Card is being a bit naive here, especially as, when reading his fiction, Michael Collings suggests that "Card takes his place beside C.S. Lewis, who is one of the rare writers in Science Fiction and Fantasy who used the genre to give shape to his deepest religious beliefs."[2] I'm not sure that Mormon beliefs are as evident as Collings suggests, but they are certainly there. I have spent long and interminable conversations arguing about religious beliefs in the writings of J.R.R. Tolkien; I cannot take myself out of the reading, and whether Tolkien

---

[1] "OSC Answers Questions," *Hatrack River* (29th January 2003), www.hatrack.com/research/questions/q0110.shtml.

[2] *In the Image of God: Theme, Characterization, and Landscape in the Fiction of Orson Scott Card* (Greenwood, 1990).

meant what many people see can never be proven. However, when I read the Ender Saga I find myself in a much better position. As a Latter-day Saint myself, when I read something that seems to set my Mormondar off, I am not just encountering what I think might have been Card's conscious or subconscious telling, I am experiencing a religious belief that I hold dear.

In this way, two ways of reading *Ender's Game* collide. First, trying to explore Card's motivations and meaning, and second, what Card himself has called, an "epick" approach to criticism where a person or group finds relevance for themselves in a particular story.[3] This approach involves author and reader engagement with the text. I do have to caution, however, that the themes I see in the Ender Saga may not be what Card intended, nor may they be what other Mormons see.

Ender as the Messiah

I'm not convinced by the argument that Ender is a Christ figure; he is however the hero of the story. Actually he's one of my heroes, but part of my attraction to him is his vulnerability and his unChristlike imperfection. He begins *Ender's Game* with very different relationships; with Valentine, with Peter, and with the bullies at school; his inability to get on with some people is much more human than the perfect Christ of Mormonism. In some ways Christ seems to be an ideal that people are striving towards, whereas Ender is a possibility that is in all of us. Each of us has people we love, people we dislike; but we also have the potential within us (or hope we do) to do heroic things that are asked of us.

Within Mormonism there are numerous examples of imperfect "types" of Christ—people who exemplify elements of Christ's character and actions but are nonetheless only human and imperfect—and it's possible that Ender could be considered one of them.

The Chosen One

In the opening lines of *Ender's Game*, this shadow is immediately evident to me as a Mormon: "I've watched through his

---

[3] "Fantasy and the Believing Reader, Science Fiction Review" *Hatrack River* (Fall 1982), www.hatrack.com/osc/articles/fall82.shtml.

eyes, I've listened through his ears, and I tell you he's the one." This conjures up images of what Mormon's describe as the "Grand Council in Heaven" where Christ is identified as the one; the only begotten of God who will perform a mission to save humanity from physical and spiritual death. In distinction to Ender, however, Christ was the only possibility, there was no Bean waiting in the wings to take over should Christ fail (see *Ender's Shadow*).

The Mental and Physical Sacrifice

If this was the only parallel between Christ and Ender we might be justified in saying the link is tenuous at best. However, there are other elements that make the parallel obvious. In the original novella, the Christlike nature of Ender's mission is laid out in unequivocal terms:

> "At least we know that Ender is making it possible for others of his age to be playing in the park."
>
> "And Jesus died to save all men, of course." Graff sat up and looked at Anderson almost sadly. "But we're the ones," Graff said, "We're the ones who are driving in the nails."[4]

Although this passage was removed from the novel, this theme is particularly evident in Ender's struggle before the final battle. Combined with his physical and mental exhaustion, his self-doubt and dreams and visions we read:

> Late one night he woke up in pain. There was blood on his pillow, the taste of blood in his mouth. His fingers were throbbing. He saw that in his sleep he had been gnawing on his own fist. The blood was still flowing smoothly.

The Gospels tell of Christ's experience of Gethsemane as a prelude to his death and atonement on the cross. However, within Mormonism, Gethsemane takes on an added importance as more than just a preparation; it is a part of the sacrifice that Christ goes through. In Mormon scripture Christ describes the agony he endured here:

---

[4] "Ender's Game," in *First Meetings in Ender's Universe* (Tor, 2004), p. 112.

> For behold, I, God, have suffered these things for all, that they might
> not suffer if they would repent; . . . Which suffering caused myself,
> even God, the greatest of all, to tremble because of pain, and to bleed
> at every pore, and to suffer both body and spirit—and would that I
> might not drink the bitter cup, and shrink.[5]

In this passage we see the theme from the novella that Ender
and Christ sacrificed of themselves for the freedom of others,
and that both shrank from the enormity of the task demanded
of them. The blood of Christ is an incredibly important symbol
within Mormonism as it is through the blood that humanity is
cleansed. The employment of blood as an element in Ender's
battles outside of the physical encounters with the Formics
evokes an image very relatable to the events of Christ's life.

But . . .

There is always a matter of debate; what I see as clear-cut
Christlike references might be someone else's clutching at
straws. I have avoided what I have seen as tenuous links,
though his actions and the effect he has on others can be
likened to a Mormon's relationship to Christ:

> He [Ender] turned to Bean, took his hand. To Bean, it was like the
> touch of the finger of God. It sent light all through him.[6]

There are also huge distinctions that should be made; not least
that Christ was fully aware of his mission, while Ender was
not. Christlike qualities are not limited to Ender; perhaps sur-
prisingly, another type of Christ can be seen in aspects of the
portrayal of the Hive Queen.

The unqualified and selfless forgiveness she offers Ender
for the destruction of her entire species could be seen to be similar to the events of the cross where Christ forgave those who
nailed him there. She is not any form of savior figure though
she could be an imperfect example of Christlike forgiveness
that is expected of humanity. It is perhaps, only in this one act
that she shows Christlike qualities; this makes her less a type

---

[5] *Doctrine and Covenants* 19:16, 18.
[6] *Ender's Shadow*, p. 285.

of Christ and more an example of how to live his teachings. However, as with Ender's imperfections, there are many elements of the Hive Queen that don't fit into any Christlike analogy. For example, Christ died to save humanity, whereas the Hive Queens on the home planet died rather than destroy humanity—a quite striking disanalogy suggesting that this type of analogical thinking can be taken too far.

The Importance of a Child

Throughout the Ender Saga the reader cannot help but be struck by the importance of the child genius. In his 1991 introduction, Card noted that "Ender's Game is a story about gifted children." Although not distinctively Mormon, the importance of the child is a theme that runs through Mormon history. One of the arguments often used to explain Joseph Smith's relatively young age of fourteen when he was called as a prophet surrounds the innocence of youth, in not being encumbered by the prejudices of adulthood. As a child he did not know "that there were no such things as visions or revelations in these days; that all such things had ceased with the apostles, and that there would never be any more of them."[7] Another example is the prophet Mormon being called to lead the Nephite armies at the age of fifteen, when he also records that he "was visited of the Lord, and tasted and knew of the goodness of Jesus."[8]

Graff's description of Ender's father shows a similar line of thinking in the Enderverse:

"You're forgetting the research we've been conducting. It may not be final in some technical scientific sense, but it's already conclusive. People reach their peak ability as military commanders much earlier than we thought. Most of them in their late teens. The same age when poets do their most passionate and revolutionary work. And mathematicians. They peak, and then it falls off. They coast on what they learned back when they were still young enough to learn."[9]

---

[7] *Joseph Smith History* 1: 21.

[8] Mormon 1:15.

[9] "The Polish Boy" in *First Meetings in Ender's Universe*, p. 56.

This is a theme that's repeated through Ender and Bean specifically, and through Peter and Valentine as they adopt the pseudo-identities of Locke and Demosthenes. This is also continued in *Ender in Exile*, the immediate sequel (in terms of the in-world time sequence) to *Ender's Game*. Here the abilities of the child Ender are sharply contrasted with the ambition and ignorance of Admiral Morgan.

Whether Card had this in mind when he began writing the Ender Saga is doubtful; but as a subconscious contributor to the development of the story this would have certainly added to the possibility, and certainly wouldn't have detracted from it.

The Nature of God

God is seemingly absent from *Ender's Game*, and in the Shadow Saga, Bean seems to be an atheist and society appears post-religious. Card, himself, has said "God cannot be a character in the stories."[10] The children in the Battle School leave (or are supposed to leave) all elements of religion behind. However, *A War of Gifts*, a later Card novel taking place in the same time span as *Ender's Game*, suggests that this is not necessarily so.

The most obvious exploration of the nature of God is in *Xenocide*, where the Gods of the Path (the Path being a world colonized after the defeat of the Formics), and the associated religious devotions, are explained away as genetic "enhancements" and the result of an extreme form of OCD. Taken in isolation this presents a negative impression of religions. I might liken elements of this view of religion to Marx's critique of religion as a tool to subjugate the masses; or a Feuerbachian mirror where, as a creation of humanity, God is only a reflection of what we desire and fear; or many other religious critiques. Ender's critique of the gods of the Path gives a description of God that is distinctly Mormon:

> "So let me tell you what I think about gods. I think a real god is not going to be so scared or angry that he tries to keep other people down. . . . A real god doesn't care about control. A real god already

---

[10] "Questions and Answers" *Washington Post* (3rd November 2010), http://live.washingtonpost.com/orson-scott-card.html.

has control of everything that needs controlling. Real gods would want to teach you how to be just like them."[11]

Although people from many religions may read this and at first glance suggest that this is the God which they believe in, the various nuances make this distinctly Mormon. The crux of this description comes in the last line where Ender argues that "Real gods would want to teach you how to be just like them." Within Mormonism this belief is described in varying ways, whether in a way that describes humanity as "joint heirs with Christ"[12] or in the couplet; "As man is now, God once was, as God is now man may be."[13]

For Mormons, existence is seen to be a three-stage process, commonly described as the plan of salvation. There is a pre-mortal existence where humanity were created as spirit children of God, moving onto mortality or the earthly existence which then culminates in death and a post-mortal existence where humanity is resurrected and have the potential to become like God. Humanity and God are on the same continuum of existence, just at different stages. What this means and how this happens is actually one of the dominant themes in Ender's Saga.

A Philotic Connection-Creation

Ender's Game lays the basis for a much greater exploration of a theme that becomes crucial in the rest of the saga. References to the ansible as a means of communication and the independence and initiative the computer evidences when creating the game beyond the killing of the giant is the only indication of a possible computer based intelligence in *Ender's Game*. However, this is developed slowly in the subsequent novels. When we read of Jane, the initially virtual character the computer goes on to become, the importance of the interconnectivity of things isn't made explicit, but for a Mormon there are parallels to their belief in the pre-mortal existence:

---

[11] *Xenocide,* p. 391.
[12] Romans 8: 29.
[13] *The Teachings of Lorenzo Snow,* p. 1.

Almost from the moment of her [Jane's] creation, her memories extended back to a much earlier time, long before she became aware."[14]

What this means becomes clearer in *Xenocide* when humanity, and other sentient races, become applied to this eternal existence:

"And we aren't some soul that God created out of nothing. We're free because we always existed. Right back from the beginning of time, only there was no beginning of time, so we existed all along. Nothing ever caused us. Nothing ever made us. We simply *are*, and we always were."
"Philotes?" asked Miro.[15]

This passage may seem atheistic; humanity is in essence eternal and always existing. However, within a Mormon worldview, while God is the creator of our spirits and bodies (at different stages), he created spirits from an eternal pool of intelligences: "man as a primal intelligence is eternal. Likewise the spirit-elements that compose his Divinely-sired spirit and the matter elements that compose his physically-sired body are eternal."[16] When humanity is seen to pass through a four-stage existence beginning as intelligence (or as a philote, to use Card's terminology) the parallels between the belief and the books are clear.

The creation of a spirit child of God can be seen to be mirrored in a description of creation by the Hive Queen:

"So when you make a Hive Queen, you already have the biological body, and this new thing—this philote that you call out of the nonplace where philotes are… it takes on that identity and possesses the body and becomes the self of that body—"[17]

However, within Mormonism, it is believed that this type of existence as an intelligence (philote) or spirit (aiúa) is not sufficient. It's important that humanity has the opportunity to progress to become like God. A necessary stage in this development is the gaining of a mortal body as a prelude to the immortal body in the resurrection. The desirability and necessity of

---

[14] *Speaker for the Dead*, p. 175.
[15] *Xenocide*, p. 367.
[16] Truman Madsen, *Eternal Man*, pp. 23–24.
[17] *Xenocide*, p. 446.

the body is explained when Jane receives her body in *Children of the Mind*: "She was astonished with the wholeness of this body. She realised, now, that until this moment she had never been a self before. What she had for all those centuries was an apparatus, not a self. She had been on life support, waiting for a life."[18] Although Mormons wouldn't see the pre-mortal existence as purely a time of waiting, more a time of learning and progression, the fulfilment of that existence with a body is a very Mormon concept.

It seems undeniable to me, that even with the differences, Mormonism's plan of salvation was used, by Card, as a conscious or maybe subconscious influence for the development of philotes and the nature of humanity and the progression of the self. There might even be a similar parallel found in the three-stage existence of the piggies in *Xenocide*.

So Is the Enderverse Mormon?

Yes and no. There are certainly ideas throughout the Ender Saga that have parallels within Mormonism, some of which I have not had space to address here. I don't think that the themes and story as it stands could, or would, have been written by anybody but a Mormon. However, *Ender's Game* and its sequels are not works of theology, neither are they statements of belief or proselytising tools, rather they are works of science fiction that are written for entertainment and enjoyment. That is as it should be; I love to read the stories, and I don't need to reference any religious beliefs to be gripped or make them Mormon for them to have relevance.

Card writes in an introduction to *Ender's Game* that there are many readings of the book as a "transaction between storyteller and audience." The one I have outlined above is the one that I have created in my mind, "guided and shaped by [the] text, but then transformed, elucidated, expanded, edited, and clarified by [my] own experience, [my] own desires, [my] own hope and fears."

Do I think Card will agree with my identification of some of the Mormon ideas I've found? I hope so, but if he doesn't, then they are no less valid for me.

---

[18] *Children of the Mind*, p. 236.

Masks and
Deceptions

12
They're Screwing Around with Us!

DON FALLIS

Manipulation of gravity is one thing; deception by the officers is another.

—ANDREW "ENDER" WIGGIN

Manipulation—and not just of gravity—is central to *Ender's Game*. Colonel Hyrum Graff and the other teachers at the Battle School constantly manipulate Ender Wiggin in order to turn him into a "killer," into "the best soldier possible," into the new Mazer Rackham. They limit and control his contact with the outside world to make him more self-reliant. Moreover, as Ender notes, the one letter that he does receive from his sister Valentine is also "part of their manipulation." To make him more inventive, once Ender becomes a commander, his army is assigned to battles at an unprecedented rate, without sufficient notification, and against unfair odds. As Ender tells his troops, the teachers are "screwing around with us." (Little does he know how much!)

Ender is not the only one who is manipulated in *Ender's Game*. The teachers manipulate the other students as a means of *indirectly* manipulating Ender. For instance, Graff turns the rest of the kids in Ender's launch group against him by singling him out for praise. And almost everyone on Earth is manipulated when Ender's siblings take on fake identities on the nets. Without the common enemy of the Buggers to keep it united, the world might easily have sunk into chaos. But by pretending to be adults (Locke and Demosthenes) rather than young children, Peter and Valentine are ultimately able to wield great power and to bring peace to the planet. With the "Locke Proposal," Peter is able "to use Demosthenes' influence with the mob and Locke's influence with the intelligentsia to accomplish something noteworthy. It forestalled a really vicious war that could have lasted for decades."

Even though he is usually the victim of manipulation, Ender himself engages in manipulation at least a few times. When Bonzo Madrid and his friends corner him in the shower, Ender gets Bonzo to fight one-on-one by taunting him: "Your father would be proud of you. . . . He would love to see you now, come to fight a naked boy in the shower, smaller than you, and you brought six friends. He would say, Oh, what honor." By singling him out for praise, Ender also manipulates Bean in exactly the way that Graff manipulated him.

The most notable instance of manipulation is revealed toward the end of the novel. It turns out that, in order to get Ender to completely destroy the Formics (*aka* the Buggers), Graff and the old Mazer Rackham have fooled Ender and his jeesh into thinking that they are still just playing a game.

> "There were no games, the battles were real, and the only enemy you fought was the buggers."
>
> "I didn't want to kill them all. I didn't want to kill anybody! I'm not a killer! You didn't want me, you bastards, you wanted Peter, but you made me do it, you tricked me into it!"

Is any of this manipulation morally justified? While the most important ethical question is probably whether humanity is morally justified in eliminating an entire alien race in order to protect itself, whether it is okay to manipulate a six-year-old child into doing it for us is certainly a close second. I'm going to argue that it is okay. But in order for me to do so, we need to begin by getting a better grip on what *manipulation* is.

What Is Manipulation?

Basically, you *manipulate* someone when you get him to do something that he otherwise wouldn't have done. Still, there has to be more to it than that—there are many ways to get someone to do what you want that do not count as manipulation. For instance, you might *persuade* him with a rational argument to act differently. While Graff's prepared to lie in order to get Ender to join up in the first place, he ends up having to tell the truth. "We're allowed to do that in emergencies," he says. He convinces Ender to sign up for Battle School by being open with him about what the situation with the Buggers is.

Such rational persuasion does not count as manipulation because it does not *violate people's autonomy*—in other words, it doesn't interfere with their ability to make their *own* choices about their lives. Giving someone *reasons* might very well change her mind about what to do. But she still gets to make the choice. Almost all moral philosophers agree that the distinctive wrong of manipulation is that it takes away this choice.

Manipulation is also different from coercion. You *coerce* someone when you change her behavior by eliminating some of her options—or at least by making those options extremely unattractive. For instance, I might threaten to shoot you if you do not give me all of your money. There's not a lot of coercion in *Ender's Game*; nobody is forced at gunpoint to attend Battle School or to accept promotions. As Graff explains, "conscripts make good cannon fodder, but for officers we need volunteers." Even so, Ender does coerce his commander Bonzo into allowing him to practice with the Launchies.

When Ender is transferred to his unit, Bonzo won't let Ender train with the Salamander Army because "he don't want a totally untrained little kid to screw up his precision maneuvers." So that he has some opportunity to become a better soldier, Ender starts training with his friends during free play. But Bonzo orders Ender not to practice "with those little farts" because "I won't have any soldiers in Salamander Army hanging around with Launchies." In response, Ender *threatens* to go to the teachers: "if you try to control my free play, I'll get you iced." As a result, Bonzo is coerced into rescinding his order: "Galling," we read, "and yet he had no choice. No choice about anything."

While we might want to say that coercion is simply an extreme type of manipulation, manipulation is typically much more subtle than coercion. Coercion does violate someone's autonomy, but in a different way than manipulation does. Whereas coercion works by openly restricting someone's choices, manipulation changes her behavior by messing with her ability to make her own (informed) choices.

Manipulation often involves deception. For instance, Graff and Rackham get the kids to destroy the Buggers by fooling them into thinking that they are still just playing a game (even after Ender's father had explicitly told Graff, "let's not have any deception here!"). Peter and Valentine also resort to deceit in order to get people to do what they want—their alter-egos would be much less influential commentators if the public knew that they were just a twelve-year-old boy and a ten-year-old girl.

Manipulation, however, need not involve deception as when a manipulator simply plays on a psychological weakness. This is what happens when Ender gets Bonzo to fight one-on-one. Ender doesn't need Bonzo to acquire a false belief about anything. He knows that, after his mocking remark, Bonzo's pride won't allow him to do anything other than make it a fair fight. In fact, when Graff tells Ender the truth, it might also be manipulation of this sort. Given young children's vulnerability and their lack of experience with the world, a statement that counts as rational persuasion when the audience is an adult might count as manipulation when the audience is a child. (Of course, Ender is certainly not your typical child.)

Either way though, the person who is manipulated may not be *consciously aware* that he is being manipulated. Indeed, the manipulator himself may not always be aware that the manipulation is going on. When Ender manipulates Bean by singling him out for praise, he does not realize what he's doing and why: "Why am I doing this? What does this have to do with being a good commander, making one boy the target of all the others? Just because they did it to me, why should I do it to him?"

Now that we have a better grip on what manipulation is, we can ask whether screwing around with people in this way is ever morally justified.

Some Manipulation Can Be Morally Justified

It is usually wrong (all things considered) to manipulate people. For instance, there is not much to be said for the sort of self-serving manipulation involved in the marketing of "scareware." We are all frightened of computer viruses, so we worry about turning on our systems and finding messages like the following marching around the screen:

COVER YOUR BUTT. BERNARD IS WATCHING.

—GOD

I LOVE YOUR BUTT. LET ME KISS IT.

—BERNARD

By playing on our fears and by lying about the effectiveness of their products, con artists make millions of dollars every year selling antivirus software that doesn't do anything to address the problem. In fact, the scareware itself often turns out to be a virus of sorts.

Even so, it's sometimes okay to screw around with people. For instance, parents typically have trouble getting their kids to eat vegetables, so they often resort to deceit. In fact, Jessica Seinfeld has written a cookbook called *Deceptively Delicious*, which contains recipes that are "stealthily packed with unseen veggies, puréed so kids will never suspect." While it is rarely okay to manipulate adults for their own good, nobody thinks that there is a problem with this sort of paternalistic manipulation of children.

Manipulation can also be justified if it's done in self-defense, but there are limits to what you can justify by claiming that you acted in self-defense. In particular, philosophers claim that legitimate acts of self-defense must satisfy a "proportionality requirement." For example, if someone walks toward you in a menacing way, but without a weapon, blowing his head off with a laser gun would be "excessive force." Ender's manipulative taunting of Bonzo, on the other hand, seems like a perfectly reasonable way to avoid getting beaten up by a *whole group* of older kids.

More generally, manipulation can be justified if there is no other way to achieve some morally important end. While messing with people's autonomy *is* pretty bad, this badness can sometimes be outweighed by what philosopher Shlomo Sher calls "redemptive moral considerations." Screwing around with people is only *prima facie* wrong—everything else being equal, it's a bad thing to do. However, manipulation is not necessarily wrong *all things considered*.

It would be better if parents could get their kids to eat vegetables just by explaining to them the long-term health benefits of consuming leafy greens, thereby avoiding the moral cost of manipulation and deceit. The problem is that it's just not possible to get many kids to eat vegetables using rational persuasion. Thus, paternalistic manipulation is arguably justified here. It is for the children's own good.

Similarly, it would have been better if the attack on Ender in the shower could have been avoided, or at least scaled back, without the use of manipulation. But that just wasn't an option. Dink Meeker tries to stop Bonzo by giving him *reasons* not to attack Ender: "Because he's the best, that's why! Who else can fight the buggers! That's what matters, you fool, the buggers!" But this attempt at rational persuasion only spurs Bonzo on. Ender thinks to himself, "You've killed me with those words, Dink. Bonzo doesn't want to hear that I might save the world."

So, some instances of manipulation are morally justified. But it is one thing to trick a kid into eating his vegetables. It's quite another to trick a kid into destroying an entire species. Was it really okay for Rackham and Graff to manipulate Ender in this way?

Can the Manipulation of Ender Be Morally Justified?

We might try to justify the manipulation of Ender on the grounds that it was part of an act of self-defense. Graff and Rackham manipulated Ender and the other recruits because it was the only way to save themselves and the rest of humanity from the Buggers. As Graff later explains to Ender, "it had to be a trick or you couldn't have done it." But there is an important difference between Graff and Rackham manipulating Ender and Ender manipulating Bonzo. Ender was manipulating the very person who was about to attack him. But Ender is not going to attack Graff and Rackham. It is the Buggers who are about to attack them. So, why should they get to manipulate Ender?

We might instead try to justify the manipulation of Ender on the grounds that it was done for the greater good, and there was no other way to bring about this good. In 1941, Franklin D.

Roosevelt recognized that Adolf Hitler—much like the Buggers—was a serious threat to all of humanity. But public opinion in the United States was strongly opposed to entering the war. So, in one of his fireside chats, FDR told the American people, "we have sought no shooting war with Hitler. We do not seek it now." At that very moment, he was actually doing everything he could to provoke the German military into firing on American ships so that he would have an excuse to declare war. Given what was at stake, such manipulation was probably justified. As the presidential historian Robert Dallek writes, "in light of the national unwillingness to face up fully to the international dangers facing the country, it is difficult to fault Roosevelt for building a consensus by devious means."

The idea that this sort of manipulation for the greater good might be okay goes back to Plato's idea of the "noble lie." In the *Republic*, Socrates says that the rulers of a city should tell the people that the gods have placed a certain sort of metal (gold, silver, or iron) in each person's soul. This metal determines the person's station in life (rulers, those who help the rulers, farmers and other craftsmen, respectively). According to Socrates, "this tale would have a good effect in making them more inclined to care for the state and one another."

Even though it's done for the greater good, this sort of screwing around with people still seems pretty creepy. After all, even the "vicious, nasty" sociopath Peter Wiggin (*aka* Locke) claims that he is trying to "save mankind from self-destruction." And even if FDR's manipulation and Peter's manipulation were justified, it arguably sets a very bad precedent. In the future, it may be easier for leaders to resort to manipulation and deception when the ends *don't* justify the means. (Remember George W. Bush and those bashful WMDs in Iraq.) Nevertheless, the end of saving the entire human race from total destruction is probably good enough grounds to justify a little bit of devious manipulation of Ender.

Even if the stakes are really high—as they are with the threat of the Buggers and the Nazis—not everyone is going to be convinced that the ends justify the means. Immanuel Kant, for instance, claims that it is *never* okay to treat someone simply as a means, even if doing so will bring about very good consequences. However, Ender is not being used simply as a means. Just like the kids who are tricked into eating their vegetables, Ender is manipulated by Rackham and Graff for his own good. Unless the Buggers are destroyed, Ender and his family will die along with everyone else. As Ender notes, "the only reason that I'm here is so that a bugger won't shoot out Valentine's eye, won't blast her head open like the soldiers in the videos of the first battles with the buggers."

Even though Ender himself benefits from the defeat of the Buggers, that's clearly not the main reason that Graff and Rackham manipulate him. But we don't manipulate children simply for their own good either. For instance, we don't primarily use rational argument to get them to internalize various social norms, such as not hitting, offering apologies, and saying "Please" and "Thank You." True, getting a child to obey these rules benefits the child just like getting him to eat his vegetables does, but we are also thinking of the larger society when we engage in this sort of manipulation. We don't want to inflict monsters like Peter Wiggin on the world.

In my argument that Rackham and Graff's manipulation of Ender is okay, I keep appealing to the fact that the everyday paternalistic manipulation of children seems to be okay. It might be suggested, however, that there are important differences between the two cases. After all, the paternalistic manipulation of children is usually done *by the parents*. Even if it's okay to manipulate your own kids into eating vegetables, it's not okay to screw around with *other people's* kids in this way. While Graff is not Ender's biological father, there is an important sense in which Graff *is* Ender's father. Being a "Third," Ender is essentially a ward of the state. As Graff explains to Ender's parents, "we already have your consent, granted in writing at the time conception was confirmed, or he could not have been born. He has been ours from then."

Now, maybe I have ignored some morally important distinction that shows that everyday paternalistic manipulation of children is okay, but that Graff and Rackham's manipulation of Ender is *not* okay. At the moment, however, it seems to me that his instructors at the Battle School and at the Command School have pretty good grounds for screwing around with Ender.[1]

---

[1] I would like to thank Adam Arico, Andrew Cohen, Tony Doyle, Victor Kumar, Laura Lenhart, Kay Mathiesen, Lucinda Rush, and Dylan Wittkower for many helpful suggestions.

13
The Lying Game

RANDALL M. JENSEN

Everybody lies. A kindly nurse tells a young Ender it won't hurt when his monitor is removed from the back of his neck. The International Fleet (I.F.) removes the monitor to make Ender think they are no longer interested in him. Peter tells Ender that someday in the future he will kill him and get away with it by pretending to grieve. Colonel Graff has no problem lying to Ender to convince him to leave his home for Battle School. All this before Ender even leaves the planet!

After Graff's cruel treatment of Ender on the shuttle ride to Battle School, Ender confronts him. "I thought you were my friend," he says. Why did Ender think this? Because Graff "didn't lie." Graff was fully prepared to lie if he needed to and told the truth only because it suited his purposes, but Ender was convinced that friends tell the truth.

When he arrives at Battle School, Ender learns how important it is to be a skillful liar. He's grateful to Peter for forcing him to learn how to put on "the lying face" and hide his feelings from others. He also quickly discovers that "the adults are the enemy, not the other armies. They do not tell us the truth." Ender now believes that some lies are hurtful and thus evidence of enmity, while other lies are simply a necessary part of doing business and no reason to get upset. Some lies are even "more dependable than the truth."

Ender's exhausting journey from Battle School to Command School is filled with lies, deception, and manipulation, culminating in the biggest lie of all: Ender is told he is still in school, still running a training simulation, when in fact he is commanding the real invasion. He sends soldiers to their death and eventually presides over the destruction of the Bugger home world, all without knowing what he's doing. This is a terrible lie, and yet perhaps Graff is right when he tells Ender that "it had to be a trick or you couldn't have done it." A lie saves the world!

Ender's story cries out for more reflection on what it means when we lie. What is a lie? Are all lies wrong? Can we lie out of love and friendship rather than enmity? Is it wrong to tell a lie when the stakes are enormous?

What's in a Lie?

Graff lies to Ender. We have here a liar (Graff), a lie (the claim that this is still just a game), and an audience (Ender). What makes this a lie? It isn't merely that what Graff says is false. Not every falsehood is a lie. Ender's jeesh also speaks as if they're still playing a game, but even though they're mistaken, they aren't lying—except for Bean, of course, who knows the truth.

What makes Graff's falsehood into a lie is that he *knows* it isn't true and that he *intends* that Ender believe it is true. Whether a statement is a lie thus has more to do with the mind of the liar than with the content of the lie itself or the effects on the audience. While a lie in the *strict* sense might require that someone make an explicit statement with intent to mislead, a lie in the *loose* sense might not involve directly telling a lie. Someone might plan for an audience to acquire a false belief without uttering it directly. This creates space for lies of omission and other kinds of deceptive strategies. As Valentine is forced to realize in her relationship with Peter, a very clever person can deceive even while telling the truth.

Very few people would quarrel with the notion that there's something wrong with lying. Immanuel Kant believes that lying is immoral because when I lie, I fail to see you as a person like myself and look at you instead as a thing, a means to an end. Simply put, I use you. In gaming language, when I lie to you I treat you as an NPC (a non-player character) rather than as another player.

Through lies and deception, Graff makes Ender his tool or, more accurately, his weapon—a weapon of mass destruction, even, "like the Little Doctor." Ender himself explicitly makes this connection between lying and using someone: "Graff was only acting like a friend... everything he did was a lie or a cheat calculated to turn Ender into an efficient fighting machine." And though Ender sees the need to become a weapon, he vows that he "won't be fooled into it." In Kant's language, Ender is striving to see himself as an end and not merely as a means, even if Graff doesn't see him that way.

Kant is committed to an *absolute* rule against lying: lying is always wrong, with no exceptions. This is hard to swallow. Aren't there situations in which lying is called for? In *The Republic*, Socrates considers the idea that morality is a matter of following simple rules such as "Pay your debts!" and "Speak the truth!" and makes the plausible suggestion that such rules will always have exceptions (lines 331b–d). Socrates asks if we should follow such rules when dealing with someone who is out of his mind. Does Ender owe the truth to Bonzo or Peter?

Whereas Kantians locate the wrongness of lying in the will of the liar, *utilitarians* believe that lying is wrong—when it is wrong—because of its harmful consequences. Modern utilitarianism, founded by British philosophers Jeremy Bentham and John Stuart Mill, is based on the simple thought that morality consists in bringing about the greatest happiness for the greatest number of people. If Graff were simply to tell random lies to Ender, it would break down their relationship and serve no useful purpose. Success in battle obviously depends on the accurate communication of data and orders.

A rule of thumb against lying makes sense, then. However, a lie can be very useful not just for achieving our own ends but also for bringing about some good or averting some evil for others. In such cases, utilitarians think that a lie will be the right thing to do. Presumably that's how the many adults who lie to the children in Battle School justify their dishonesty. Perhaps they're using their students to achieve their own ends, but for a utilitarian their end might be important enough to make it okay to do this.

These two moral perspectives—Kantian and utilitarian—differ about what makes lying wrong and consequently about when lying is wrong. Since most of us are likely to feel the pull of both points of view, it's no surprise that we're sometimes torn about whether we ought to lie or not. As Graff says, the idea that "human beings are all tools, that the others use to help us all survive" is "just a half truth" rather than an outright lie as Ender claims.

Plato's Game

In the *Republic*, Plato famously sketches an account of an ideal city ruled by an elite class of guardians. These guardians must be carefully created through an elaborate process of breeding, testing, physical training, and a meticulously controlled education of the mind and heart. The I.F. seems to have read the *Republic* very carefully, and Plato's ideal city obviously requires a Battle School!

One of the key issues in the education of these young guardians is the stories they are told. Like Graff and the others who run the Battle School, Plato realizes that it's crucial to control the flow of information. Stories help form character, so guardians should hear stories that will make them virtuous rather than vicious. (Plato focuses on stories because he doesn't have access to a fantasy computer game that can help assess and shape the character of his trainees.)

Guardians mustn't be told false stories. And even if a story is true but might corrupt the young, then we should take it out of circulation. Plato believed that many of the well-known stories of his day were both false and pernicious because they tell of "gods warring, fighting, or plotting against one another" (lines 377b–378e). By depicting the gods in this light, these tales encourage the young to follow suit. Such stories would ruin the young guardians in much the way that the I.F. is worried that certain information might ruin Ender and render him unfit to command the fleet. Just as Graff and his superiors worry that Ender will turn out to be too much like Peter or too much like Valentine, the founders of this ideal city must make sure the guardians become neither too savage and harsh nor too gentle and soft (lines 410c–412a). The solution in both cases is for the perfect commander to be at once both hard and soft, to be courageous and decisive and yet also sensitive and self-controlled. And that's just who Ender is—or is it rather who he becomes under Graff's careful manipulation?

While Plato insists that his guardians not be told false stories that might corrupt them, he later explains that their education and training may require certain lies. Indeed, the ideal city itself is built on a lie as its very foundation. This is the famous "myth of the metals" in which citizens are told that:

> All of you in the city are brothers . . . but the god who made you mixed some gold into those who are adequately equipped to rule, because they are most valuable. He put silver in those who are auxiliaries and iron and bronze in the farmers and other craftsmen. (line 415a)

This myth supports the hierarchical meritocracy of the ideal city, helping to keep those who are only fit to be a farmer or a merchant from trying to rule. It will work only if the inhabitants of the ideal city believe in the myth—much as the battle system in Battle School only works if the cadets believe in the importance of the standings that report the results for each army and each soldier.

Later, Plato describes another key deception crucial for creating the proper guardians. The city will have a breeding program hidden by a system of festivals and contests designed to make sure that "the best men have sex with the best women as frequently as possible, while the opposite is true of the most inferior men and women" and that "the former's offspring must be reared but not the latter's" (lines 459d–e). This seems an awful lot like a low-tech version of the I.F.'s strategy for creating brilliant children such as the Wiggins. In both cases, a cultural myth (or bias?) will obscure what is really going on.

At first, Plato seems to have an inconsistent attitude about lying. No false stories allowed in the education of the guardians, but the city itself is built on falsehoods! Plato explains by drawing an important distinction between a "true lie," in which one is "false to one's soul about the things that are," and a lie in words that is only a pale imitation of this true lie (lines 382a–e). From his point of view, what we say with our mouths is not what's important, but what we believe in our souls. This distinction creates the possibility that someone might lie in words but nonetheless create truth in the souls of the audience. That is what Plato thinks the founding myths of the city do. Such a lie he refers to as playing a medicinal role in the city; it is "useful as a form of drug" (line 459d) and even a "noble falsehood" (line 414b).

This kind of lie is arguably not best seen as a lie at all. It is rather a myth. And it doesn't seem that a myth must inevitably fall prey to the Kantian objection that the mythmaker is treating the audience as a means to his or her own ends. Kant presumably doesn't mean to deny that we can tell certain kinds of truths through fiction, and myth seems to live on the border between fabrication and fiction.

A mythic story is just as likely to be shameful as noble, just as likely to create falsehood as truth in the souls of the people. Thus Plato thinks that only the rulers of the city will be in a good position to tell such a lie, for only they can properly judge the effects of their words on the souls of the citizens. Who are the rulers of the ideal city? Why, it's the philosophers, of course. Plato's legendary figures the philosopher kings (and queens!), who know and love the truth, will be able to craft myths that create truth in the souls of the ruled. Are Graff and his ilk up to this job?

We're Saving the World, After All

Is Graff's lie a noble one? It doesn't seem to be the kind of lie Plato has in mind. Plato isn't merely thinking with the utilitarians that a lie might be permitted simply because it has good consequences. Rather, his paradoxical idea is that a lie, if it's a myth, might actually tell the truth.

Graff's lie doesn't seem designed to help Ender see a deeper truth in the way a myth can. Graff simply wants Ender to slaughter Buggers and sacrifice pilots without having a clue that's what he is doing. However, some of the other lies surrounding Battle School may fall into this category, as the leaders want this school to be the entire world to their students, and such a world is inevitably driven by myth. Certainly they have developed some expertise in how to mold their students, even if the truly exceptional children like Ender and Bean can see through their efforts and run circles around them.

The most likely justification for Graff's big lie to Ender is utilitarian. At his trial, Graff tells us that he argued that he did what he believed "was necessary for the preservation of the human race, and it worked . . . the prosecution had to prove beyond doubt that Ender would have won the war without the training we gave him . . . The exigencies of war." Graff's lie thus serves the greater good.

Or did it? Utilitarianism instructs us to bring about the best possible outcome. For whom? For human beings? No: for all sentient creatures. Graff's calculations should include the effects of his actions on the Formic species as well as the human species. Once this is taken into account, the claim that the lie is a lesser evil becomes less clear. For the lie causes Ender to exterminate a species. One world is saved but only at the cost of another. In the future, Ender Wiggin will be known simply as the Xenocide and he will be remembered as the perpetrator of an atrocity rather than the savior of humanity.

Of course, this evaluation of Ender's actions and Graff's supporting role in them is an oversimplification.

- First, while it is later discovered that the Buggers were actually no longer a threat to humans, this wasn't known at the time. Many versions of utilitarianism encourage us to do what is *expected* to lead to the best outcome. It did seem reasonable for humans to believe that the Buggers remained a threat that could not be ignored.

- Second, there was no xenocide, for after the battle Ender receives the cocoon of a hive queen and will eventually find a new home for her and her children.

- Third, and most interestingly, it is difficult to know how utilitarianism should handle a hive species. Does the pain or pleasure of each individual Bugger get weighed in the same way the pain or pleasure of each individual human is? Does an individual Bugger even experience pleasure and pain? How should our ethics make room for a hive species?

Speaker for the Dead

In the sequel to *Ender's Game*, more than three thousand years have passed since the Bugger Wars, and yet because he has spent most of that time in interstellar travel, Ender is still in his thirties. No one thinks to connect Andrew Wiggin, an itinerant Speaker for the Dead, with the monstrous Ender the Xenocide, or with the venerated founder of the order of

Speakers, the author of *The Hive Queen and the Hegemon*. Yet these three apparently different people are in fact one and the same man.

The Speakers for the Dead are a kind of secular religion whose vocation is "the pursuit of the true story of the dead" (*Speaker for the Dead*, p. 141). After having spent much of his young life being the victim of lies and deception, Ender now spends his time uncovering the truth and speaking it in love. "I'm a Speaker for the Dead. I tell the truth, when I speak at all, and I don't keep away from other people's secrets" (p. 224). This speaking of the truth is difficult work and is often far from pleasant. "There was always pain after a Speaking, because a Speaker for the Dead did nothing to soften the truth" (p. 294). Yet this sometimes hard truth is meant to heal the hurts caused by toxic lies and to liberate people from the deceits woven by others and by themselves. "He doesn't tell us what we want. He tells us what we know is true. He didn't win our affection, Mother, he won our trust. . . . I thank God for the Speaker. He was willing to speak the truth, and it set us free" (p. 312).

Speakers aren't interested in creating myths about the dead. "He wasn't telling the Truth, with trumpets, he was telling the truth, the story that you wouldn't think to doubt because it's taken for granted" (p. 280). No noble falsehoods for a Speaker for the Dead, nothing but the plain and simple truth about those who are gone, and thus about those who are left behind as well.

Is this because Ender has come to believe that lying and deceit are absolutely immoral and so he will have no part in them? Probably not. Perhaps it's because he has learned the hard way that lying and deceit do more damage than we can imagine, that while they might sometimes seem necessary for our survival, they will never help us flourish. Most of all, it seems that Ender has reaffirmed the connection between friendship and the truth. When he comes to love the Hive Queen, he is able to tell her story. Likewise for the Hegemon, who is his brother Peter.

As one of the children of a dead man for whom he Spoke puts it, "I think you can't possibly know the truth about somebody unless you love them. I think the Speaker loved Father. . . . I think he understood him and loved him before he Spoke.

. . . I know he loves me. And when he shows me that he loves me, I know it's true because he never lies to anybody" (pp. 312–13).

In the end, Ender speaks the truth not out of some Kantian sense of moral obligation or out of a utilitarian demand for the greatest good, but because truth is the only language love can speak.

14
And Who Is Demosthenes?

ALEXANDER HALAVAIS

Who I Am

As regular readers are aware, I do not waste time writing about myself. This has not stopped others from writing about me, however, and this has come to be an unnecessary distraction. Especially when world events demand our collective attention. Indeed, it may be that this distraction is intentional, meant to draw debate away from the impending global train wreck.

The core of many of these criticisms is that my ideas are worthless because you do not know my real name. This is, of course, nonsense. My ideas live and die on their own merit. You do not need to know who I am to know I speak the truth. I provide facts, backed by evidence, the logic that ties them together, and recommendations for action. Look back on the sentences I have written thus far. Will the signature that follows change what you think of those words? If so, the problem lies not with me.

Why, then, do I not write under my own name? I write pseudonymously for the reasons heroes—real and imaginary—have often worn masks: to protect themselves and their loved ones. Many people have found the truth of my words inspiring and have come to call for the changes I have promoted. But many others, including those who call themselves friends, would rather see me silenced. My identity makes me and my family targets, but you cannot silence the voice of someone when you do not know who they are. You cannot arrest an idea.

And so I rely on technology to provide us with a shared space for ideas. The nets give me voice and safety from reprisals. The founders of the United States were lucky enough to have access to printing presses, which allowed them to produce pamphlets signed not with their own names, but the pseudonym "Publius." That they did not sign their own names and serve themselves up to the forces amassed against them did nothing to diminish the truth of their words. I do not compare myself to James Madison, or Alexander Hamilton, or John Jay. But I proudly compare myself to Publius.

—Demosthenes

People in Masks

At the end of the twentieth century there was a popular film called *The Princess Bride* in which one of the characters notes "People in masks cannot be trusted." Later, the protagonist is questioned about his mask-wearing, and explains "It's just they're terribly comfortable. I think everyone will be wearing them in the future." Here we are in the future and I find myself writing from behind a mask to answer someone who has sent another missive to the nets from behind his own mask.

Both of us have donned masks, I suspect, for the same reason. At least initially, we represented voices in opposition to structures of power. These voices could be easily crushed by pressuring us as authors, since we did not have the protection of an audience, and represented a challenge to entrenched structures of power. These days, though, Demosthenes represents not a single voice in the wilderness, but the voice of a growing movement with growing influence.

To pretend Demosthenes's motives have nothing to do with personal biography is folly. Although the logical soundness of an argument is important, the individual story that has led to that argument is also important. Unlike the Buggers, we value individualism and the personal histories we each create. Our words serve mainly to recapitulate our life paths. Because every argument omits as it includes, it is important to know why the argument is being made and whether we can trust the person making it. It is true: people in masks cannot be fully trusted.

In part, this is because arguments made from behind a mask require relatively little in the way of risk from the author. Particularly for those speaking out against government and mobs, the risk might simply be too great to bear. While I do believe in the positions I present to my readers, I also value my future ability to participate in the conversation, which requires my true identity remain concealed. Demosthenes is not in the same position. He has gained such a broad following that his safety would benefit by making his identity known, as would his credibility. We rightly put more trust into those who stand behind their arguments with real, physical bodies, and who believe enough in their message to risk their personal safety.

This ease of raising and killing off our avatars in public space was always an issue with the nets, but it becomes far more of an issue when real lives are at stake. Demosthenes claims he proffers only ideas, but those ideas have real results, and put all of our lives at risk. There is a reason that in the real world power is always built on the threat of death and dishonor—because those who will follow you must risk their own as well.

I enjoy my mask. It's comfortable. But as readers, we should not trust those in masks. History has taught us that for every hero in a mask, there are a dozen about to rob your store, sabotage your factory, or bully your child. It is time we discover what sort of person stands behind the mask called "Demosthenes."

—LOCKE

Names and Ideas

Surely Locke does not mean to suggest that I am a bully or a thief. Because my life, as Demosthenes, is an open book. You may read everything I have posted to the nets, the bumbled mumblings of fumbled eloquence. And that, Dear Reader, is all you need know; at least for now.

My detractors face the unenviable task of mounting *ad hominem* attacks on the lack of my personhood. But "Demosthenes" is not a person, and if anything, attacks on the source of these ideas are even more objectionable than arguments against the person. Milton can be found arguing a congruent point in his classic screed against censorship, *Areopagitica*:

> For Books are not absolutely dead things, but doe contain a potencie
> of life in them to be as active as that soule was whose progeny they
> are; nay they do preserve as in a violl the purest efficacie and extrac-

tion of that living intellect that bred them. I know they are as lively, and as vigorously productive, as those fabulous Dragons teeth; and being sown up and down, may chance to spring up armed men. And yet on the other hand, unlesse warinesse be us'd, as good almost kill a Man as kill a good Book; who kills a Man kills a reasonable creature, Gods Image; but hee who destroyes a good Booke, kills reason it selfe, kills the Image of God, as it were in the eye.

Those who disagree with me should not be so eager to do away with my *nom du nets*, to shoot the messenger. My ideas do not need the foundation of a writer. I am a whistleblower. I sound the alarm and alert you to the dangers we all face. You decide whether to take action, hopefully by applying your own wisdom to the issues at hand. And here I share a desire with the seventeenth-century philosopher John Locke—ironically, the namesake of one of my detractors, who calls upon me now to reveal my identity. Locke—the real Locke, that is—held that good government is the result not of granting people authority based on their names or their biography, but on the basis of good ideas. People read my postings not because of who I am, but because of what I say.

This idea that men, in a state of nature, are essentially equal, grounds the *Federalist Papers* published by "Publius," and in turn undergirds many of the Founding Fathers' ideals in the United States. For John Locke, an appeal to ancestry, to religious privilege, to wealth, or to power should not be grounds for gaining more influence within government. The search for truth is what is important, no matter the source of that truth. It is in the best interest of all citizens to protect individual rights, to provide space for the expression of ideas, and to make decisions based on the best ideas, not based on who presents them.

I feel a particular affinity for the second of the *Federalist Papers*, written by John Jay, but drawing very heavily on the ideals already articulated by John Locke. *Federalist* Number Two asks New Yorkers to think about how to create a new constitution, and how to convince those who prefer to remain a colony to change their minds. It suggests that like proselytizing in religion, forced changes in attitude are ineffective. The better path is an appeal to the true nature of things, and the conviction that revealing that truth to the nonbelievers in an open and honest way is the best way to change their minds. It also argues, and eventually demonstrates, how during certain periods of uncertainty, the right words can change the world.

The nets provide us with space for making our ideas heard without recourse to our wealth or background or who our parents might have been. There have been other technologies that have done this to a lesser extent. The salons and coffee houses that Jürgen Habermas describes, and the community of letters that used the printing press to extend this public sphere, for example. A combination of social influences during the period, including the emergence of a bourgeoisie that was literate, politically interested, and had time to discuss the shared problems of the day, leveraged new social conventions and technologies to—however temporarily—overlook differences in pedigree, wealth, and power, and to come to some consensus without appeals to character or standing.

The nets are our coffee houses, providing an intellectual space where good ideas win out no matter who brings them to the fore. On the net, it doesn't matter if you are a retired garbage man, or a teenage girl who is still in school, or a recruit on the front lines who sees more than the military structure will allow him to speak about. The nets make them all equal and with that equality comes democracy.

Michel Foucault was once asked why he sought anonymity. It was, he said,

> a way of addressing the potential reader, the only individual here who is of any interest to me, more directly: 'Since you don't know who I am, you will be more inclined to find out why I say what you read; just allow yourself to say, quite simply, it's true, it's false. I like it or I don't like it. Period.

I would go further and say that all those who wish to be taken seriously should speak in public using a pseudonym. We don't need to know who you are to know what you stand for. Tell us what you stand for. Remove your trappings of government authority or the wealth made in commercial enterprise and show us that your ideas make sense.

—Demosthenes

War and Deception

I am so very glad to learn, given our most recent epistle from Demosthenes, that my pseudonym should be presented as a mark of civic-mindedness. Barely hidden in his posting are hints to his identity. Which of those three was the real Demosthenes: the garbage man, the teen, or the rebellious trooper? All represent fairly tame possibilities. He ignores some of the other potential hands at the keyboard. Is he the Hegemon's right hand, testing the waters for a shift in the global order? Is he an *agent provocateur*, an old Russian bear egging us toward a fight that will likewise reshape the future? Or perhaps just the concoction of an arms dealer's public relations firm, written by an army of eager interns? For all we know he may not be human at all!

Or perhaps he writes under other names as well, testing different identities and different positions to see which will win out in the end. Maybe these identities help to reinforce one another, providing a straw man or a foil or the source of unbridled praise. All we know for certain is that he aims to deceive, by not revealing the full truth of all that he is.

It is said that the first victim of war is truth, but the relationship goes the other way round as well. War is built on deception and on lack of transparency. We know how important deception is to the prosecution of war, to the grand strategy that brings us to war and to the tactics that end it. And if politics is war by other means, we might expect those who engage in political action to be equally likely to deceive. In fact, if Michael Walzer is to be believed, we require our politicians to have "dirty hands," even as we should condemn them for the same. So, perhaps Demosthenes sees the concealment of his identity as akin to the "noble lie"—a deception in service of the public good.

Although in the original formulation by Walzer, and indeed in its precursors in Machiavelli and elsewhere, the dirty hands can include misleading the public, later Walzer applies it more directly to immorality in warfare: particularly the destruction of civilian targets. While he suggests that there is no exception that allowed for the civilian targeting of Hiroshima or Dresden late in the Second World War, earlier attacks on civilian targets were justified by "supreme emergency"—an existential threat to social life in the Allied nations. Certainly, Demosthenes's heated rhetoric suggests that he sees his enemies as more than merely combatants, but as existential threats to humankind. Perhaps this justifies his willingness to mislead.

Or perhaps he is precisely what he says he is. But given not just the possibility that he might be misleading us intentionally, but a structure of reasoning that might allow him to do so while seeing it as a necessary evil (or even not an evil at all, since it is in the service of human survival), asking him to give up his mask seems like a small concession.

Indeed, we might draw on his own example of the public sphere. A number of theorists have rejected Habermas's version of the story of the coffee house, and Habermas himself recognized that the "public sphere" that emerged was ideological— based on the false idea that educated well-off Europeans represented "the public" as a whole. There may have been an understanding that people should "bracket off" issues of social position. It may even have been made explicit with rules of conduct in some places. But in the end, non-male, non-white conversants were unlikely to be heard, and social position was only "bracketed off" among those of a certain class and background. This bracketing served a particular purpose: universalizing those who already had power and making them feel as though they could speak for everyman. If Demosthenes is a voice that is not normally heard, his point has been made. He can come out now and reveal himself. But he may just be another person with power, adopting the mask as a way to bypass discussions of privilege.

Since Demosthenes has called on the source of my pseudonym, I feel justified in doing the same with his. The real Demosthenes found himself disputing lies given in a legal case, and in his speech "Against Evergus and Mnesibulus" he argues that knowing the character of the witnesses is enough to judge the veracity of their testimony:

> I shall devote a larger part of my speech to exposing the character of these men than to proving that their testimony is false. As to my charge that the testimony to which they have deposed is false, they seem to me to have given proof by their own actions, and there is no need for me to produce any other witnesses than themselves.

In the end, we must judge Demosthenes not only by his words, but by his character. That character may be worthy of trust, but in a free society trust can only survive if everyone is willing to reveal themselves equally. When one person feels justified in lying, concealing, and deceiving, others are placed in the position of assuming that everyone is lying, concealing, and deceiving. There can be no civilization when only some of us get to hide our true selves.

—LOCKE

True to Our Selves

I will admit I find this talk of "true selves" a bit confusing. When I write here, I write as Demosthenes. Perhaps it's impossible to wear an identity without becoming what you pretend to be. Because, despite Locke's insistence that my body is the determining factor in my character, the more I write, the closer I feel to Demosthenes.

Here's the trick, though. Demosthenes does not exist without Locke. We are two sides of a many-sided conversation, and we write ourselves into being. Much as Locke may wish to draw distinctions and root our true selves in the bureaucratic trappings of identity, we are what we become when we dress ourselves up in words.

We may already come to this sense of self in our early interactions with our brothers and sisters as small children. We are in some sense defined by how our family sees us. But the nets constitute a new global nervous system, a way for us to think collectively and come toward consensus. I do not wish to prevail as an individual, but rather to unveil the true path that best serves our planet. I am as much Locke as Demosthenes, and in the end, for us to move forward as a species, we will need to find ways to recognize that our most important contributions have nothing to do with our name, and everything to do with how we come together as "us."

—DEMOSTHENES

Child Development

15
Every Breath You Take

Ashley Shew

"I've watched through his eyes, I've listened through his ears, and I tell you he's the one."

How significant are the differences between the monitors used on children in *Ender's Game* and the monitoring devices employed on children today? "Monitoring" children seems an essential part of childrearing, but most of us also share an uneasy feeling about the scrutiny Ender endures as a Battle School trainee and as a child under observation before he's sent to school. The adults of the I.F. seem to be overstepping, going too far, but is their justification different in character from the stories we tell ourselves today about our own monitors?

In the rooms of my two children, I have audio "baby" monitors that help me listen in on my children as they talk and sing and sleep. My eldest daughter used to talk to herself for an hour every night and every nap time before falling asleep. I loved to listen in on her conversations and her thoughts, to know what was on her mind when she thought she was alone. My youngest does more singing and falls asleep more quickly, but it's always fun to pick up on what she says to herself when she assumes she is alone.

I often wonder how long is too long to monitor one's offspring. My eldest just turned four years old, but, even this morning, we used the monitors wisely. We could hear her walking around in the upstairs of the house, asking "Where's my family?", and so we knew to go upstairs. The ease and simplicity of the technology make it so that I don't often consider the intrusion into their lives that the monitors represent. But would it still be appropriate to use this technology on teens or pre-teens?

Ender's Game and the world it presents make me feel uneasy about my ready reliance on monitoring devices for children. The monitoring of children exists as commonplace, accepted, and reinforced in this generation, more than any other. Better, cheaper devices make it so that many parents now can have video monitors (instead of just voice monitors) to watch over their children and to keep them safe. Baby monitors (video and voice), nanny-cams, surveillance cameras in schools, internet web-monitoring, cell-phone tracking, and RFID tagging currently serve to enhance a parent's ability to protect, control, and monitor children of all ages. Parents and teachers view monitors as necessary safety devices.

While in many ways unlike the monitors of Ender's generation, our current systems of monitoring share both a name and an ethos with Ender's monitor. Monitors—by their very nature and both in his world and ours—share information, allow for a view (or an ear) to the conversations and movements of, in these cases, children, and give the illusion of privacy where none exists. They allow adults to watch over children, to protect them or intentionally choose not to protect them, to change their behavior in desired ways, to curiously watch or listen, and to be both away and present at the same time.

Deterrence

Ender's Game starts with the removal of a monitor from the back of Ender's neck. Ender's monitor connects to his senses, and its removal causes trauma. In the words of his doctor, "We could have unplugged his brain for all time." The removal dazes Ender, and he soon encounters Stilson without the device. The monitor kept him safe because the other children knew they would be observed bullying Ender. But the device's removal emboldens Stilson to attack Ender, very much to the detriment of Stilson.

After the encounter, Ender believes that, with his monitor off, he is just like his psychopathic brother Peter, ready to cause violence and pain. He explains his aggression to his parents and Colonel Graff: "I wanted to win. . . . So they'd leave me alone. . . . You took away the monitor. . . . I had to take care of myself, didn't I?" Monitors serve as deterrence—from bullying (being the cause of violence) and from bullies (deterring the violence of others). Observation allowed Ender to be less cautious of his own welfare.

When we consider monitors, we recognize two primary functions: 1. keeping a person from harm by deterring the unwanted behaviors of others and 2. keeping a person from performing unwanted behaviors. In Ender's case, monitors served to deter older boys, including Peter, from physically and verbally attacking him. Even after the monitor in his neck was removed, adults were highly aware of Ender's movements and thoughts. Though Ender was not clued in to all the types of monitoring, Bean figured out (in *Ender's Shadow*) that the clothes they wore had sensors for monitoring heart rates and tracking movements while in Battle School. Bean recognized that he could move freely if he was naked. Ender knew that the teachers watched, but he never tried to escape them. Monitoring is accepted as normal and regular, just like my four-year-old knows that I can hear her in her room and uses the technology to let me know when she needs a glass of water in the middle of the night. Bean took the monitors as intrusion, an assertion of the superiority of the adults who tracked him like an animal, while Ender reflected on the way the monitor controlled the behavior of the kids around him.

Proponents of monitoring justify the intrusion by appealing to deterrence; crimes and offenses that would otherwise take place don't happen because someone can so easily be caught. New Jersey's saturation in cameras and subsequent dip in crime bears out this theory, but we also witness this change in the case with child-specific monitoring. Web-monitoring software keeps young adults from surfing into content that they should not for fear of getting caught; nanny-cams ensure that babysitters and older siblings remain kind to their charges (like Peter when monitored); cameras and metal detectors in high schools prevent violence.

The value and costs of deterrence receive a lot of public attention in discussions of gun rights, capital punishment, and nuclear arms. The value of the deterrent effect of monitors on children is less explored. Most parents and administrators in schools justify monitoring by appealing to safety. Fights are prevented because students know they will be seen. Deterrence makes people safer, but it comes at the cost of freedom. Bean saw the monitors for what they were—the assertion of authority, reinforcing a hierarchy between the watched and the watcher. While we justify monitoring based on safety for a child (deterrence from harm by others or themselves), at the same time we keep that child from acting freely (keeping them from performing behaviors they otherwise would want to).

Warped Drive

Monitors warp behavior, and the idea that people need to be monitored for their own good can be insulting as children grow. We value authenticity—getting to be our true selves—but how are we to know who people (including children) really are if we are never in situations where they can relax and act "normally"? Being on camera, knowing about the gaze of someone unseen, changes how we act. Though these changes can be positive (like a teen less likely to steal something from a locker), they also force people to be aware of how they are perceived by others at much younger ages. We think not only of how we are acting, but also about how it *looks like* we are acting, editing our thoughts and deeds while performing them.

And we don't just use monitors on children. Other creatures receive our intrusive gaze. Wildlife monitoring—by hunters, by conservation groups, and by amateurs—has witnessed an explosion in the past twenty years. Camera traps, infrared trip wires connected to cameras that take a picture (or video) when tripped, catch animal poachers and smugglers, help wildlife and conservation experts keep track of the numbers of endangered species, enable photographers in snapping amazing photos, and aid hunters in tracking prized game. With these devices, we're privy to areas and experiences that are otherwise inaccessible. Jane Goodall, the famed primate expert, spent forty-five months embedded with chimpanzees in Gombe before she ever witnessed the common practice of ant-dipping by those chimps. The presence of an outsider, a watcher, an adult, or other observer can warp behavior. Animals have been known to attack camera traps. There's very little debate about the appropriate use of these devices, but it seems to me that a conversation about the monitoring of children goes along with a debate on trap cameras. We take trap cameras as helpful safety devices in both cases. We see ourselves as acting in the best interest of animals and children, our charges. The World Wildlife Federation is a huge proponent of their use because the monitors can help stop poachers as well as gather some amazing photos for promotional materials.

Knowing you're being watched changes how you act—for children, animals, inmates, and would-be felons. But even if the gaze of monitors isn't felt—isn't realized and recognized—the intrusion is still there. Monitors don't always warp; we can gather authentic child and animal behavior when the child is unaware. The only way I know my shy two-year-old knows her ABCs is because she sings the song to herself when she assumes no one is listening. But, the intrusion remains, whether or not the subject realizes it.

Violence

The intrusion of monitoring exists as a type of violence. While we often justify the use of monitors as deterring violence, they present a sort of violence. Art Historian James Elkins in his book *The Object Stares Back* (1997) writes that:

> Seeing is effortless and mercurial, or so it seems, and it appears we prefer it that way. But we cannot permanently forget the harshness and pressure of seeing. Seeing is at the very root of our way of getting along in the world, and a single look can have all the force of hatred and violence that may end up being expressed in more brutal ways. (p. 25)

In Ender's case, we can see hatred and violence built up in his monitoring. While not hatred toward Ender himself, hatred and fear—of the Buggers and of death and of failure—loom in the act of monitoring. Monitors (people watching the monitors) have objectives, motives, and desires that play out on their screens, that inform their decisions, that intrude and extract and tear. What's done with Ender through his monitors—through the fantasy game monitoring his thoughts and the suits monitoring his movements—pushes him and controls him and acts to reinforce the belief that he is not his own.

Monitoring exists as a purposeful activity and never merely looking on. The data that the commanders collect gets used to fully shape Ender into what Peter and Valentine could not be—both deeply compassionate and terribly violent. While these exist within Ender, the Battle School cultivates them by isolating him and pushing him and testing him. Being seen alone, feeling the full force of a gaze, stigmatizes and pushes into Ender in a way not witnessed by any of his other schoolmates, with the exception of Bean.

Elkins illustrates the violence of looking with an example of a doctor's report on a medical case where a eunuch experienced unusual dreams:

> This is the violent side of seeing, where the mere act of looking—an act that can also be the gentlest, least invasive way to make contact with the world—becomes so forceful that it turns a human being into a naked, shivering example of a medical condition. . . . The seeing is aggressive: it distorts what it looks at, and it turns a person into an object in order to let us stare at it without feeling ashamed. Here seeing is not only possessing (the doctor "owned" the case, he got to lecture about it, he had the reproduction rights to his photograph and his article); seeing is also controlling and objectifying and denigrating. In short, it is an act of violence and it creates pain. (p. 27)

Ender too is a naked, shivering example. The tracking of his movements and of his mind present a violation; the act of monitoring is aggressive. The commanders want Ender for what he could do and what he could become. He remains the object of their gaze, their specimen to push, and all the other students exist as similar experiments for the use and consumption of the commanders who console themselves with the idea that such intrusion is for the public good.

How, then, does the monitoring performed on our children compare? Our ends are less grisly. We justify the use of monitors on our children by the desired outcomes of our intrusive gaze; we hope to keep them safe and happy and good. In the case of newborns and infants, monitors—voice, video, and those crib devices that track movement—make a great deal of sense. We don't worry about the freedom and authenticity of babies because their lives are completely dependent on their caretakers. But at what point should our children be allowed to have private lives of their own? At what point does a gaze move from care to violence?

Separating "good looking" from "bad looking" is often difficult (and not just on hotornot.com!). Some monitoring can be useful, but it should not be pervasive in every part of a child's life. When older children get upset at a parent looking at a diary, or when a child wishes not to perform something publicly, or when high schools install cameras to monitor hallways, we feel deep moral ambivalence. We recognize some "bad looking," monitoring gone too far, when we see adults manipulating children into "reality" TV ("Toddlers in Tiaras" and other child acting), into people who represent themselves differently from how they feel (represented, for example, in the reluctance of some people to "come out"), and into people who feel shame when none should be required (when I pull out a wedgie in a store with CCTV). We recognize that we should feel weird about watching older children with the same level of attention that we do younger children. We value trust, and monitors make it so that trust cannot be established. Monitors presume that no trust exists. Similar ideological problems do not exist for monitoring inmates and areas rife with crime because these situations already involve distrust.

We see Ender suffer as a result of the "bad looking" he receives; we see the violence conferred by the gaze of the commanders. Parents and teachers are equally capable of violence—of over-scrutiny, of detrimental shaping and shame, of pushing and prodding. While parental involvement is incredibly important, the deep ambivalence we feel about Ender's monitors should inform our treatment of monitoring devices in our own lives, especially as we encounter new and easy monitoring devices. While we might enjoy the ease of monitoring, engagement treats our children more fully as the good human beings we want them to become.

Outcomes

The reaction of the upcoming generation to monitoring, so far and from what I can see, involves more openness, but not necessarily in a positive way. Facebook, Twitter, and other social sites allow for more sharing and allow users to present themselves as they see fit, though these sites often come with the surrender of information to corporations, and not parents. Though this self-induced monitoring, a voluntary surrender of information, is preferable to the contents of a diary being distributed without consent, issues still persist.

Ender and his classmates willingly surrendered their thoughts to a computer game that monitored them, while Bean refused to play, the only one to do so. Bean recognized the intrusion, the violence, the assertion of hierarchy implied in the treatment of students and refused to play. In this way, he was able to be freer and more fully realize and choose his actions than any other student. We witness this in the final battle.

In an age of YouTube videos, Google Streetview, and *Here Comes Honey Boo Boo*, knowing the appropriate levels of sharing, of monitoring, and of performance are difficult to ascertain, even for many adults.

The monitoring we see in Ender's case produced children who knew they had no privacy, no private lives, no things of their own. Devices and programs that monitor and share challenge values we hold as important, like trust, autonomy, authenticity, and private possessions. The increased cheapness and ease of camera traps on wildlife, RFID tagging, and that feature on my phone that allows me to show everyone where I am, mean that we are likely to feel increased tension about safety and privacy—and good parenting.

Ender's Game helps illustrate why we should worry about what counts as "good looking." The line between parenting and monitoring has never been less clear.

16
Being and Learning

Stephen Aguilar

When I was six years old, I was a kindergartener learning how to write my name with an oversized crayon. When Ender Wiggin was six years old, he was a Battle School launchie and was learning how to fight mock wars in zero-gravity battlerooms.

By age twelve, I was in middle school, struggling with pre-algebra and wondering who I would sit with at lunch. Ender? By age twelve, he had finished Command School and successfully led the third invasion against the Buggers, (mostly) killing them all in the process.

I'll admit it. I have Ender envy. Sure, I take solace in the fact that he and I are both "thirds," but that doesn't make up for the fact that I'm not a genius leading the fight against intergalactic space bugs.

I was a student like Ender. Most of us were. Like Ender we were "trained" in schools meant to prepare us for the "real" world. Yet, who hasn't asked themselves questions like: "when will I *ever* use this?" during a particularly boring algebra lesson, or scoffed at attempts like the following meant (somehow) to make math *less* abstract:

> Bob is training to be a forest tour guide. As part of his training, he must climb a slanted rope net into a tree that is 45 feet high. To the nearest hundredth of a foot, how far away from the tree did he anchor the net if the net is 100 feet long?

I'm pretty sure we're meant to use the Pythagorean theorem here, but let's be honest, this calculation has nothing to do with learning how to *climb a slanted rope net*. Plus, I somehow doubt that someone screaming "Hey Bob! Do you know how far that rope is from the tree? Let me tell you!" will be of much use to him if he falls to his death because of the distraction. More to the point, how does this help me learn that math is useful? No offense, but I don't even know Bob and don't really care about his rope climbing.

There were no fictional "Bob-like" examples mucking up the Battle School curriculum. The name of the game was *battle*, and if you wanted to excel you had to learn how to *play*. That's why Colonel Graff and Major Anderson weren't interested in making their students work on abstract problems. Ender, Bean, Petra, Dink . . . they were all learning how to use their light guns, running formations, leading their toons, and figuring out innovative strategies—like how to quickly change directions with the help of a cable in order to confuse and intimidate their enemies. I say "enemy," but at the Battle School their enemies consisted of other students who could learn as much from defeat as they could from victory (unless they were punks like Bonzo). In short, the Battle School worked because every student learned by *doing*.

The notion that human beings can learn, and be understood, by examining how we do things is not specific to a science-fiction universe. Within the past century two philosophers—one American and one German—also wrote extensively on the subject and grounded their theories on a shared understanding: that to be human is to be engaged in our world through action, not abstract thought. The Battle School taught this implicitly; John Dewey and Martin Heidegger wrote about it explicitly.

John Dewey: Promoting Experiential Learning

The Battle School isn't just fascinating—it makes both pragmatic and philosophical sense. In the United States, a version of the Battle School could have taken place. The American philosopher and psychologist John Dewey experimented with methods and ideas aimed at infusing school with real life. Dewey wanted school to prepare students for life in an authentic way. He pioneered ideas centered on turning schools into buildings where students would engage with complex ideas in "real-world" ways, as opposed to demonstrating their knowledge via tests. He founded a "lab" school to test these ideas. Students in his lab school would learn about photosynthesis by caring for plants in a greenhouse and watching them grow, for example. Dewey's school still exists today and is located near the University of Chicago.

Dewey was a pragmatist—and I mean that in a technical sense. He was a member of the intellectual community who believed that theory and practice are tightly interwoven. Pragmatists like Dewey held the view that theory followed from the examination of practice—the examination of *do*ing things.

Ender, for example, didn't think really hard about how light guns worked, develop a theory of light guns, and then test that theory during combat. Instead "he aimed the gun at the floor and pulled back on the trigger. He felt the gun grow instantly warm; when he let go of the trigger, it cooled at once. Also, a tiny circle of light appeared on the floor where he was aiming." Ender *used* light guns and then developed a theory about how to *better* use them. This is the heart of Pragmatism: do, theorize, and think about what you just did, then do some more. He made good use of this way of thinking when he first arrived with his fellow launchies:

> . . . they kept making stupid mistakes, which suggested things to do that no self-respecting, well-trained soldier would even have tried. Many of the things they attempted turned out to be useless. But it was always fun, always exciting, and enough things worked that they knew it was helping them.

Ender's experimenting embodied Pragmatism, and eventually led him to the knowledge that soldiers would be smaller targets if their legs were bent and frozen, and that frozen soldiers could be used as shields for other soldiers. This practice of trial and theorizing led to knowledge that would not have been achieved any other way.

Battle School was the perfect environment for this kind of experiential learning. I would wager that if Dewey had designed it from the ground up that it wouldn't have changed very much. Subjects like math and science were important, but they were tackled by Ender and the rest of the students at their own respective paces on personalized desk computers. Classes were spoken of, but they weren't important. What was important was what happened when two teams were pitted against each other in the battleroom.

Everything students learned at Battle School came from direct experience and experimentation during the battleroom games. During these intense events the lines that separated cheating from playing fair were blurred—only victory mattered. All of these experiences served to educate Battle School students as to the nature of war. This understanding would not have been possible to demonstrate on paper—students had to *show* their understanding through the game.

The games pushed Ender and his friends to their limits, and prepared them so well that when they left the Battle School and fought similar battles in Command School they were unaware of the fact that they were *actually* killing the Buggers the entire time. There was no energy wasted on pointless abstraction, and every lesson was learned by engaging with tasks directly related to what they would be expected to do so that the transition between commanding ships and commanding fleets was seamless. Dewey would be proud of such a learning environment.

Not Your Father's Occupation

Ender referred to himself as a tool for humanity, and in many ways this is an accurate way to describe his role, but another way to think about Ender's role (as well as the role of each of his fellow students) within the Battle School is that they were all embedded in *occupations*.

Like "pragmatism," the term "occupation" has a more specific meaning for John Dewey. As he mentions in *The School and Society*, an occupation is "a mode of activity on the part of the child that reproduces, or runs parallel to, some form of work carried on in social life."

Dewey believed that children weren't simply vessels to be filled with abstract knowledge. The schooling experience many of us are familiar with—one where students are expected to sit still and demonstrate competencies through exams—would make Dewey turn over in his grave. He believed that traditional schools organized in that way fostered a sense of selfishness in children. (We've all met the child who says: "I know something *you* don't know" in a sing-song voice, haven't we?) Selfishness aside, Dewey believed that schools organized in what we can call the "traditional" manner aren't pragmatic, and disrespect children.

Think about it: traditional schools test for the presence of knowledge, but who's to say that the student actually knows what to *do* with that knowledge? If a student aces their chemistry exam, does that meant that they are capable of actually working in a lab with hazardous chemicals? Probably not. Not only is this not pragmatic (why bother learning something that can't be used?), but it is also disrespectful (why did we just force a child to demonstrate knowledge that is only useful on paper?).

Instead of empty vessels to be filled with knowledge, Dewey believed that occupations were a way to be true to the idea that children are people too. It's an obvious point in some ways, but by organizing a school around the concept of an occupation children are allowed to *engage* with the world. They see a problem, experiment, and solve the problem. In this way schools are a truer reflection of life and allow children to become better prepared for life.

Ender's occupation was Bugger annihilation. He was a *soldier* in a Battle School, and a *commander* in Command School. The Battle School was pragmatic. Every learning objective that Major Anderson and Colonel Graff created for Ender pushed him, but the objectives also forced him to be engaged in a world that he would have to face eventually. Imagine a world where there was no battleroom, no game, only a traditional school. Ender would have never truly interacted with the world he was expected to command later on.

The beauty of both the Battle and Command School were that they seamlessly prepared their students for the "real" world—the Third Invasion. Every game and every challenge that Ender and his friends faced were accurate representations of the war they would have to fight. This, Dewey would argue, is the ideal way to teach children.

The Enemy's Gate Is Down

Fifty years later and an ocean away, we turn to Martin Heidegger. This may seem disorienting, but remember that philosophy is a lot like the battleroom. When you first enter it you may be off-balance, but that's only because philosophy sometimes asks us to abandon our preconceived notions and re-examine our perspective in relation to the contexts we find ourselves in. We have to find our objective—our "enemy gate."

The good news is that all philosophy is written to make sense of something we all experience, and all philosophical concepts are tools that can anchor our thinking to something we want to make sense of. For now, Martin Heidegger and his philosophy are our enemy gate, and his gate is down.

Heidegger cared about *being*. The philosophical term for this is "ontology": literally, "the study of being." For him it was necessary to study ontology in a manner that respected the contexts human beings found themselves in. Ever heard of "I think therefore I am"? Change it up to "I *do* therefore I am," and you'll begin to see what Heidegger was about.

He believed so much in this, in fact, that he made up his own word to discuss human beings. That word is *Dasein,* and is literally translated to "being here." Where's here, you ask? It's where you are *right now* in a physical sense, but also a conceptual and experiential sense. He believed that the best way to understand us human beings was to think about us in relation to our context, our environment, and what we *do* in our environment. Want to understand Ender Wiggins? Then we'd best understand the context where Ender found himself.

Null Gravity for the Very First Time

Have you ever been in null gravity? Me neither, but I imagine that it would be just as, if not more, disorienting for me as it was for Ender and the rest of the launchies:

> They filed clumsily into the battleroom, like children in a swimming pool for the first time, clinging to the handholds along the side. Null gravity was frightening, disorienting; they soon found that things went better if they didn't use their feet at all.

Why are new things and experiences so . . . noticeable? Heidegger would argue that it's because they're obtrusively "present-at-hand" rather than "ready-to-hand"—or, in other words, we're not used to them yet, and have to think *about* them rather than simply thinking and acting *through* them.

Have you ever picked up an instrument without knowing how to play it? That instrument is present-at-hand because you notice it rather than play it. It doesn't quite make "sense" to you because the knowledge of what to do with it isn't there quite yet. By contrast, once you learn to play the instrument, it fades into the background as it becomes ready-to-hand. This transition enables you to think about expressing yourself through the melody and performance rather than getting stuck on thinking about how to produce this or that note or chord.

For those launchies and Ender the battleroom was present-at-hand because they did not yet have the experience that would enable them to make sense of it in a fluid way. Consider learning to drive: for the novice driver, the car is present-at-hand and every action to use and control it is noticeable—especially for the passengers. The experienced driver, however, drives the car as an extension of his or her body; awkward movements are replaced with seamless ones that enable the driver to navigate the roads effortlessly.

New things aren't the only ones that are present-at-hand, however. Broken things are just as noticeable, possibly more so. When the parts of the battle suits were frozen by enemy fire, they immediately became present-at-hand for the wearer of the suit because they would no longer functioned fluidly. The suit no longer made "sense" as a suit—it was an impediment.

It's not just items that can become present-at-hand, however. When Major Anderson decided to modify the games to push Ender to his limits, the games themselves began to break down for Ender because he noticed that the games were being screwed up. They no longer worked the way they were supposed to, and Ender had to begin to think *about* the game instead of thinking in or through the game.

Ready-to-Blast

In general, our every day experience is filled with things that are *not* broken. Did you notice that you're flipping through a collection of bound pages with printed characters on them? That is has a weight, and its pages have a texture? Of course not: you're reading, and those things are only noticeable if you take a moment and think about it. (Don't do that, keep reading!) Items like pens, pencils, doorknobs, and light guns go unnoticed until they break. In fact, most objects or tools we use with great frequency are "ready-to-hand" because they are ready to be used without much thought, and this "readiness" renders them invisible to us.

Every tool that we use to engage with the world is ready-to-hand, and for good reason. If we always noticed the tools we used it would impede our ability to use them. If I constantly noticed the keys on this keyboard I would never be able to type fast enough to keep up with my thoughts, and if you noticed each individual word you wouldn't be able to focus enough on their meanings to make sense of things once you get to the end of a sentence.

Ender could not have saved all of humanity at Command School if he had not felt that the simulator had eventually become a natural part of his body. Ender's soldiers (*any* soldiers) would not be effective if they did not feel the same way about their weapons as Ender did about the simulator. The Bugger queen would have had a useless army if that army were not ready-to-hand. That's the paradox: ready-to-handness is everywhere—until we notice it.

The Battle School, where Dewey and Heidegger Intersect

Martin Heidegger and John Dewey never met. Heidegger was German and wrote his philosophy roughly forty years after John Dewey, an American, wrote his. Despite this I like to believe that they would have most likely had a (complicated) friendship had they ever met because they both agree that to be human is to *do*. Both influential philosophers believed that life cannot be understood or prepared for in the abstract and any divisions we make between the "abstract" and the "real" are not terribly useful.

The Battle School, then, is the perfect intersection of their philosophies. For Dewey it represents the ideal learning environment because it was designed to encourage students to learn while they engaged in tasks that authentically represented the challenges they faced later on. Students of the Battle School stretched their thinking, worked as a group, and used the environment to their advantage both in and out of the Battle Room. What they learned during those initial battles transferred over to the Command School, where they finally—and unknowingly—defeated the Bugger threat.

Recall Bean's advice to Ender during the final Command School battle, "Remember, the enemy's gate is *down*," and how it perfectly mirrored the final battleroom scenario. It is for this reason that the Battle School and the Command School were both perfect instantiations of Dewey's philosophical reasoning regarding how learning environments should be structured.

The Battle School is also a window through which we can begin to understand that what students there *did* was inexorably intertwined with who they *were*. Towards the end of his journey Ender Wiggins saw himself as a tool to be wielded against the invasion because his life was defined by tasks meant to prepare him for the final battle. His own personal "ontology" was defined by being the commander who outmaneuvered his enemy at each turn. In so doing he used weapons that he had to yield perfectly—the simulator had to become "ready-to-hand," an extension of his body. The ships commanded by him and his friends had to act similarly, despite technically having a will of their own. Through this Heideggerian embodiment of the fleet, victory was all but assured.

In the end, the philosophy of Dewey and Heidegger helps us understand the how and the why of the Battle School. Through it we can begin to understand that Colonel's Graff's and Major Anderson's actions were necessary for Ender to become the commander that he did become. While he and his friends were oblivious to the lives they controlled and to the lives they ended one fact is undeniable: during their time at Battle School, Ender and his friends learned how to command well enough to save humanity.

17
Playing by the Rules

Lucinda Rush

At school, Ender drew in his notebook instead of paying attention and participating in class. His teacher knew that he wasn't following directions, but she left him alone. "He always knew the answer," we read, "even when he wasn't paying attention."

As a parent, this concerns me. Because, as an educator, I know that this happens in environments where the teachers are more focused on the children who don't know the answer, or the ones they can't take their eyes off of for a second, or the children who demand attention because they are throwing pencils or yelling out and cannot be ignored.

In these environments, kids like Ender are the "good kids," and they are left to motivate themselves because, often, teachers aren't given the time, resources, or support needed to come up with a plan for them. During the eleven years that I taught in public schools, most of my time was spent in schools with great administrators and kids with involved parents, and even we felt the pressure. But we've all heard about schools that have a ton of problems, and at these schools the good kids are pretty much ignored, left to be just some good statistics on paper, because there were so many other things to deal with, and I have firsthand experience in this type of environment as well.

As a Third, Ender was born with a job. Ender was to wear his monitor, in hopes that he would be selected for a greater cause. Later on in Battle School, he had a real job—to train himself and others his age to save the world. Good kids in schools today have a job, too. They need to do their job to make their schools look good, so they can get accreditation and accolades from the media and funding from the state, and the teachers and administrators get to keep *their* jobs that they have worked so hard for.

Oh, and we also hope that they're intrinsically motivated enough to learn that they'll reach their own greater possibilities. But what are we asking them to learn? We're asking them to master forty percent of the material on a standardized test. When they do this, they get movies and parties and stickers, and two weeks to do some "fun learning" that might be challenging to them and will hopefully make them life-long learners.

Jumping through Hoops to Win the Game

Ender was able to work around the Battle School system by using "free time" to form a group of other launchies who couldn't do what they needed to do by following "the rules." He was able to meet his intrinsic desire to learn and succeed by working around the system. In his case, by working around the system, he was meeting the expectations of the adults in charge. They were manipulating him so that he would learn how to manipulate the system. Dink knew what was happening, and he tried to warn Ender early on in Battle School. He refused to be promoted, refused to be manipulated by the adults. "It's the teachers, they're the enemy," Dink says, "They get us to fight each other, to hate each other. The game is everything."

What's important to Graff and the others is to test Ender and the lauchies, so they can observe and decide whether or not they are up to the task of saving the world. The adults pushed Ender to his limit, until he didn't care about the rules anymore. "Forget it, Mazer," he says in the end, "I don't care if I pass your test, I won't let you beat me unfairly—I'll beat you unfairly first."

But not all good kids learn how to manipulate the system. Good kids like Ender and his siblings and fellow launchies meet their benchmarks, pass their tests, and are then left alone. They may be completely fine, or they may be deeply troubled, or somewhere in between. The teacher lets them out of class to go to the bathroom, and they return an hour later and it doesn't matter, because they are good and they can learn in five minutes what the teacher has been talking about for the past two days. The teacher has been so busy dealing with the kid who is lying on the floor, refusing to get up, while making sure that all of the objectives for the day are written on the board in case the principal walks in with his check sheet, that there is no time to even think about what that good kid was doing out in the hallway for all of that time.

Unlike Graff, Mazer Rackham and the other adults "in charge" of Ender and the other launchies, teachers in our world often don't have the technology or support to monitor the good kids to make sure that they're becoming self-motivated learners. On graduation day, the good kids receive their diplomas with honors from the school principal who has probably never laid eyes on them before.

These good kids go to college and fail, because they aren't used to needing to study or work hard to get good grades. Or, these are the kids who, out of nowhere, hack into the school computer, or lash out at the school bully, killing him in the process. Can we better prepare our children for dealing with bullies, going to college, and handling what comes after? Could the adults in Ender's life have better prepared him for what was to come? Instead of pushing him to see how far he could go before he broke, manipulating him and making up rules that he would bend and change, perhaps they could have given Ender, and his fellow child geniuses, a bit more credit and control over their lives.

No Child Left Behind: Changing the Rules as We Race to the Top

In the world of education, whether it's Battle School, K-12 schools, or our colleges and universities, there are unwritten rules that both adults and children know and follow. Children know what the unspoken rules are, and how to manipulate situations to meet their desires and innate needs.

They're already quite good at this by the time they finish elementary school, and by the end of high school they're experts. What do I need on my transcripts to get into college? What do I need to do to get an A in this class? How can I avoid running into these bullies today? Wearing the monitor and being a third made Ender a target for bullying at school and at home, but the adults in his life had other things to worry about. Stilson and his buddies knew that they could get to Ender after school.

Once Ender's monitor was out, and no adult was watching, they didn't have to follow any rules. Ender knew this too. He knew that if he didn't teach them a lesson right then and there that they would continue to make him miserable for the rest of his life. Sure, there were probably rules and dos and don'ts about bullying. But everyone knew that those rules weren't always followed. We can't protect our children from everything.

Teachers and administrators learn to navigate around the rules as well. Those of us who have been in the world of education for a while know that over the years the rules change, but kids and their basic needs haven't changed that much. We do what we can to do the best at teaching and inspiring our students to learn, while meeting the expectations of everyone else. We fill out the proper forms, make the phone calls, attend meetings, and in those small minutes of "spare time," we continue to expand our content knowledge and learn about the latest trends and pedagogies, and hope that we get a chance to try them out before the end of the school year.

The teacher thinks: how can I get this student to pass the test and move on, even though I know he can't sit still for ten minutes, much less for this forty-five-minute test? Maybe I'll let him stand up and jump around in the middle, even though technically I'm not supposed to. The administrator comes up with a plan: how can I motivate (or threaten) these teachers so they get these kids to pass the test so I can keep my job? What can I say to the parents of these good kids, so they won't go to Disneyland for a week in February so my school gets ninety-eight percent attendance this year, and we get an A on our school report card?

Everyone learns how to work the system. It didn't take long for Ender to figure out that the Giant's Drink game was rigged, and that no matter which drink he chose at the end he would lose. He was forced to find another way to the end of the game. Ender's teachers use an interesting form of problem-based learning, by manipulating and creating rules that were designed to be broken, to turn Ender and his peers into the best soldiers that will save the world.

In the age of school report cards, standards, and high-stakes testing, educators and students have learned how to follow the rules, while bending and breaking them when they perceive it's necessary. Recently, in Atlanta, thirty-five teachers and administrators, including the former superintendent, were accused of conspiring to cheat on state tests and have been indicted on charges including racketeering and theft.[1] They're accused of changing test answers to improve scores—test scores that influence school funding as well as teacher pay and bonuses. Schools in Washington DC have been investigated because of a high number of erasures on standardized tests, which could indicate cheating.[2] A survey recently conducted by The National Center for Fair and Open Testing revealed that test score manipulation is widespread in US public schools.[3] This is widely attributed to the use of test scores to determine things like teacher raises and school funding.

We wonder why some of these kids can't pass standardized tests, when they had a bag of chips and a Mountain Dew for breakfast, and stayed up all night watching Teen Mom, or worse, having eaten nothing at all and stayed up all night listening to their parents party or fight. These kids deal with all of this, and still they come to school and have an extra job to do, and teachers get blamed if the students don't do their jobs. We do what we can to meet our intrinsic desires to grow and learn in a way that satisfies us, while still being able to pass through the system without making too many waves.

Even before Battle School, Ender had to do his job, and try to pass the test despite dealing with constant mental and physical abuse at the hands of Peter and the bullies. All of the grown-ups in *Ender's Game* do this too. They're faced with an unbelievable amount of pressure. They have to find the good kids, the smart kids, the mentally strong kids, who are going to be able to save the world.

Graff, like real-life teachers, was under a lot of pressure too. He felt that he had to cheat the system and manipulate the kid soldiers into being the best that they could be, so that he could do his job. Even though he knew that he might be held respon-

---

[1] E. Peralt, "Grand Jury Indicts Dozens of Atlanta Educators Over Cheating Scandal" National Public Radio. http://www.npr.org/blogs/thetwo-way/2013/03/29/175728192/grand-jury-indicts-dozens-of-atlanta-educators-over-cheating-scandal

[2] J. Gillum and M. Bello, "When Standardized Test Scores Soared in D.C., Were the Gains Real?" USA Today. http://usatoday30.usatoday.com/news/education/2011-03-28-1Aschooltesting28_CV_N.htm.

[3] National Center for Fair and Open Testing, "Standardized Exam Cheating in 37 States and D.C.; New Report Shows Widespread Test Score Corruption," www.fairtest.org/2013-Cheating-Report-PressRelease.

sible for the deaths of children, he did what he had to do to supposedly save humanity.

Lies: More Dependable than Truth

Ender figured out at a very young age, that when it came to adults "sometimes lies were more dependable than the truth." When he had his monitor taken out, the "monitor lady" assured him that it would not hurt. Ender knew that it would hurt. The trauma that he experienced reaffirmed his lack of trust for adults, and his knowledge that everyone, including adults, lie and bend the truth. Ender knows that what he does in school isn't important, because the job that he was born with has nothing to do with school.

After Ender has his monitor taken out, he's led to believe that no one is watching him and that he was not selected for Battle School. If he'd known the truth, could this have saved another child's life? Could this have prevented Ender from the emotional trauma that he experienced when he realized that he may in fact be "just like Peter"?

When he arrives at Battle School he's quickly reminded that adults can't be trusted, when Graff isolates him from everyone on purpose. But Graff and the other adults have their reasons for this manipulation of Ender and the others. Graff says "he can never come to believe that anybody will ever help him out, *ever.* If he once thinks that there is an easy way out, he is wrecked." Their "big test" is to save humanity. It doesn't really matter what it does to Ender and the other kids, as long as they pass the final test. After Ender beats the Giant's Drink game, General Levy is concerned. Graff tells him he is being too compassionate when he pleads with him, "don't hurt him more than you have to."

In the world of education, we lie for all kinds of reasons. We tell our students that everything that they learn in school is important, and passing standardized tests is the most important and greatest accomplishment of the year, even though to ourselves we wonder about the credibility of the lawmakers who come up with these rules, and we know that the passing scores represent the bare minimum of what students should learn. In Battle School, similarly, Graff and the other commanders present the scoreboard as the most important aspect of the students' training. Ender, Dink, and his comrades—the "good kids," left perhaps too much on their own—realize that the scoreboard means nothing, and that it is learning through experimentation, sometimes through failing, that means the most.

Most of the teachers that I know and have worked with do not have a problem with common core standards. The problem is the emphasis that is placed on the tests, the time that they are forced to spend collecting data and paperwork and defending their profession. Should students have to spend hours learning the art of passing the multiple-choice test? How does this prepare them for college or life after school? Just like Ender and the rest of his crew, who figured out that the *real learning* took place during free time, away from the scoreboard, teachers know this, and students figure it out soon enough.

Why do the adults in Ender's life lie to him? To protect him from harm, because they know that they will need him later to save the world? To protect him from himself? If Ender had known that he had killed Stilson, would he have even gone to Battle School and then (supposedly) saved humanity from the Buggers? If they had told him that he was actually fighting and killing the Buggers and that human soldiers were dying, would he have been able to save the world? The lying and manipulation that happens to Ender is not for Ender's sake, it is for the sake of something more important.

What If?

In my second career as a university librarian, I see what happens to the good, yet ignored kids who fall in the middle somewhere when they come to college. They are shocked when they're ignored by a professor, but from out of nowhere get a failing grade at the end of the semester. Usually, no communication from a teacher is a good thing, right? They don't know why the five-paragraph formula that gave them the passing scores they needed on their writing tests for the past five years doesn't get them an A on a college paper. With high-stakes testing that forces us to focus on the passing of the test, and not the process of learning, we have enabled these brilliant kids to coast through the "games" set up for them, and stifled their creativity, and they pay the cost later in life.

Like Ender and his fellow launchies who entered Battle School after years of being (as far as they knew) ignored, and only silently observed by the adults in their lives, these good kids that I speak of are not prepared for what awaits them. It's like putting them in the Battle Room and asking them to figure out how to walk with no gravity. Ender and his friends may have been able to save humanity and the Buggers, had they been given the opportunity.

What if the adults in control of Ender's life had treated him differently, during the six years that he had his monitor in, before he went to Battle School? What if he had been encouraged to do more than just go to school, stay out of the way, and be observed to see if he could pass their tests?

Yes, he did end up completing his mission, but he was manipulated into doing so, killed two other kids along the way, and injured others, not to mention what it did to him mentally. What about the boy who committed suicide over the game? Could that have been prevented? Maybe they could have done more to prepare Ender for what was to come, so that he would have been able to deal with what happened in the end. Or better yet, maybe he and his baby-genius friends could have figured out a better solution, had they been given the chance. Ender was on the right track, during a conversation that he had with Mazor Rackham, and he was cut off. "So this whole war is because we can't talk to each other. . . . Maybe they didn't know we were intelligent life. Maybe—".

Rackham cuts him off and says that they've been over all of these things, but who knows . . .? Ender and his buddies may have thought of something the adults hadn't. Giving kids the freedom to explore and develop ideas is a good thing, and children who are able to think and explore for themselves are able to discover and create things far beyond anything that a board of education and or teacher could contain within any standardized assessment-driven program.

18
Snakes and Ladders, Not Squad Attack

Louis Melançon

A battle has raged and is over. Regardless of which side is the victor and which is the vanquished, there is destruction, there is injury, there is death. Among all this devastation is a boy, perhaps twelve, standing alongside instruments of destruction. But not just any instruments of destruction, these are his instruments that he personally used in the battle to deprive others of life or limb.

We could be talking about a scene from the Yugoslavian break up or Burundian Civil War. Or perhaps this describes Colombia, Uganda, or the Central African Republic today. Or perhaps it describes the culmination of Ender's efforts against the Buggers in the Third Formic War.

For all but the last example, it is almost universal that heads shake, tongues cluck, the act of using children in war is disavowed and shame is cast upon those who violate this taboo. You, as a fan of *Ender's Game*, might also wag a finger at the League for such actions. Or there might be a niggling part in the back of your mind that feels perhaps it might be okay to make this small exception, just this one time. This little doubt brings us a key question: Is it really that important that a society prevent children from participating in war? Perhaps the League's actions provide us, as outside readers, a perspective on our own society's actions.

Little Drummer Boy

War is a social activity. Unfortunately not in the cocktail party sense, but in that it is two or more societies interacting in a fashion that is loud, boomy, and destructive. Highballs and gimlets may or may not be involved.

All members of a society are involved in a war when that society is involved in a war. In modern western societies there is a pretty large "air gap" with participation being mainly passive or highly removed: paying taxes, a portion of which will go to funding the war effort, or consuming news reports from the front lines. In other societies and in the more recent past this gap is not quite so large. Like two elephants waltzing, fighting armies will trample everything around them. Sadly enough, war can become all too real and present for non-combatants; like those who perished during the Scouring of China in the First Formic War. Not to sound callous, but we won't be spending time on the plight of these children in this chapter. Their victimization is tragic, but not our focus here.

Likewise, we won't focus on the use of children as auxiliaries in war. Children have filled roles such as messengers, squires and pages to warriors, or battlefield musicians, to give a few examples. While exposed more closely to the traumas of combat, they were not intentional inflictors of death and destruction. Let's go ahead and put it on the table that witnessing the violent deaths of adults through organized violence isn't an optimal maturing experience for children. Before you think, "Well, Bruce Wayne witnessed his parents being killed by street thugs and he's Batman!" I would like to point out that that is random violence, not organized, and his vigilante antics (as well as his treatment of his wards) open a whole other set of concerns.

So which children are we concerned with here? Where's the problem? It revolves around children who are active participants in the fighting: that population of children under arms in the battlefield and using these tools to bring about the deaths of others; like Ender and his cadre at Command School. Having a child take the life of another (adult, child, or even sapient alien) presents an unacceptably high risk of damage to still not fully-formed moral fiber.

The children we want to think about here are those who enter a field of battle to perform deliberate acts of violence. We're not bothered about cases like a child who's attacked and kills their attacker just as Ender did to Bonzo. While the loss of another's life in trying to preserve your own is an unfortunate result, if the child didn't react they would lose their own life. So according to Thomas Aquinas's Doctrine of Double Effect, killing someone while really just doing what you can to defend yourself is ethically okay. [1]

Or what about a child auxiliary, say a knight's squire who defends an unarmed serf from a rampaging Viking? In cases like this we can agree with Augustine of Hippo, who maintained that violent acts on behalf of those who can't defend themselves are ethically acceptable—and perhaps even required.

The children we're going to consider are seeking to deprive others of life and limb through their actions. These are not children swept up in the winds of war, they are part of the wind.

From Playing Soldier to Being One

There are few acts which are considered forbidden in every culture. The taking of human life by another is a central matter in this land of forbidden activities. In the case of the taking of human life (which we will expand here to include sapient alien life), a society cannot form or function without some sort of control on this activity. The taking of life must be placed within some sort of framework: reserved for religious leaders (in a culture with human sacrifice), those going against another society (warriors and soldiers), or those who may take life in self-defense or in defending the lives of others. Ethical standards about the taking of life are now born for that society. At that point, those who take life outside these frameworks must be addressed by the society.

Understanding and incorporating societal frameworks, including this particular one about taking life, comes from that common human experience called growing up. Making the usual exceptions for progeny of Zeus, Odin, or other ancient pantheon heads, none of us springs fully formed into this world. Understanding what's appropriate, especially in terms of the taking of another's life, is a learning experience as we interact with and observe the society in which we live over time.

What happens then to that still-forming individual when aberrant behavior is repeated based on encouragement or

---

[1] For more on the Doctrine of Double Effect, see Chapter 02 in this volume.

coercion from a source of authority? The inappropriate lesson is learned and incorporated into the moral fiber of the individual. There are many studies and experiments which look into children's development in emotional intelligence, ethics, and social stratification. The upshot is that we can say: If ethics are learned, and the most basic forbidden task is regularly and repeatedly performed before ethical standards have been learned, moral damage will have occurred.

The practical outcome is that it may be hard for these children to become functioning members of society. After all, what they learned and observed growing up was killing. At the end of the Third Formic War, Ender's cadre realizes they will have difficulty returning to society. Part of this recognition is gleaned from the plans of various covetous governments, but part is the recognition that they are no longer children. They lost their childhoods the moment they started at Battle School. They have a lot of catching up to do: an ethical framework consisting of inappropriate behaviors has to be unlearned and the appropriate framework learned. Meanwhile their peers have only had to learn and practice just one, the appropriate, framework.

Another implication of using children to fight wars is that it violates the ethical requirement, explained by Immanuel Kant, that human life be treated as an end in itself. We should interact with each other on the basis that each person has inherent and absolute value. We ought not to utilize—and thus devalue—another individual merely as a means to achieve our own goals. This is where the League, the I.F., and Colonel Graff fail spectacularly.

Lord of the Flights in Zero Gravity

A soldier *qua* soldier, whether child or adult, is a means to achieve an end: to do violence against others so that the collective will of one society is accepted, through force, by another society. But the individual soldier can still express some amount of free will and simultaneously be an individual of inherent value. You might think of the soldier-poets of World War I, as an example, expressing their free will through the medium of the written word.

But there are more tangible examples to illustrate the principle. Consider the individual soldier who acts beyond what is required of him in battle; think of the phrase "above and beyond the call of duty." Alvin York's silencing of German machine guns in 1918 highlights this. Having already achieved his assigned goals, he continued his attack to provide relief for soldiers under his command coming under fire from German positions. These actions, which led to Alvin York becoming the most decorated American in World War I, were undertaken to ensure that the remaining soldiers under his command would be able to continue to develop as ends in themselves. Of course, the Germans whom Corporal York killed were treated as means, not as ends. Even here, though, York sought to kill as few of the enemy as possible and with his seven soldiers took over 130 prisoners alive—giving them a chance to continue on as ends at the conclusion of the war.

Though not easy to achieve, having more experience at simply being alive makes this kind of accomplishment somewhat easier for an adult than it would be for a child. A child soldier simply does not have a solid enough understanding of their society's ethical framework to determine how they may simultaneously be a means for the larger society while also attempting to develop themselves and others as ends. Ender and crew face an even larger obstacle in the form of Colonel Graff. The International Fleet actively works to suppress individual development in its child soldiers.

The atmosphere which Colonel Graff establishes in the Battle School is not conducive to the ethical development of children in a fashion that would generate positive growth. While a loose framework of adult supervision is present, for the most part the children of various ages are left to their own devices to form proto-societies within the launch groups and cross-age range "armies." It doesn't reach *Lord of the Flies* level, but at certain moments, the school appears to be short only one decapitated boar's head on a stick.

Every child who enters that school is treated merely as a means for the International Fleet, even if Graff and Rackham harbor some hidden, inner warmth for the kids. Though there are non-martial educational opportunities, soon every child recognizes the only thing that matters is The Game: their army's standings, their personal rankings, victories, "kills," shot accuracy. Few realize there is something else in life beyond this training for killing. The adults under Colonel Graff not only did nothing to allow the children to develop this part of themselves, but actively sought to suppress it in certain cases—Ender being the most obvious, but not the only example. For others, like Bonzo, the results of this suppression and devaluation to a mere means were more permanent. Why did the I.F. feel it was justified to behave this way and think that child soldiers were necessary?

But, But . . . Aliens!

Ender clearly suffered at the hands of Graff and his staff. Every chapter's transcripts of discussions between Major Anderson, the Fleet Provost, or any of a host of other high ranking individuals showed an explicit understanding of the fact they are inflicting moral damage on Ender. These transcripts also show why they feel they must do this: they believe that the Formics and the human race cannot exist in the same universe. If not for the luck of having Mazer Rackham in the previous Formic Wars, humans would already have been eradicated. The Formics are a threat to humankind's existence. Extreme measures must be taken to prevent the achievement of Formic goals.

The League needs a concept to allow it to make decisions and undertake activities which it would otherwise find distasteful or ethically problematic. Enter philosopher Michael Walzer and the concept of the supreme emergency. According to Walzer, a society, if its very existence is under threat, can take otherwise ethically distasteful actions to survive beyond the crisis. Michael Walzer lives in our world, not the Enderverse, yet the League has bought into this concept lock, stock, and barrel. It could be debated whether the threat of the Formics is as dire as it seems. Do they truly remain a threat to the very existence of humankind, after their defeat and withdrawal in the Second Formic War? The League and the Fleet's strategy is founded on the assumption that they do, causing the League and Fleet to travel down some ethically problematic paths.

The invasion of Formic space implies the goal of absolute victory, with the extinction of the species from the universe. Then there is the policy of creating child soldiers, taking them from their families at an early age, and placing them in Battle

School to be shaped by Graff and his staff into tools they feel are the only hope for the survival of the human race.

Declaring a supreme emergency is always a risky proposition, as Walzer himself points out. An obvious problem is identifying when the emergency has passed. In the fight against the Formics, the League set a pretty clear goal—extinction. In the long run, a society may find it ever easier to take those unpleasant steps it felt it was compelled to take to survive that first emergency. There are foreshadowings in intra-League maneuvers and Earth-side combat at the end of the Third War. This isn't fully addressed in *Ender's Game*—but is something to be kept in the back of our minds. Finally, there is the problem of possibly taking a too unpleasant step in the heat of the moment. This is that moment of clarity in the harsh light of the morning after the emergency, when it is brought home to a society exactly what unpleasant things they did and what values they sacrificed in order to survive.

The Trial of the Century

At the conclusion of Ender's unwitting xenocide and the League War, we see Colonel Graff brought up on charges for the events at the Battle School, with special focus on his decisions, which more fully shaped Ender into the Fleet's desired tool. He is acquitted.

Monitoring the courtroom activities, Ender believes that the trial is actually about him, not Graff, and how human society (specifically the American society from which Ender and Graff originate) will come to terms with what he is and has done on their behalf. But Ender is mistaken. Society is placing itself on trial here, and this can provide reflection on our own choices.

Successfully and repeatedly fulfilling Kant's ethical rule—always to treat individuals as ends in themselves—is difficult. Merely seeking to fulfill it is a really hard task, but even the struggle to attempt it is important. Western societies claim to take up this challenge: avoiding the devaluation of the individual as mere means and allowing the development of the individual as an ends is a cornerstone ideal. Ender's America and the League at large didn't just fail in this struggle; when the supreme emergency is declared they entirely throw Kantian values out of the airlock with the founding and running of the Battle School.

The threat passes, as threats do, and society looks in the mirror. Society realizes it needs to judge what it has done. Perhaps Graff's acquittal signals that society doesn't really place stock in achieving the ethical values spelled out by Kant. Or perhaps it signals an acknowledgment of the evil they have inflicted upon these children and a realization that punishing one individual for this collective sin merely compounds the failure. It could be interpreted either way. Personally, I'm on the bubble.

It also gives us an opportunity to reflect on what values our own societies hold and how tightly we may wish to adhere to or discard them in difficult situations. There's something to be said for deserving to exist. It would seem the Formics understood this as they faced the human counter invasion of the Third Formic War. While Thomas Aquinas and Augustine of Hippo allowed for the use of violence in defense of the self or others, there are lines which cannot be crossed. Even to achieve a good end, means which produce bad results beyond the Double Effect should be avoided.

The League chooses to set this aside in using children to carry out its invasion of Formic space. This calls into question whether Enderverse-humanity deserves to exist at all. Here in the real world, we should use this example to consider how much or little compromise of values in the name of protecting a thing may destroy its value.

Oh, and we should still say no to using child soldiers.

A Question of Character

19
Peter's Game

JASON P. BLAHUTA

Many of the children who live in the world of *Ender's Game* and its sequels appear to be embodiments of the Machiavellian ideal of leadership put forth in *The Prince*. All are cunning, obsessed with victory, possess a flexibility of mind particular only to the young, and all are capable of being ruthless. Of the dozens of child-soldiers in this world, three stand out as the most formidable: Ender, Bean, and Peter.

But Ender, who we come to know the most intimately and root for the most, is the least prince-like of the three. Rather, it's Ender's menacing older brother Peter who is the best leader, the fullest embodiment of the Machiavellian prince. To understand why Ender never attains the status of being a great leader, despite winning the Formic war and saving Earth, we must not rely on popular assumptions about what Machiavelli says, but must consider what Machiavelli actually says of leadership in *The Prince* as well as in his other works.

Niccolò Machiavelli is one of the most misunderstood thinkers of all time. Although he received a humanist education and had penetrating insights into ethics, politics, and history, by profession he was not an academic but a devout civil servant dedicated to his hometown of Florence. This left his work with a distinctly practical flavor, and often meant that he cut corners when defining some of his terms and explaining the background for some of his key ideas, making him partly responsible for the many misunderstandings of his works.

There are two other reasons why Machiavelli is poorly understood: a smear campaign against him after he was dead and a failure by later generations to understand the context in which Machiavelli wrote. The smear campaign resulted from the fact that Machiavelli pissed off the Roman Catholic Church, because he treated the papacy as simply another secular power (the Church had its own army that would frequently engage in wars, often calling upon allies to lend their troops to its campaigns) and also because he was brutally honest about what success in politics required.

The Church took offense at both of these points and placed Machiavelli's *The Prince*, which was published posthumously, on the list of banned books known as The Index. Machiavelli himself was labelled a teacher of evil. The Index was a precursor to today's best-seller lists, and once you found yourself on it, your place in history as a great writer was secured. Needless to say, everyone who was anyone immediately got a copy of *The Prince* and devoured it. This is also a problem for understanding Machiavelli, for many readers of *The Prince* forget that as much as Machiavelli wasn't a professional philosopher, he was a complicated and nuanced thinker who in writing *The Prince* was vying for the attention of Florence's reinstated masters, the Medici family.

So Machiavelli writes to catch the attention of the Medici with shocking one-liners such as "It is much safer for a prince to be feared than loved" (Chapter 17) and his assertion that the prince "does not even worry about incurring reproach for those vices without which he can hardly maintain his position," (Chapter 15). In the context of *The Prince* as a whole as well as Machiavelli's other works, both philosophical and literary, these controversial statements are more often than not watered down to commonsense views. It is only within this broader context that we can now get a proper understanding of Machiavelli.

The Machiavellian Prince

In *The Prince,* when the prince encounters Fortune, Machiavelli's version of the Roman goddess, she appears as a raging river and as a lady. The qualities of the prince are defined in part by how he responds to her: the prince cannot defeat a raging river, so he acts prudently when the river is quiet, building dams and dykes that allow him to channel her destructive force when the river does flood. When Fortune appears as lady, the prince is to be audacious: throwing all etiquette and conventional morality out the window, he is to take her, by force if need be.

This last image, a thinly veiled sexual assault, has made Machiavelli the target of many critics, but it must be remembered that in the context which Machiavelli is writing—one in which Florence and the rest of the Italian powers are still very aristocratic in mental outlook—Machiavelli is not so much glorifying and advocating sexual assault, as he is criticizing the lameness of the aristocracy which would dictate that a "lady" of the court could only be approached by an acceptably well-bred suitor and only according to the rules of court etiquette. Machiavelli is saying that in times of crisis, the luxury to wait for a member of the upper classes who has enough merit to solve the problem is not always available. The state needs someone—anyone—who is capable, and it needs them now.[1]

Afterwards, Machiavelli remarks that Fortune appreciates such audacity, and favors young men who act this way as opposed to their older and more conservative counterparts. This emphasis on youth in terms of leadership is crucial, for it speaks to another quality in addition to prudence and audacity that a leader must have: flexibility. In his poem *The Tercets on Fortune*, Machiavelli offers a third version of Fortune, as an all-powerful and sadistic goddess who takes great pleasure in raising men up only to destroy them once she's used them for her purposes and had her fun with them. Machiavelli's advice to the prince when faced with this bitch-goddess is to remain flexible and able to anticipate and adapt to Fortune's ever-changing plans.

Machiavelli claims that what he teaches isn't really new, that the ancients taught the same doctrine, albeit secretly, when they claimed that their princes were sent to be educated by Chiron the centaur. The hidden message, according to Machiavelli, is that a leader must know how to fight both as a man and as a beast, and specifically, Machiavelli claims that when fighting like a beast he must embody the strength of the

---

[1] This argument is made in much greater detail by John Freccero in his "Medusa and the Madonna of Forlì: Political Sexuality in Machiavelli," in *Machiavelli and the Discourse of Literature* (Cornell University Press, 1993).

lion and the cunning of the fox, for the lion can scare off adversaries and the fox can sense traps.

What many readers overlook is the first part of the image where Machiavelli says the prince must also fight as a man, that is to say, through laws. Fighting as an animal is never enough for Machiavelli; a true prince must also be a legislator and be capable of organizing a society through crafting political institutions and laws. The importance of this is made evident in Machiavelli's praise of rulers which occurs in the *Discourses* (Book 1, Chapter 10), a significantly larger work devoted to the question of how republics should be constructed and governed. Machiavelli claims that the greatest states are those that outlive their founders, and they can only do so if they've been well designed in terms of laws and institutions. For if a state relies only upon the skill of its leader, when that ruler dies, the state's ability dies with him. So, a ruler must fight like a beast and like a man, and must have a sense of vision that extends beyond the immediate circumstances of his life and into history.

Ender the Xenocide

At first glance, Ender Wiggin seems an ideal candidate to be a Machiavellian prince. He is young, cunning, audacious, and flexible. He's capable of being tough, even ruthless, but only when he has to be—as is evidenced by his brutal attacks on Stilson and Bonzo, which are defensive but definitive. Ender also has a certain amount of vision and is capable of inspiring those he commands.

Ender, despite coming from a well-off family, is also a third child. This means he is a social outcast and is anything but part of the aristocracy. Ender learns this lesson painfully at the hands of his big brother Peter who bullies him mercilessly with games of Astronaut and Bugger, and whose position he usurps when he is chosen for Battle School.

Unlike Bonzo and many of the other cadets, Ender has vision that exceeds his own self-interest. He does not look at Battle School as a place for his own advancement, but as a necessity for winning the upcoming war with the Buggers. While the other commanders take offense at their losses in the battleroom, every confrontation for Ender marks a step closer to the real war that is coming, and his only concern is how to win that war.

Ender's obsession with victory comes out most clearly in how he adapts to the changing rules of the battle simulations, even when the new challenges come from Bonzo's shower-room assault as opposed to the teachers. The teachers keep trying to throw Ender off his game, partially because they're testing him to see how adaptive and resourceful he really is, and partially because with the International Fleet's starships approaching Formic planets, they're running out of time. Ender's commitment to the war effort is also evident in how central a place Battle School takes in his life; he literally lives for the battle. All his spare time is spent practicing, constantly making himself ready for battle, or studying the battle tactics of other military leaders, such as the legendary Mazer Rackham, who defeated the Buggers in the last war. Studying history in an effort to learn from the successes and failures of previous great leaders was Machiavelli's advice too.

Despite all this, Ender never seems to fully live up to the Machiavellian ideal of the prince. Ender does his job supremely well and, within the confines of Battle School, shows initiative by disobeying his commanders, finding his own way, and forging his own corps of loyal soldiers—but he never actively seeks out glory or advancement; he merely responds effectively to everything the teachers and the other students throw at him.

In this respect, Ender is like the Roman general Cincinnatus, whom Machiavelli praises in the *Discourses* (Book 3, Chapter 25). Cincinnatus was retired and was called upon by the Senate to rescue the Roman army, which through the incompetence of its leaders, had become trapped. Cincinnatus obliges, leaving his plow in the field to answer the call of his state. He succeeds, saving the army and Rome, and then gives up all power and returns to his tiny farm and his plow. A laudable man and a great general, but not a prince.

What makes Ender less a prince than anything else is what initially raises him above the other child-soldiers. He is in Battle School to win the war, not out of self-interest—but the prince needs to have a healthy self-interest invested in all things, for this is the source of his ambition. Machiavelli's prince wants to go down in history as a great leader who founded a state or rejuvenated a state that was in trouble, but

Ender has no concern for his legacy. In the wake of his victory, Ender becomes obsessed with the fact that he has practically committed xenocide and devotes the rest of his life to atoning for this act; he desecrates his victory by disparaging his own defense of Earth and accepts the slur of Ender the Xenocide.

Even though all knowledge at the time pointed to the war as an act of self-defense against an alien aggressor, Ender chooses to wallow in his own guilty conscience rather than continue his service to the state, a very un-princely thing to do. This is not surprising, though, for Ender never sought his place in Battle School, and is so psychologically frail (as nearly all the children are) that he has to be lied to about the fact that in Command School he is no longer fighting simulations, but is remotely commanding actual space fleets that will kill or be killed unquestioningly at the command of Ender and his toon leaders. In fact, Ender has to be protected from the reality of many of his decisions, such as his killing Bonzo in the shower. Ender is so soft, that he even feels haunted by his victory over the giant in the Giant's Drink videogame, and feels that he's become a murderer—fears he's becoming like Peter.

Bean the Shadow

Bean is far more pro-active then Ender. Even before he is rescued from the streets by Sister Carlotta, he is constantly advancing his position, first through working his way into Poke's gang, and then by turning the bullies into Papas to secure entry into the food kitchens. Once in Battle School, the first thing Bean does is explore the air ducts and perform valuable reconnaissance on his teachers. Not only does Bean show audacity by exploring the air ducts, but he also refuses to play the Giant's Drink. Eventually Ender recognizes Bean's daring nature and picks him to lead a toon with the purpose of designing radical strategies that are so audacious that they will defy conventional logic and confuse the enemy. Bean has more ambition than Ender does, but it is still an ambition of a limited nature.

Bean is not quite human, not at the start of his story at least. His first experiences of life were of a cut-throat world where morality did not exist, survival was the name of the game, and self-interest was the only motivator. This leaves

Bean unable to understand something as genuine as Sister Carlotta giving him a hug; he can only explain it to himself in terms of her self-interest and what she gets out of the act. And it prevents him from understanding how Ender commands, or why the others respect him. This is why despite studying military history more extensively and likely more intelligently than Ender, Bean still cannot command others on his own. Bean simply cannot understand the human component of leadership. Despite the fact that he can never lead the way Ender does, Bean is superior to Ender in other ways. Not only is he more audacious than Ender, but he also possesses a grander sense of vision. Whereas Ender is focused on the war, Bean can already see the bigger picture, and anticipates what will happen on Earth if the Formic war is brought to a successful conclusion. Such issues are beyond Ender's horizon—he is a general, not a politician.

Throughout his story Bean does grow as a person, but he never grows enough to be fully human, and his growth is often awkward and reveals weaknesses in his development. He successfully traps Achilles, but his growth has made him soft. Instead of killing Achilles like he wanted to do when they first met on the streets of Rotterdam, Bean leaves him to the authorities. This decision allows Achilles to escape the legal ramifications of his numerous crimes in the political turmoil that erupts at the end of the war, and results in further danger for Bean, Peter, and Peter's family years later. The consequence, for Bean, is that he can never be Machiavelli's prince, because he can never lead—he's incapable of securing the loyalty and respect of those he commands—and Bean knows this. He attributes this to his tiny physical stature, and others suspect it stems from his genetic code, altered at the hands of a criminal scientist. The truth is much more banal: Bean is simply too emotionally scarred from his tough years on the streets of Rotterdam.

Peter the Great

Peter seems the least likely to be a Machiavellian prince. He isn't even deemed worthy of Battle School. One of the reasons for this—his inability to get people to like him—might seem to rule him out as a candidate for prince. A prince does not have to be liked, it is enough to be feared, but he does have to get people's attention by displaying his leadership skills. Peter's initial failure to persuade the leaders of the Battle School of his merit merely makes his rise to power all the more impressive and illustrates the changing nature of power in a technologized society.

When Peter is denied entry into Battle School, he doesn't wallow in self-pity or resentment at the indignity of his baby brother being pegged as the savior of the planet while he's stuck at home; instead he starts his online commentary of Demosthenes and Locke to influence events surrounding the war. In a world of sound bites and planet-wide multimedia computer nets, you don't need others to like you or the blessings of the powers that be, all you need to do is create a likeable avatar and possess the audacity to circumvent the standard avenues to power.

Just like Bean, Peter knows that he can't presently acquire power and command others in the real world, but unlike Bean, who is unable to overcome his inability to understand humanity, Peter's problem is his age, and he cloaks himself in the anonymity of the computer nets in order to overcome this temporary limitation, building his following and command through his words and his avatar. Peter also has the vision and foresight of Bean, for he too has figured out how the international peace on Earth will implode the moment the Formics are defeated. And he surpasses Bean in terms of his ruthlessness, for he will use anyone—his sister Valentine, Ender, anyone—to advance his plans.

In his quest for power, Peter shows himself as exhibiting prudence the most. His manipulation of events and rise to power are evidence of this. But he has cunning too, as seen in *Shadow Puppets,* where he is able to detect the trap Achilles sets for his family, and fakes their deaths by allowing Achilles to blow up a shuttle they aren't on. His resolve is also firm, as he has no issue with seeing Achilles die in the aftermath of the failed coup.

History's Verdict: It's Peter's Game

In Machiavelli's mind, history is the final judge of a prince's success and worth. From the vantage point of the history of the world Ender lives in, it is only Peter who is worthy of being considered a Machiavellian prince of the first order, for his accomplishments were remembered positively by history for centuries more than those of Ender and Bean. Ender and Bean are necessary and play their parts well, but for Machiavelli they are ultimately the supporting cast in Peter's game.

20
Sympathy and the Perfect Soldier

D.E. WITTKOWER

Sympathy is at the heart of Ender's story, even from his origin as Third. Peter had too little; Valentine too much—Ender was permitted to be born in the hope that he would turn out as he did: having his sister's sympathy, but the ability to act like his brother when circumstances demanded.

We see how Ender uses this sympathetic orientation to better understand the Buggers, watching films of battles over and over again, and later, on Eros, living within spaces designed for them and in which they felt at home. Living in the house of your enemies is not so very far from walking a mile in their shoes.

And yet we might still ask why this was so very important to the I.F.—indeed, why this was important at all! Surely if the intention was simply to train Ender to be able to destroy the alien home world, sympathizing with the enemy can only be an impediment. Similarly, feeling strongly for the soldiers he commanded might prevent him from making the hard sacrifices needed to win the final battle, and every battle along the way.

But then, this is why he was lied to. He needed to be able to use his sympathy to organize action which, however, was thoroughly unsympathetic in the way it was carried out. The great lie transformed him into a perfect moral monster: able to use his morality to most successfully achieve morally questionable ends, untroubled by any actual questioning of the morally questionable.

In the hands of the I.F., morality itself became just another weapon.

Ender's Sympathy

Sympathy is the ability to put oneself in the place of another, the surprising moral periscope that allows us to see things from someone else's perspective. The displacement of self into the perspective of another certainly involves relating to the feelings and values of others—considering them as if they were one's own—but it need not necessarily involve going through those feelings along with another.

This is the distinction usually drawn between sympathy and empathy: in sympathy, we understand the feelings and perspective of others by putting ourselves in their place, whereas in empathy we undergo those feelings on behalf of another. Obviously, though, these are difficult to separate cleanly—to understand another's perspective, we have to at least imagine and feel the weight of undergoing those feelings along with them; conversely, even if we respond empathetically to someone's situation, undergoing feelings on their behalf, we might still think that they're in the wrong, and may still turn the insight of empathy to our advantage.

The way that Card presents sympathy as nearly definitional of Valentine's character, in *Ender's Game*, if not throughout the series, fits uncomfortably snugly with the misogynist view of women as users of emotional leverage to manipulate others—both in her normal life as a child, negotiating family relationships, and in her extraordinary life as a world-political demagogue and debater. But Ender, too, knows how to manipulate those around him, and uses his sympathy to build an effective team, and to recognize and navigate around those who seek to harm him.

Stilson is met with force, but we shouldn't ignore the way Ender deals with Bernard. After sending a homoerotic message under his name, Ender reflects that "tampering with the system had done its work. Bernard was contained, and all the boys who had some quality were free of him. Best of all, Ender had done it without sending him to the hospital." In this first moment in the assembly of Ender's jeesh—through which he became friends with Shen—Ender knew that Bernard's bullying exposed his weakness. He knew that a quick message would put Bernard's ridicule of Shen, for walking in what he thought an effeminate manner, into a sexual context, making it impossible for Bernard to shame Shen for his effeminacy without appearing sexually interested and therefore effeminate himself.

It's also sympathy, not strength or violence, that allows him to survive his bathroom encounter with Bonzo. Only his understanding of Bonzo's way of viewing himself and his moral world allowed Ender to equalize the playing field by convincing Bonzo that his honor demanded he shed every advantage and fight individually and naked.

But sympathy is not just the way a cat understands how a mouse will attempt to escape—sympathy is also at the core of the way Ender builds his alliances. He knows and respects the intimate bond represented by Alai's whispered "Salaam." He gets where Petra's coming from, and has a real sense of what it must be like for her to be a girl in this very male environment. Although he's tough on Bean, he always has his eye on where he can bring him; how he can bring Bean to his highest potentials. Sympathy is the key element that Ender uses to assemble a team that is able to work organically as a unit, in a moral and emotionally-rich simulation of the Queen's fleet, whose unity is instead literally organic, and who feels instead no concern for any one of the soldier-bodies in her hive mind.

How ironic, then, that the skillful tactics and fluid collective orchestration in battle that Ender's jeesh accomplishes in the Third Invasion is so similarly uncaring for each soldier sacrificed in the process.

Loyalty and the Philosophical Animal

Sympathy is needed, it seems, to build a team cohesive enough to wage war against a hive mind. And yet the conduct of war requires a kind of unsympathetic application of sympathy, devaluing both the enemy and the soldiers to be sacrificed for the war effort. In *Ender's Game*, the great lie can resolve the contradiction, but in the real conduct of war, it's not so simple.

We know today about post-traumatic stress disorder (PTSD), which comes not just from having suffered violence, but also from the trauma of having inflicted it. Ancient rituals were once used to purify the warrior returning from battle: even when the killed was an enemy on a battlefield, the need was felt for a bright line of penitence and ritual washing in order to separate the stark moral landscape of war from those greener pastures of civilized life.

Plato considered the difficulty of bringing together these seemingly contradictory attitudes in the guardians of his ideal city. In Book II of *The Republic*, Socrates says the guardians must be "dangerous to their enemies, and gentle to their friends; if not, they will destroy themselves without waiting for their enemies to destroy them," then asking Glaucon "How shall we find a gentle nature which has also a great spirit, for the one is the contradiction of the other?"

While Glaucon is at first nonplussed, Socrates leads him to consider the nature of the dog as a kind of exemplar of the kind of approach to the world which holds each of these seeming contradictions at once, and not in conflict with one another. "A dog," Socrates says, "whenever he sees a stranger, is angry; when an acquaintance, he welcomes him, although the one has never done him any harm, nor the other any good." Socrates goes on to say that this makes the dog "a true philosopher" because "he distinguishes the face of a friend and of an enemy only by the criterion of knowing and not knowing."

Just as the dog takes familiarity or unfamiliarity as the criteria for either love on the one hand or hostility on the other—rather than the dog's own feelings, which might lead the dog to care for the stranger or turn against a cruel master—so too must the guardian value all citizens of his or her city for this reason alone and devalue all foreigners, similarly for this reason alone. The guardian, like the dog, must act on the basis of an idea in order to allocate his or her emotions properly for the greatest benefit to the state.

As we find out later, the idea that serves this function in the guardians is Plato's "Noble Lie," similar to the great lie in *Ender's Game*, as Randall Jensen discusses in "The Lying Game," Chapter 13 of this volume. In the Noble Lie, the guardians are made to believe that they, along with all other citizens of their Republic, were birthed by the earth that makes up the Republic's territory, and so that they are all brothers and sisters, with their land as their shared ancestor—a literal "Motherland."

Today, in the wake of the terrors of the twentieth century, we may be far more wary than was Plato of the deployment of fascistic and nationalist ideology as a method of directing the emotional responses of soldiers—something like Plato's Noble Lie led to xenocide in Ender's world and genocide in ours.

Sympathy in the Field

The difficulty in bringing soldiers to violence at the right times, and only at the right times, is no merely conceptual issue. In an article in the *Journal of Military Ethics*, Ronald Arkin noted the difficulty of creating "true warfighters."[1] Summarizing several studies, he points out that interviews found that of Army soldiers in World War II who had the opportunity to fire on enemy positions, only 18 percent had done so; that of F-86 pilots in the Korean War, 50 percent never once fired their guns; and that less than 1 percent of pilots in World War II were responsible for over 30 percent of the total enemy planes downed. In an interview, Arkin speculates that "combatants may not fight well because they lack a built in aggressiveness and may be incapable of following certain orders."[2]

At the same time, Arkin notes some alarming statistics from a 2006 Surgeon General's report on soldiers in Iraq,[3] including that "10% of Soldiers and Marines report mistreating noncombatants," that "only 47% of Soldiers and 38% of Marines agreed that noncombatants should be treated with dignity and respect," and "17% of Soldiers and Marines agreed or strongly agreed that all noncombatants should be treated as insurgents."

How do we account for these seemingly contradictory findings? Perhaps the difference has to do with facing soldiers rather than insurgents. A combatant might find it difficult to seek out the death of a soldier just like themselves—just as ambivalent, often, about the cause; just as kind to their families; just as human and humane—on the basis of often quite abstract conflicts between governments. When facing an insurgent, it may be easier to think of the enemy as a hateful killer

---

[1] "The Case for Ethical Autonomy in Unmanned Systems" (December 2010).

[2] "Ethical Machines in War: An Interview with Ronald Arkin." OWNI.eu (23rd April 2013) http://owni.eu/2011/04/25/ethical-machines-in-war-an-interview-with-ronald-arkin.

[3] Surgeon General's Office, Mental Health Advisory Team (MHAT) IV Operation Iraqi Freedom 05-07, Final Report (17th November 2006).

rather than a regular person stuck in the middle of a conflict having perhaps little to do with their own beliefs and desires. Here we can see sympathy as a barrier to the conduct of war, but also a preventative force against atrocities and wrongful killing of non-combatants.

Perhaps some soldiers are basically Valentines and others basically Peters. We can easily imagine a Peter, even one who doesn't believe in the cause and is not acting out of fear, having little trouble killing where more humane soldiers would hesitate.

While both of these considerations surely have some truth to them, it seems like other factors must be at work as well. It is tempting to look to technology as an explanation, as it is intuitively obvious that our natural sympathy has less to work with, so to speak, when we drop a bomb or fire on an airplane rather than engage with an enemy on the ground. When we look carefully at the 'distancing' features of technology, though, things get even more complicated.

Moral Distance

David Hume discusses sympathy in his *Treatise of Human Nature*, where he holds that sympathy is a kind of human instinct—a natural and emotional response to others. It is, in fact, foundational to our moral responses to others. The similarity of others to ourselves awakens this instinct, whereby we imagine ourselves in the place of others. This instinctual identification, then, brings about a transfer of our natural concern for our own welfare and happiness to an awareness of and concern for the welfare and happiness of others. Through the instinct of sympathy, the happiness of others is able to bring us happiness as well, and their suffering brings pain upon us as well.

Even a setting is enough to awaken this sympathetic instinct—looking around someone's home, we see artifacts that attest to the activities of their days and we find ourselves drawn into their perspective. Similarly, Ender's time on Eros must have given him sympathy for the Buggers, as he became accustomed to the proportions and spatial organizations that made sense in their mind. And so too must presence on the ground in a foreign land bring about a kind of understanding of, and presumably an increased valuation of, the lives of enemy combatants.

The 'moral distance'—the lack of a shared context of daily life—embodied by many technologies may baffle the instinct of sympathy. The drone pilot in a bunker in Nevada will not feel the same sorts of connection to those they target as would a soldier on the ground, just as Ender, or even Bean, cannot feel a moral proximity to their enemies in the "simulator"—or even to their own troops, who appear similarly distanced.

And yet this insight, while surely true, can't possibly account for the facts at hand. Soldiers on the ground in World War II reported that they felt the battlefield to be a lonely place, feeling disconnected from the enemy even by the lower-tech technology of the rifle, where firing on an enemy 'position' felt abstract and difficult to be motivated by. It may have been the 'moral distance' of the rifle that contributed to the *reluctance* to fire, even though it surely also contributes at other times to a willingness to kill with relatively little guilt. Nor can we point to a distance of race and ways of life, for we must account for both the low rate of pilot engagement with enemies in the Korean War and the high rate of atrocities in the Vietnam War. Further, the experience of being on the ground in battle leads to a "fog of war," in which confusion, hatred, and fear easily lead soldiers to indiscriminate killing. And surely we can't ignore Abu Ghraib, in which soldiers cohabitating with prisoners—it's hard to imagine a closer moral proximity in Humean terms—engaged in systematic inhumane abuse.

Perhaps we have compensated for natural sympathy and the reluctance to commit violence by training soldiers in dehumanization of the enemy. We can see this in how the term "Buggers" is used to insultingly depict the Formics as mere insects, and, tellingly, the resonance with "the Bugs" in Robert Heinlein's *Starship Troopers*. Heinlein's Bugs are often read as a depiction of Asian communists, and the dehumanized view of Asians in mid-century America fits well with the image of ants: the racist claim prevalent at the time was that Asians and communists viewed individuals as of value only for the collective, and entirely willing to sacrifice themselves and one another for the collective. (If this is all a bit too abstract to convince you of such a serious charge, take a look at Heinlein's *Sixth Column*, which is straightforwardly about the Red Threat and the Yellow Menace, and has plenty of racial slurs to boot—plus a weapon programmed to kill only Asians.)

The 'moral distance' of technology may enable relatively guiltless killing but also may help free combatants from the forces of hatred, fear, and prejudice which lead to atrocities. Some emotions lead us to a more moral conduct of war, others away. But it seems we can't have one set of emotions without the other. Perhaps, instead, we should attempt to disengage the emotions entirely from the conduct of war, leaving sympathy to play a role only at the planning levels of politics, strategy, and tactics.

Beyond the Fog of War

This is Ronald Arkin's solution. He advocates the use of autonomous military robots, able to make decisions on the fly about whether and when to engage with enemy combatants. This has clear advantages. First, just as it makes sense to use robots to do industrial labor in dangerous conditions, surely it makes sense that, if circumstances require someone to be in the line of fire in order to neutralize an enemy, it might as well be "someone" who isn't alive. A robot need not fear death and is not subject to racism, hatred, and revenge. A robot can be free of the fog of war, making choices about engagement in a purely mechanical-rational manner.

The concerns here may be obvious. Our sympathetic instinctual engagement with those around us and with their social and material context seems invaluable in distinguishing a combatant from a non-combatant; a soldier from those (perhaps with a weapon) seeking only to defend themselves; and even a fellow soldier from an infiltrator or turncoat. Arkin believes computational advances can overcome these difficulties; I am less certain. And, it's worth adding, I find it hard to imagine that an American robot army, killing autonomously while soldier-programmers are free from threat, cannot but present a horrific vision to the world; the height of technological arrogance and disrespect for human life, even if those robots are remarkably successful at killing only enemy combatants.

This horrific vision wouldn't be prevented if autonomous robot combatants were only used in defense, or if a robot army were up against only other robots, but here, war begins to become thin and disappear—it might nearly as well, it seems, be waged in a true simulation rather than in violence articulated in the form of metal plating and integrated circuits. We might be reminded of Philip K. Dick's 1953 short story "The Defenders," in which humanity has retreated underground, leaving robots to carry on the war between the United States and the Soviet Union.[4] The robots soon enough find an easier way to satisfy the humans' desire for destruction and hostility: rather than waging war, they begin to construct miniature models of various cities and send video underground of the sets being destroyed. As the robots explain:

> "You created us," the leady said, "to pursue the war for you, while you human beings went below the ground in order to survive. But before we could continue the war, it was necessary to analyze it to determine what its purpose was. We did this, and we found that it had no purpose, except, perhaps, in terms of human needs. . . . It is necessary for this hatred within the culture to be directed outward, toward an external group, so that the culture itself may survive its crisis. War is the result. War, to a logical mind, is absurd. But in terms of human needs, it plays a vital role."

Perhaps Dick is right that this would be the proper vision of the fully rational warfighter waging war in a fully rational manner—a manner in which war fades away into a simulation manufactured to satisfy the emotions of the less-than-rational decision-makers far removed from the field of battle.

But if dispassionate, mechanical-rational conduct of battle is desirable only if and when it takes place in defensive positions only, or in a fully automated pseudo-simulation of combat only between things and no longer between people, then this is hardly a solution to the reconciliation of sympathy and violence in soldiers—it is much closer to either police action on the one hand or to a sort of state-sponsored demolition derby.

The Perfect Soldier

What's the solution to this problem? How can humans wage wars both effectively and sympathetically—how can we have a

---

[4] This plot was also later adapted for Philip K. Dick's novel, *The Penultimate Truth*. Copyright on "The Defenders" has lapsed, and it's easy to find online, and there are several excellent recordings of it that can be freely downloaded from *Librivox.org*. My favorite is Megan Argo's, available here: http://librivox.org/short-science-fiction-collection-24.

military able to clearly and unhesitatingly kill enemies without disinhibiting our natural sympathy by the dehumanization that leads to atrocities and wanton killing of non-combatants?

The ideal solution is embodied in Ender: he's able to both understand and kill the enemy; he can love and value his soldiers while sacrificing them; he's the innocent child who can yet preside over countless deaths; he can do what is necessitated by the situation, even commit atrocities, without being subject to fear, hatred, and the fog of war; he can be both Xenocide and Speaker for the Dead. But he can be and do all this only because he is fractured—only because deception has systematically separated his moral virtues from their immoral application.

Outside of the realm of fiction, there's no "solution" to this problem, and the case of Ender shows us how monstrous any so-called "solution" would be. The conduct of war is and should be a horror. Moral conduct of war, insofar as this is not already a contradiction in terms, is and must be fraught with moral and psychological damage. The alternatives are a descent into psychopathy, or the alternative of mass-produced rationally-allocated slaughter—or peace, if we want it.[5]

---

[5] Many thanks to David Bzdak, Elizabeth Farrington, Patrick Lin, Sean McGaughey, and Joleen Westerdale for their thoughtful comments on a draft of this chapter.

21
Ender's Power

DELIA DUMITRICA

I'm your tool, and what difference does it make if I hate the part of me you most need?

Enter Ender Wiggin, the child-soldier expected to deliver Earth from the threat of Buggers. From a lonely and bullied child to the ultimate military commander, Ender's journey represents an on-going struggle between the desire for freedom and the reality of the mechanisms of control and the forms of constraint making up the very fabric of society. The legendary rise of Ender is a beautiful science-fiction novel: after all, the only Buggers we know of belong to the class of insects. Nevertheless, Ender's story has a lot to tell about power.

Asked to think about power, we often describe it as unrestricted freedom to act. As ability, power seems to be something we possess. But in reality we're often restricted by cultural, legal, and social boundaries. Sometimes power appears as an ability to influence others. Freedom, power, control, constraint—the terms seem to refer to each other in a circular way: freedom as an instance when you have power, power as a form of having control, control as the imposition of constraints, and we're back to freedom as the absence of constraints.

All social relations depicted in *Ender's Game* can be understood as relations of power: relations between children and parents, relations between recruits and the Battle School training staff; relations between citizens and ruling elites; relations among children, recruits, and soldiers; and, not least, Ender's own relation to himself. All of these are essentially spaces where power is learned, exercised, and resisted. It's within these spaces of power that Ender's character develops.

Power, argued French philosopher Michel Foucault, is not merely a repressive system. It also produces identities and knowledge. This may sound quite reprehensible, for the freedom to be whomever we want and the objectivity of knowledge are the two things we hold most sacred in the Western world. Not for Foucault! Power, he argued, "traverses and produces things, it induces pleasure, forms knowledge, produces discourse."[1]

Ender's own journey is one about understanding how power is exercised, but also how it produces the individual. Caught between family, colleagues, teachers, and the threat of the Buggers, Ender has to constantly negotiate, adjust, and rethink who he is and who he can be. By following him, we enter a story about the ways in which power relations mold character and behavior.

The Power of the Fist

When we first meet Ender, he's just about to get hurt by a bunch of school bullies. The timing of the attack is significant. Our hero has been carrying a heavy burden: the stigma of being a third child in a society with harsh population-growth restrictions, and the envious position of possibly being the best of all. Needless to say, Ender is not the most popular lad!

The bullies take advantage of their physical strength to push Ender around and harm him. The only thing that had stayed in between Ender and his nemeses had been a monitor implanted into Ender's brain, through which Ender's life and thoughts had been watched by a stronger (and far more threatening) force: the I.F., the ultimate protector of Earth against the alien threat. The monitor itself had been Ender's protection: it forced the bullies to restrain themselves, as their actions could be watched by a higher authority. The bullies may have been stronger than Ender, but parents, schoolteachers, the government and ultimately the I.F. could hold them accountable and punish them.

---

[1] Michel Foucault, *Power/Knowledge: Selected Interviews and Other Writings, 1972–1977* (Pantheon, 1980), p. 119.

Ender's monitor represents a punitive form of power: parents admonish or ground their children; the government fines you or throws you in jail. What gives these actors the ability to punish is their control of resources (parents, for example, can take away your Internet privileges; the government controls the prison system), as well as the general consensus that they are within their rights to restrict behavior deemed unacceptable and to make you pay for failing to respect social and legal norms. They are, in Foucault's terms "technologies of behavior," managing individuals by drawing boundaries between what's right and wrong, and punishing individuals when they cross the boundaries of acceptable behavior).[2]

The consequence of this form of power is that the bullies who never seem to give Ender a break have to repress their desire to hurt Ender. But they will only do so as long as they believe they can be punished. With the monitor gone, Ender's life is no longer public. With no one observing, the bullies can finally have their day and take their revenge on Ender. Yet, their power goes only as far as the fear that they can instill in others. Physical strength works only to the extent that it is able to produce and maintain fear.

In itself, fear is insufficient for this type of power to be sustained at length. Fear can be easily undermined by instilling even more fear. That's exactly what Ender does to Stilson and his gang: the fear of being harmed makes Ender conclude that "To keep them from taking him in a pack tomorrow, I have to win this now, and for all time, or I'll fight every day." By the time Ender is done with the bullies, nobody fears them anymore. Physical strength can be outwitted by the smaller, but smarter, child; at the same time however, this type of power affects Ender, prompting him to modify his behavior in response to anticipating his colleagues' reactions. Furthermore, the effects of this behavior haunt Ender, altering not only his understanding of what the world wants from him, but also his relations to others.

Yet, paradoxically, Ender's victory over the bullies also reinforces the type of power made possible by fear; that is, a form of power that represses desires or actions. Reflecting on his

---

[2] Michel Foucault, *Discipline and Punish. The Birth of the Prison* (New York: Vintage, 1995), p. 294.

final encounter with Bonzo, Ender realizes that the power (but also the willingness) to kill replaces fear by fear. But is it an enduring form of power? And is this the whole story about the ways in which power forms identity?

The Logic of Punitive Power

There's a certain sense of justified retribution that both we, the readers, and Ender feel as the bullies are punished. The bullies—like the Buggers—are crossing over the limits of acceptable use of physical strength: they seem not to respect other people's freedom and seek to annihilate anyone whose presence gets in their way. Yet, this feeling is also undermined when we ask who has the right to punish and how commensurate is the punishment to the deed.

In a controversial book entitled *Just and Unjust Wars*, Michael Walzer has described some of these dilemmas. Decisions in war often appear to leaders as a matter of necessity. Precisely because their task is to protect the collective, leaders feel justified in placing collective survival above anything else. Yet, this does not mean that these leaders are necessarily right, free of guilt, or absolved of responsibility. Ender feels he has no choice but to fight. Because he sees himself at a physical disadvantage and because he has assessed the situation in terms of a 'win or die' logic, he deals the enemy the ultimate blow.

Yet, after the war, Ender finds out that the Buggers did not intend to destroy Earth, realizing that the punitive logic of the I.F. was based on the wrong premises. Similarly, there is no way of knowing if indeed Stilson, Bonzo, or Peter would in fact have killed Ender. Arguing that a specific form of power—punitive power—has been on the rise in the Western world from the eighteenth century on, Foucault suggests that at its heart lies a new way of understanding bad or criminal behavior: "One must take into account not the past offense, but the future disorder. Things must be so arranged that the malefactor can have neither desire to repeat his offences, nor any possibility of having imitators."[3]

---

[3] Michel Foucault, *Discipline and Punish: The Birth of the Prison* (New York: Vintage Books, 1995), p. 93.

This is the perspective taken by both Ender and the I.F.: they are entrenched in the belief that the past behavior of the bullies or of the Buggers is a sign of their desire to exterminate others. From this perspective, ensuring that the bullies or the Buggers cannot strike again appears to them as the only rational solution.

Ender's beliefs, views, and actions rest on this punitive logic; yet, this logic is not Ender's own creation. He didn't simply wake up one day deciding that others are out to get him, have the means to get him and will eventually get him! To a great extent, Ender, like his brother Peter and like the I.F., are taking for granted that the world is a 'win or die' scenario, where total victory over the 'enemy' is the only possible solution. Total victory appears as the only way to ensure survival, to avoid abuses, excesses, or further violence. By allegedly preventing future costs, extreme punishment becomes morally justified.

So, Ender's deadly actions never appear before a court of law. In fact, collective judgment of the I.F.'s actions is suspended until after the war is won. The desired outcome works as an excuse for manipulating Ender, for shaping him into the deadly weapon that he has become. The only ones who truly get punished for their crimes are, in fact, the bullies and the Buggers! The question of whether the punishment they have received is a just one is only hinted at, yet never fully developed in the book, leaving the reader to reflect for herself—or to avoid reflecting altogether—on the moral implications of Ender's unexpected findings about the Buggers.

In a system based on punitive power, the strategic calculation of the possibility that the bullies or the Buggers would retaliate becomes the ultimate justification for action. More importantly, it's a justification that remains taken-for-granted and never truly questioned. This taken-for-granted logic represents what Foucault called the 'regime of truth' (or, in other word, what can be conceived of or imagined as the 'truth') of society. The 'win or die' logic of Ender's world leaves no alternative, no possibilities: the only 'truth' that can be imagined is that of 'kill or be killed'. The form of power rooted in such a 'regime of truth' is by far more difficult to make effective than the power of the fist in shaping your understanding of the world, and, consequently, who you become!

Formative Power

How does this 'regime of truth' shape Ender? Throughout his training, we see Ender's inner struggle between a desire to win, which often appears as something stemming out of Ender's character, and a desire to please others and conform. The struggle is not alien to us at all, for, as children, we have often experienced similar processes whereby, like Ender's sister Valentine, we have told ourselves: "We may be young, but we're not powerless." We play by the grown-ups' rules long enough, "and it becomes our game."

The hope that we can indeed transform the game takes us back to the relation between Ender and the I.F. This is, after all, a relation of power: Ender is the world's only hope. And, as he rises to the expectation, his prestige, skill and sacrifice earn him the respect of his colleagues and the adulation of the masses. But, the world—and more clearly, the I.F.—also shapes Ender into becoming precisely the weapon needed to destroy the enemy. Constantly isolating Ender from the rest, sometimes even pushing the others to hate Ender, Colonel Graff creates the ripe environment to further legitimize Ender's 'win or die' logic. Ender becomes convinced that he is on his own, in a world where strength is unrestricted.

At some point, Ender realizes "what he hated so much. He had no control over his own life. They ran everything." Yet, the mere process of realizing this also indicates that control over one's life is never fully total. For the thought to emerge, one needs to recognize that one is subject to control. The question, as Foucault put it, is that of how "human beings are made subjects."[4] Power, he argued, was not merely about limiting our desires and actions, but also about opening up possibilities for new desires and behaviors. This is the formative aspect of power: a power that produces us, as individuals, by providing the models and values through which we can imagine ourselves as 'subjects', while simultaneously 'subjecting' us to this 'regime of truth'.

Ender's journey is not merely an initiation rite, whereby a young boy discovers who he truly is. In spite of what the novel may suggest, Ender does not have a hidden identity or essence

---

[4] Michel Foucault, "The Subject and Power" in *Critical Inquiry* 8:4 (1982).

inside himself. His identity is a process of production. Ender, Peter, Valentine, and all the other children become who they are by being shaped by relations with peers, adults, and the Battle School, by the looming threat of the end of the world, and, ultimately, by the 'regime of truth' of a society imbued with a 'kill or be killed' mentality. We can argue that Ender's training had begun long before the Battle School, as Peter acted like the omnipresent enemy ready to strike down. With Peter nearby, Ender's life becomes about survival. Yet, at the same time, Peter is his brother and he loves Ender; there is no irrefutable proof that Peter would truly kill Ender!

Once Ender's view of the world and of himself is marked by the logic of survival, Graff's mission is merely to convince Ender that there simply is no alternative to this logic. Graff creates an environment where survival becomes the rational course of action. "We're bringing him to his full potential," Graff remarks. In turn, Ender responds to this call and starts scrutinizing others from the vantage point of survival, to anticipate their next moves. He also scrutinizes himself to ensure that he is, indeed, taking the best course of action within this logic. When he thinks of his family and realizes that the thought weakens him, Ender toughens up and never allows himself those thoughts again. He constantly reorients himself, through external and internal observation. Observation is an ongoing process: Graff and the I.F. observe Ender, Ender knows he is observed, while at the same time he also observes his colleagues and himself.

The more Ender observes, the more he adjusts. In the beginning he tells himself that his adjustment is an act of rebellion against the teachers. He sees right through their tricks and outsmarts them. Seemingly beating the grown-ups at their own game earns Ender the respect he never had before. As this happens, Ender becomes powerful and can tell himself that he is different from Peter or the adults: his power is one "born of excellence, not manipulation." Yet, Ender's success and actions are precisely what the I.F. expects of him. Up to the last minute, Ender fails to see that he is not outsmarting his teachers; he is merely doing what they want him to do. He adjusts to what they expect of him: Ender "made no complaint, though. Mazer had told him that there would be no pity and his private unhappiness meant nothing to anyone. Most of the time it meant nothing even to Ender." In the end, the conditions laid out by the teachers have been internalized and Ender has become the weapon he was expected to be.

This is the process through which Ender becomes a subject, in Foucault's sense. He brings himself into being by learning who he's supposed to be, by internalizing what is being expected of him, and, most importantly, by never questioning the taken-for-granted logic of 'kill or be killed'. This brings us back to the notion of formative power. Foucault, for instance, wondered about the relation between the individual and the 'regimes of truth' mentioned earlier, asking "How does the subject fit into a certain game of truth?"[5]

We can understand Ender's journey as one in which he literally makes himself as an individual, by using the logic and the 'regime of truth' that Peter, the bullies, Graff, and perhaps the world have provided him with. In the process of crafting himself, Ender acts in a seemingly free way: he makes his own choices, he draws his own conclusions. Yet, in another sense, his actions are not entirely his own but make use of—and are constrained by—the "models that he finds in his culture and are proposed, suggested, imposed upon him by his culture, his society, and his social group" (p. 34).

Power and Identity

Does this mean there's no escape from the grip of the 'regimes of truth'? Is Ender the result of his own actions, or are his actions the result of Graff's clever manipulation? Upon being released from his duties, Ender comes to realize the arbitrariness (or perhaps the errors) upon which the I.F.'s edifice of power had been constructed: the Buggers were not the enemy, their first attack on Earth had been a mistake: "We did not mean murder," the Buggers cry out to Ender, "We thought we were the only thinking beings in the universe, until we met you, but never did we dream that thought could arise from the lonely animals who cannot dream each other's dream. How were we to know? We could live with you in peace."

---

[5] Paul Rabinow and Nikolas Rose, *The Essential Foucault. Selections from the Essential Works of Michel Foucault: 1954–1984* (New York: The New Press, 2003), p. 32.

Peace, of course, had never been an option to consider within Ender's or the I.F.'s 'win or die' logic. It is this logic, more than anything else that marks Ender's journey, his transformation into what Foucault calls a 'subject'. This word is meaningful, for it plays upon its two layers of meaning: Ender is *subject to* the military regime of the I.F.; this regime, with its goals and agendas, seeks to control Ender's development and transform him into a military leader. But Ender is also a *subject* or a self-conscious individual questioning and working on his own identity. For Foucault, in the process of becoming subjects, we're simultaneously constructing an identity for ourselves, through the stories and the means at our disposal, and being ascribed such an identity by other people.

Power is never simple. Just like us, Ender, Peter, Graff, Ender's parents, and all of the others, are caught in between their efforts to make their own choices and lead their lives according to their own beliefs, and the fact that these choices and beliefs remain produced by the very networks of power which they try to use. Like us, they can occasionally question, resist and even subvert these networks of power. Or, at least, that's what we would like to believe . . .

22
Weaponized Virtue

David M. Wilmington

"I'm crazy," said Ender. "But I think I'm OK."

"When did you decide that?" asked Alai.

"When I thought you were about to kill me, and I decided to kill you first. I guess I'm just a killer to the core. But I'd rather be alive than dead."

They laughed and agreed with him.

Anyone who loves *Ender's Game* would risk showering with Bonzo Madrid if it meant getting the chance to spend a week fighting in the Battle Room, exploring the computer Fantasy Game world, and playing in the holographic game room. Despite our awareness that the I.F. Battle School is an insanely unhealthy place for children—or as Dink Meeker believes, it even destroys childhood—the compelling idea of a three-dimensional, zero-gravity, constantly changing space for training soldiers in "the combat of the future" is far too cool not to love.

Since the Battle Room itself was the basis for everything that became the Ender series, and remains a central "set piece" of the Ender novels, it's not hard to understand why it wins out as the strongest among all our other images of the story. Still, the entire training experience—from the bunk bed barracks, to the Giant's Drink, to the mess hall, to the 3D video games, to frozen-limbed launches floating helplessly toward a "star"—is irresistible to fans of every age, and has been for years, as the book gains new generations of fans.

As Orson Scott Card describes it, the inspiration for inventing the original story about Ender and the Battle School came from two main sources: curiosity about the crucial role of military leadership for historical and future wars, and fascination with the "children" who did most of the killing and dying in war. So it's no surprise that *Ender's Game* became a novel describing a military campaign that was unique—not just because of the science-fiction settings or technology, but because of the unique kind of child leader created and shaped by the training of the Battle School.

As with all athletic, musical, and military training, the central idea of the Battle School is to create people capable of performing certain tasks and making decisions that accomplish specific goals in specific ways. The training has to fit the goal, so a lot of thought has to go into the definition of the goal and the proper ways to train people so they can achieve that goal. If you want to create a great jazz musician or soccer player, training a kid with Bach flute sonatas or badminton might succeed in developing a *good* musician or a *good* athlete, but not one capable of improvising like John Coltrane or scoring goals like Lionel Messi. You will not achieve your actual goal unless the kid practices the habits of seeing or hearing, thinking, performing, and improvising that are specific to jazz or to soccer.

Graff has to adapt the usual training program of the Battle School, because although the world needs Ender to become a great leader, he does not want to create the usual great leader. He remains convinced that only a uniquely brilliant, violent, intuitive, and ruthless leader can lead the fleet in the only mission that will save humanity. Furthermore, it's not enough that this leader be willing to think about and sometimes act in ways that are ruthless—the leader has to *be* ruthless, deep down in the core of his character.

The epic coolness of all the technological and military trappings of Battle and Command Schools helps to disguise something vicious: Ender's training turns him into a monster.

Greeks in Space?

Although the enforced seclusion and manipulation of Ender does recall Plato's idea of a "guardian" who is excluded from the life of the city even while he protects it, Graff's approach to creating this ideal leader is even closer to key ideas of character formation in Aristotle's virtue ethics.

Aristotle's *Nicomachean Ethics* was written from the political and moral perspective of the Athenian Greeks of 330 B.C., but many modern philosophers, theologians, and educators have returned to his approach in the last several decades. Rather than trying to figure out how to identify, consider, and choose among every possible choice available in a problematic situation, Aristotle focuses on creating a kind of person. A truly virtuous person can behave virtuously, "do the right thing," simply by "acting naturally" or "being herself," because she simply *is* a virtuous person.

If you're a virtuous person, then even your desires are trained, so that you automatically desire the good. Doing the wrong thing would cease to be a temptation to you, because you actively and passionately desire only the good. At the highest level of virtue, for Aristotle (and later for Thomas Aquinas and Dante as well), the good choice will seem like the obvious choice, and a person can trust that what he wants, desires, and wills to do will be the right and good thing.

According to Aristotle and most of his modern followers, you can only create this kind of person through training in habits—a true forming of a person who becomes courageous, for example, by *doing* or practicing courageous things until the virtue of courage is ingrained into the character of the person. You practice a virtuous character like you practice scales on a piano or striking the ball in soccer. In battle, the courageous man does not debate about what to do, and both rashly crazy and cowardly acts will not even seem like options. By following his own character, he will automatically do the courageous thing.

Human Flowcharts?

This approach to ethics is quite different from most modern approaches—which essentially assume that people act like computers applying data to complicated flowcharts of possible ways of choosing and acting. The modern flowchart approach to ethics imagines that human behavior can be governed and improved by gathering more data. We then process the data, consider every possible option, identify choices that allow us to achieve a goal consistent with some higher principle, and then choose which route to follow. With more data and flexibility, the flowchart can be perfected, and good, universally acceptable outcomes will be easier to achieve.

So for example, if I had to decide whether or not to run illegal human trials of a pre-natal genetic procedure that would produce super-human intelligence in children, I might consider many pieces of data: the legal and professional risks to myself, the possible monstrous side-effects of "flipping" certain genetic switches, the potential contribution to scientific knowledge, the possibility of becoming rich, the possibility of creating the soldier who might save Earth from the Buggers, and the principle of the survival of the human species. Ideally, my ethical flowchart should include every option—including the option of protecting myself (or the reputation of well-intentioned scientists everywhere) by slaughtering all the babies to hide the evidence. The only limits or filters are whatever principles I choose as guidelines for my choices.

The problem with this (in addition to the possibility that one of the children will hide in a toilet tank and survive) is that ethical challenges are ever-new and data is always limited. No flowchart can encompass every possible development or consequence such that correct moral choices will result. Furthermore, as the last two centuries of world history have shown, it's more and more difficult to agree about which principles are the highest and which should win out if there's a conflict (whether in law, culture, or religion).

The recent return to virtue ethics, whether centered on Aristotle or other philosophers of virtue, focuses on the cultivation of character: train up a person to habitually do good things for good reasons, and she won't have to agonize over the vast flowchart of possible choices. If she sees a wallet or a wounded squirrel on the sidewalk, she won't even consider stealing the cash and using the credit cards or nailing the squirrel to the ground and watching it die.

When faced with the scientific experiment example above, the virtuous person would simply not see genetic experiments on a dozen human children as a live option at all. Like a saxophone player who doesn't have to think about the fingerings for each note, the virtuous person will perform virtuously, with a kind of trained intuition or instinct, without deliberating over all the data and considering every physically possible option.

Whose Virtue? Which Good?

Although a virtues approach to ethics has a lot to offer in societies that are usually morally confused and incoherent, *Ender's Game* helps us recognize a serious danger in systems devoted to training habits and character. If a particular kind of training can create a person who instinctively does the good, what happens when the definition of "good" is flawed, or tragically, catastrophically mistaken? Can viciousness or evil—perhaps justified by crisis circumstances, perhaps not—be trained and ingrained as thoroughly as virtue?

The virtues tradition addresses this dark potential in part by stressing that learning to become virtuous is also learning to think critically and to deliberate about the good and the best ways of achieving the good. You have to develop practical wisdom, in order to really perform virtue. You need experience, judgment, and the ability to "read" a situation correctly in order to decide how to perform the virtuous action correctly. For example, a child who knows it's good to tell the truth might perform this virtue at the wrong time or in the wrong way ("Grandma, you're enormously fat!").

To avoid the danger of performing virtues in a way that does not serve a good end, children must observe and experience properly timed and executed behavior. Even more important, they must be invited and encouraged to think about why and how the performance of virtues serves the Good.

This is precisely what is denied to Ender and the rest of the children in the Battle School: participation in *thinking about* the ultimate Good and the means of achieving it. Instead, these are unquestioned, settled issues. If the fleet doesn't obliterate the Buggers, they will certainly come back to destroy Earth with their own Dr. Device. The Good is human survival, and the only means of achieving the Good is to destroy the Buggers.

With hindsight, readers know that if Graff, Anderson, and Mazer had invited Ender and Bean to engage with them in thoughtful deliberation of the big situation, with nothing hidden or obscured, it is possible they could have figured out the truth about the Buggers. However, instead of encouraging an environment conducive to building practical wisdom—building habits of collaborative thinking and instincts for reading the small details of a situation—Ender's training before, during,

and after Battle School seeks only to create a brilliant and brutal destroyer. The mistaken notion of the Good at the core of
Ender's training denies him (and everyone else) the chance to
become the kind of people capable of avoiding the tragedy at
the end of the book.

Firing the Weapon

Ender's Game describes a situation which confirms, powerfully
and dramatically, the power of virtues or character-based ethical
training. When Ender performs, he performs the character created
by his training, and destroys Stilson, Bonzo, and the Buggers.
Graff's plan, executed from the time Ender received his monitor,
was not simply to create a great warrior or strategic genius, but to
shape Ender himself into "Death, destroyer of worlds."

The Buggers are defeated because their opponent is "a killer
to the core" who *performs* his own character, as it was trained
in the Battle School—not because an otherwise good boy
named Ender executes strategy and tactics with the tools of
war. As he acknowledges, and even accepts willingly, Ender is
the perfect tool of the I.F. But he's perfect because he's not
merely a passive tool. He thinks, plans, reacts, improvises, and
chooses to act in ways that his teachers could never program
him to act. "You had to be a weapon," Graff admits.

From the first battle against Stilson, where Ender ignores
"the rules of manly warfare," to the fight with Bonzo when he
once again knows he must end the fight "forever," Ender is driven to win a confrontational crisis by violating the typical
rules. The Battle School and the "fantasy" video game reward
Ender not only for breaking rules but for accomplishing the
rule-breaking in the most aggressive and brutal way possible.

The solution to the final "simulation"—which Mazer
describes as Ender's final exam of Command School—comes
directly from Ender's specialized training. When Bean's
"Remember, the enemy gate is down" reminds everyone of all
the previous unfair situations the teachers created back in
Battle School, Ender remembers that his past success was
based on refusing to play by the usual "rules." He performs the
real lesson of his years of training. Total victory, for now and
forever: "If you can cheat, so can I. I won't let you beat me
unfairly—I'll beat you unfairly first."

The final battle around the Bugger home planet requires Ender to improvize—to create something new in the face of the unexpected. However, even this new performance is based on the same fundamentals and is aimed at the same ultimate goals underlying all of his training.

A Shadow of Hope?

When Bean performs, we see that his training, even before arriving at Battle School, has been different. Most readers of *Ender's Shadow* probably wonder, as I think Card intends, if things could have been different had Bean been chosen as the leader. His character is not trained for brutality, despite the fact that he grew up in a savage environment. In fact, at the critical moment of the final battle, even Bean is surprised to find himself acting according to training he didn't know he had. He gives a short improvisation on Sister Carlotta's biblical education as a way to honor the pilots plunging to their deaths through the atmosphere of the Bugger planet.

Although, like her hugs and tears, Sister Carlotta's Bible stories were mysterious to Bean at the time, his realization of the sacrifice the pilots were about to make of themselves—horrible, tragic deaths that would nevertheless mean the end of an existential threat—brings a paraphrase of Old Testament scripture out of him. Like a jazz musician quoting the melody of "Amazing Grace" while improvising a solo on "The Stars and Stripes Forever," Bean quotes King David's lament for his rebellious son ("Would God I could die for thee, O Absalom") in a gesture of honor and comfort.

Even when threatened by the arrival of Achilles ("pronounced ah-SHEEL. French") at Battle School, Bean performs a different kind of character by plotting a way to win the fight "now, and for all time" which does not begin and end with the same mode of violence threatened by his enemy. I think Card wants us to see this as a glimpse of the road not taken. Perhaps Bean's creativity could have discovered a path different from Ender's tragic solution.

We see hints of this in the final battle. Bean surveys the impossible situation, an unwinnable and suicidal confrontation, and concludes, "There *is* no strategy." Because he knows the battle is real, he weighs the cost of the pilots' lives against a hopeless last stand and concludes that it shouldn't even be fought. His additional knowledge of the situation is not complete, however, as he admits to himself when he decides that he cannot take control of the fleet away from Ender: "I'm not God, I don't see everything."

However, even Bean cannot overcome the combination of his own lack of practical wisdom and incomplete knowledge of the situation. Even he cannot overcome the mistaken idea of the Good—destroy or die—at the core of his training. Without the opportunity to participate in deliberation about the definition of the Good, and without the ability to develop practical wisdom with Ender, Graff, and Mazer, even the character whose own training allows for more creative solutions to problems cannot escape tragedy. When Bean realizes what Ender's final solution is, he performs the Battle School training as well as everyone else; the potential of Sister Carlotta's half-understood counter-training benefits only the doomed men who hear his disembodied benediction.

The Virtue of Tragedy

Like all great science-fiction writers, Card tackles problems so familiar that we can only see them clearly in an alien context. Though Ender is not Goebbels and Graf is not Mao or Stalin, the genocidal conclusion of *Ender's Game* leaves us, like Ender, with a set of familiar yet baffling questions: How could this have been avoided? Where and when was there a 'could-have-been-otherwise' moment? Can anything be done to avoid repeating these tragic mistakes?

One of the lessons we can draw is that no system of ethics can afford to bypass fundamental philosophical concerns about truth, human goods, the Good, and the means we use to pursue those things. The Battle School offers a warning via a vicious parody of virtue-ethics training. *Ender's Game* presents a warning for philosophers, theologians, and educators who are attracted to the idea of training in character development. Without a built-in and thorough consideration of the definition and relationship between the Good and the means to achieve it, without training in deliberation and discussion of the Good, training based on a virtues ethics model is merely utilitarian—it will only create tools. The tools can then be used by whoever has defined the Good and designed the habit-forming training directed to pursue that Good. As at the Battle School, the training itself will rule out discussion of what is virtuous and Good by declaring that the matter is completely settled.

The brilliance of Card's dark example—the Battle School and its most celebrated creation—lies in showing how effective training can be when the most difficult element is removed: the mystery of how to train people to do and be Good while allowing them the respect and freedom to participate in discussions about defining and pursuing the Good. Without this respect and freedom, any Ender—repeatedly affirmed as a good person by himself, Valentine, and even Graff—can be trained in habits that make him the perfect tool for a great evil.

Thinking in the Future Tense

23

Lies Were More Dependable than the Truth

COLLIN POINTON

Science-fiction author Isaac Asimov observed, "Part of the inhumanity of the computer is that, once it is competently programmed and working smoothly, it is completely honest." This is very flattering to computers, but also implies that dishonesty is essential to being human. This isn't to say that dishonesty is right or wrong, or that dishonesty is inescapable for us; rather Asimov's aphorism just implies that by nature, humans lie.

There may be dozens of reasons why we are dishonest—natural selection, practicality, the fun of manipulating others—but the fact remains that we do often lie. Maybe maturity consists in realizing that even honest people can be liars, and if so, Ender Wiggin is already mature by the age of six. And as lying presupposes some kind of knowledge of truthfulness, the topic is closely related to the questions of how to be honest in a dishonest world, and authentic in an inauthentic world. Furthermore, how can we be honest or authentic at all if we are naturally liars?

The struggle against the ease and power of lying runs through *Ender's Game*, and Card avoids presenting the challenge with the typical "lies are always bad" cliché. It isn't just the bad guys who lie in *Ender's Game* (not that identifying particular "bad guys" is even possible), everyone lies in *Ender's Game*! So many people and institutions chronically lie in the novel, that lying appears to be an addiction—and this particularly reinforces Asimov's implication that dishonesty is innate to human beings.

From the opening pages to the ending pages of *Ender's Game*, lying is shown to have both merits and flaws no matter who is telling the lies. Despite the ease of lying and the seemingly innate dishonesty of people, Ender and his sister Valentine formulate ways of becoming honest and authentic in a world of lies and deceits. Becoming truth-tellers rather than liars is not an easy path for either of them, but the two manage to devise different methods of overcoming the human addiction to lying. Val's way is to write great volumes of history, while Ender's way is the invention of the The Speaker for the Dead.

Lies for Your Own Benefit, Because We Said So

In the opening pages, "the monitor lady" tells Ender that removing the monitoring device from the back of his neck, "won't hurt a bit." Despite being only six years old, Ender knows that the monitor lady is lying:

> It was a lie, of course, that it wouldn't hurt a bit. But since adults always said it when it was going to hurt, he could count on that statement as an accurate prediction of the future. Sometime lies were more dependable than the truth.

In fact, the removal of the semi-permanent monitoring device is excruciating for Ender, and the doctor who removes it admits that the procedure could have killed Ender or left him brain-dead. This is the first of many risky situations that Ender will be thrown into throughout his life. And to make matters worse, the people around him will continue to deceive Ender about those dangers and risks.

A few examples of prevalent lies in the novel include: the secrets kept by the military, stereotypes perpetuated by society, propaganda churned out by governments, manipulations performed by individuals to force others to do what they want, and untruths characters tell themselves. The continuous stream of different lies show that *Ender's Game* is a profound study on the addiction humans have to lying. It may not be entirely unhealthy, though, if lies are indeed more dependable than the truth—yet being dependable is very different from being moral or reasonable.

The military in *Ender's Game*, known as the I.F., is an example of a vast institution built and supported by elaborate lies. Most of the I.F.'s lies take the form of secrets—a fact of no surprise to anyone familiar with militaries—indeed the very act of labeling certain information as "secret" is a judgment made about that information; which then affects who is allowed to know about it.

In *Ender's Game* it's the military leaders themselves who make judgments about "secret" information and with some dubious reasoning. For instance a colonel states, "After all this is over, the civilians can rake over our files and decide what was right and what was not. Give us medals where they think we were right, take away pensions and put us in jail where they decide we were wrong." The disturbing presumption is that officers either cannot waste time weighing moral alternatives, or worse, are not expected to at all.

In some cases secrecy is taken to the extreme in denying the freedoms of innocent people—again, a surprise to no one who follows current events. Since the "tug" pilot in *Ender's Game* will obviously know the location of the secret I.F. Command on Eros, he is required to become a permanent resident regardless of his personal freedom, at least until the end of the war. Likewise, scientists who have learned "too much" about the Buggers are mandatorily recruited into the military so that information can be strictly controlled.

There's an almost complete media blackout on all associated Bugger information; yet some tech-savvy civilians have pieced together parts of classified footage—thus with regard to information exchange between military and public, many parallels could be drawn between *Ender's Game* and our current experience with digital whistleblowers and "hacktivists."

Typically the rationale for military secrecy is the "threat to national security" because of the possibility for leaked information getting into the hands of the enemy. Yet this is not the rationale Graff gives in *Ender's Game*. Instead he tells Ender at least two explanations for the I.F.'s secrecy. The first is to prevent panic among the public. He and many other military officers are fearful of the peril humanity is in, based on the devastation the Buggers have caused in the past. They reason that if the public knew the truth of the tenuousness of their military's past victories, all hell might break loose. The second explanation is that complete secrecy prevents any civilians from questioning military decisions—presumably, if civilians could challenge the decisions of military personnel, they might feel confident enough to actually interfere with the military's operations.

David Hume was one philosopher who would find Graff's reasons problematic. Hume knew of the absolute importance of opinion for the existence of a government, and its military—as he writes in *Of the First Principles of Government*, "we shall find, that, as FORCE is always on the side of the governed, the governors have nothing to support them but opinion. It is therefore, on opinion only that government is founded." Controlling opinion becomes a matter of life and death for governments. Graff's first reason for the I.F.'s secrecy seems to assume Hume's point, but the military's sad, unethical conclusion is that secrecy is necessary because it would lose control of public opinion if the truth were known. The consequence is that rather than the I.F.'s authority being derived from the people's consent, it is only derived from their coercion through lies.

Hume would probably be disturbed at the rationale of military leaders to leave matters of justice for civilians after the war because he thought that all parts of government are necessarily founded on justice. "We are, therefore, to look upon all the vast apparatus of our government, as having ultimately no other object or purpose but the distribution of justice." In the apparatus of government Hume included: "Kings and parliaments, fleets and armies, officers of the court and revenue, ambassadors, ministers," and so on. All of them must be concerned with justice and how it is enacted.

The military leaders in *Ender's Game*, by putting off justice altogether, are risking repeated injustices. It's no wonder that the I.F. has no qualms about taking tug captains and scientists, and coercing public support through secrecy and lies, since it is concerned not with justice but only the end of winning the war by any means.

The Trauma of Lies

Imagine being referred to as merchandise, your life being so strictly controlled by watchful "guardians," that every stimulus you might encounter has already been calculated for its results in making you into exactly who (or what) these guardians want you to be. Lies on a public scale might seem tolerable, but putting ourselves in the shoes of an individual who suffers because of them, like Ender, reveals the pain involved for victims of a lie.

Besides the many secrets it withholds from the general public, the I.F. also never tells Ender that in his two boyhood fistfights, he has accidentally killed his opponent both times. If the I.F. were to tell Ender the truth, this might jeopardize Ender as the I.F's "merchandise," to use Graff's own words at one point. The same logic gets used for justifying complete prevention of contact between Ender and his family. But the most significant lie of all in *Ender's Game* is the ruse of the "simulation" battles Ender leads at the I.F. Command base.

Graff and Mazer Rackham, true role models to Ender, are nonetheless the ones who orchestrate this deception. Graff tells Ender on the way to I.F. Command that the human invasion fleets will reach the Buggers in five years. This keeps Ender under the presumption that his "simulations" are part of his training for the real battles he will command *years* away. Later, Rackham explains that he will be taking over for the battle simulator computer in order to challenge Ender. In fact, the commander of the "simulated" Bugger fleets at this point is the Buggers themselves. The great plot twist in *Ender's Game* is that while Ender is led to believe he is participating in virtual combat simulations, he is actually commanding real flotillas of ships against real enemies. Every time a ship gets sacrificed, it is a real crew that perishes, and every victory means the destruction of countless lives, Bugger and human.

While Ender has his suspicions about Graff and Rackham, his utter shock when they reveal the truth is profoundly disturbing to readers. The scale of the lie and the manipulation they put Ender through returns Ender to the memories of the physical and psychological trauma he endured under his brother Peter. This trauma lasts a number of sleep- and nightmare-filled days.

While Ender does not blame Graff for his lies and hidden agenda, we must wonder if Ender's extended social isolation is a product of psychological trauma. As older males that express care for Ender (at least occasionally) Peter, Graff, and Rackham should all be role models for Ender; yet each is exposed as a deceiver. We learn from *Speaker for the Dead* that it will not be until his thirties that Ender feels love for anyone other than his sister.

Graff and Rackham are simultaneous caring guardians and ruthless deceivers. I don't think readers are meant to love or hate them. They have noble and villainous qualities. But at least the two could justify some deceptions because they are members of an institution with goals that require deception in order to be achieved. The goal of the I.F. is to win the war, and as members of the I.F., Graff and Rackham are expected to fulfill their duty and deceive Ender if that's what it takes to win. However not all the characters in *Ender's Game* can justify lying because of a commitment to fulfill the duties of an institution.

One such character is Peter, perhaps the best liar who ever lived. He remarks to Ender and Val how simple to manipulate they are. How telling it is of the dependability and power of lies that he becomes the greatest politician to ever live on Earth! Peter's deceits and manipulations cannot be justified, like Graff's and Rackham's, on the fact that he is held to his duties as a member of some institution. While Ender trains with the I.F., Peter lies for his own gain—presumably to achieve the status of the most powerful man ever. But the great thing is, we don't encounter some cliché to explain Peter's behavior—such as his character being innately evil like Lady Macbeth or being born without a conscience. It turns out that Peter's ultimate political power doesn't result in the annihilation of Earth, but a lasting (albeit tenuous) peace. The seeming vile brother of our hero, turns out to be a brilliant strategist who might have prevented a nuclear world war. Peter's no saint, but neither is he a conniving villain bent on meaningless self-destruction.

And yet, Peter is a kind of enemy, since his cruel treatment of Ender takes its permanent toll on the youngest Wiggin. Ender has the continual struggle with himself over whether he is, inside, ultimately as cruel as Peter. He wonders whether it is just a lie he tells himself, that he is somehow different from Peter. "I am not a killer, Ender said to himself over and over. I am not Peter. No matter what Graff says, I'm not. . . . I'm not what he said."

No matter how often he says it, doubt remains in Ender's mind throughout his life, haunting his dreams, that he is just like Peter deep down. And if *Ender's Game* has not given enough evidence to doubt the idea of honesty in our lives, take a look at Val's world view:

"Welcome to the human race. Nobody controls his own life, Ender. The best you can do is choose to fill the roles given you by good people, by people who love you."

On the one hand Val presents the radical determinism of our lives. We have no control; our lives are beyond our grasp. On the other hand, she presents the possibility of freedom: we may choose among the determined roles offered to us. It should remind us of Graff's early choice presented to Ender before he leaves home: Ender may either live with his family or become a soldier. The roles are finite but the choice *is* Ender's.

Kicking the Habit

Is our fate sealed as creatures of dishonesty? Are computers the closest thing to honestly behaving entities? Even if we can select among finite roles, what free will does this really leave us with?

Val and Ender are not satisfied with a world that looks like this. Like Peter, they have great dreams, but unlike him, they do not want to participate in further machinations. They are unique in the novel because, though they both make use of lies, they also set themselves to vocations that might just wean humanity off its dishonest nature.

Val's great deception is her secretly collected evidence of Peter's cruelty. The threat of blackmail by releasing it to the public is enough to force Peter to give her the thing she wants most: her and Ender's freedom from Peter's control. Her use of deception and blackmail is one of the few examples of truly justifiable lies in *Ender's Game* because she only seeks freedom from the coercion she is surrounded by. She does not wish to perpetuate lying and deception that limit the freedom of others or otherwise cause them harm.

Over ensuing years, Val busies herself writing histories. Her history of the Bugger wars grows to over seven volumes, yet she continues writing under the pseudonym "Demosthenes" rather than her own name. In *Speaker for the Dead*, we learn that Val writes histories for every planet she visits with Ender and the books become the definitive histories of each planet, justifying her brilliance and honesty as a historian. I find her career and vocation as a historian to be her way of becoming a truth-teller. The present is too short and too emotional to establish certainties. There is insufficient time and emotional distance to weigh the various causes, let alone formulate the likely effects, of current events and decisions. Only history will tell with any clarity. That is why Val, always a possessor of great intellect, chooses to be a historian.

As for Ender, undoubtedly his greatest deception is keeping the existence of the Hive Queen a secret from everyone. Perhaps he decides to keep her hidden for the sake of her own safety. But if we believe Ender to be justified in keeping her secret from the public, this raises the question: what makes the rationale behind the I.F.'s myriad secrets different? Are all of the I.F.'s secrets justified solely on the principle that they are necessary for the public's safety? If that's the case, what gives Ender alone the right to decide what should happen to the Hive Queen? This is one ethical question I find particularly difficult to answer because though I feel Ender's decision is right, it also implies that individuals need not consult others about the fate of a species—an ethical decision of such vast importance that I also feel it ought to be made in consultation with many people.

It is the Hive Queen's communication with Ender that formulates his way to truth-telling as the Speaker for the Dead. In order to understand this new identity, we can compare Val's writing with Ender's. Both of them use pseudonyms, which are at least minor forms of lying. So is there justification for the secrecy in these cases? Val continues to use the pseudonym "Demosthenes" because it ensures widespread interest in her histories, while Ender uses a pseudonym for just the opposite purpose.

The name "Speaker for the Dead" ensures the book's popularity by its own merits, instead of its popularity being due to Ender's name alone. In addition Ender's pseudonym has a symbolic and quasi-religious purpose: it symbolizes how his identity has been left behind so that he may walk in the shoes of another, and see the world as that other person did. The *Hive Queen* is written from the point of view of a real Hive Queen. This first person view maximizes the audience's empathy with the being that she is. Of course this first-person method of truth-telling violates the kind of third-person objectivity and disinterested emotional distance important to history and science. But I do not think we are to see Val's histories and

Ender's books as opposed because they each set out with different goals in mind. The histories cover events as well as Val can research them using verified evidence. The Speaker's books are not meant to capture people objectively but rather subjectively. History teaches us what a person did, the Speaker teaches us what being that person was like: how she felt, her character and her personal intentions.

Ender's book becomes as significant for humanity as Val's histories. It forms an entire religion of Speakers for the Dead across the Hundred Worlds. Just as Val's histories are definitive for historical facts, the *Hive Queen* becomes definitive for the comprehension of Buggers as moral beings. This comprehension comes about not only by the central use of empathy (in the first person) but also in the importance of honesty for the Speakers for the Dead.

In performing a Speaking, Speakers formulate the identity of the dead "with full candor, hiding no faults and pretending no virtues." Orson Scott Card himself endorses this powerfully honest eulogizing and even hopes for one upon his death one day. A Speaking means the refusal to exaggerate or downplay any of the aspects of a person's existence. Consequently it is a whole act of resistance against the various forms of lies there are, no matter their triviality or severity.

What if Today's Truths Are Tomorrow's Lies?

We've seen that the Speaker for the Dead represents Ender's path to being a truth-teller and a possible antidote to humankind's dishonest nature. However, what evidence proves the new religion of the Speaker for the Dead to be an effective treatment? One of the great consequences of the *Hive Queen* is the historical shift it causes in humanity's view of the Buggers: from a terrible scourge to an unjustly murdered civilization.

The stereotype (another kind of lie) of the Buggers as mindless killers falls away and in its place is the view that they were equals ("raman"). Simultaneously, "Ender the hero" in the chronology of *Ender's Game* becomes "Ender the Xenocide" in *Speaker for the Dead*. Since the cause of the shift was Ender himself, he may be the very person responsible for his vilified reputation—and as such, Ender's own vilification could be another manifestation of his social isolation brought on by his childhood trauma.

For Ender and Val, the gap in time between humanity's differing views of the Buggers is a few decades but for humans on Earth it is millennia. The philosophically compelling result for readers of the *Ender* saga is insight into the fact of historical contingency: what is true now may not be true in the future. It is a concept of supreme importance, especially in the traditions of phenomenology, existentialism, philosophical hermeneutics, and postmodernism. These traditions claim that humans are historical beings—meaning that who we are, and what we think, is naturally intertwined with where and when we are born, as well as the traditions we are raised within. Sometimes called "historicity" or other times "facticity," the concept of our existence as significantly shaped by outside forces like history, tradition, language, culture, and powerful institutions supports Val's own stance: "Welcome to the human race. Nobody controls his own life, Ender."

The challenge posed to us is to take responsibility for the choices we make despite the drastic degree of limitations placed on us by forces beyond our control. Will we succumb to the ease and power of lies, or will we take the harder path of authenticity, responsibility, and truth-telling?

24

Is Ender a Murderer?

KELLY SORENSEN AND THOMAS SORENSEN

When Ender discovers that he's unintentionally wiped out an entire species, he's devastated. He feels the gravity of the consequences, even though he never felt the weight of making the decision. The adults around him made sure of that—they consistently keep him in the dark, steering him into believing he was playing training simulations.

He certainly feels regret after learning the truth about his victories: he's emotionally paralyzed, unable to leave his room for days, and then he dedicates his life to ways of asking forgiveness from a dead species. He speaks of having committed "crimes," of having "stolen" the Buggers' future, and of beginning the endless effort to repay them, all in powerfully ethical terms, under the weight of his own guilt. It makes sense. Ender committed a deep moral wrong, on one opinion: An entire advanced species is dead by his hand.

But not by his mind. He meant none of it. He had no inkling of the destruction, no idea that what he did at his computer terminal had much effect on the real world. To Ender the terminals were a simulation game—training, not war; tools, not weapons; Mazer Rackham, not the Buggers. And because he didn't know any better, according to a second (and apparently conflicting) opinion, Ender himself did nothing morally wrong.

Which view is correct? Is there even a single 'correct' view here? A key issue is this. If Ender did something wrong, then moral right and wrong depend mostly on *actual outcomes*. If not, then they depend mostly on *expected outcomes*. The problem is, there's a good case to be made for both sides.

Ender's Mind: Expected Outcomes

Let's think about expected outcomes first. If they matter most, then Ender didn't do the morally wrong thing.

What did Ender *think* he was doing? What was he intending to do, and what outcomes did he expect? He thought he was only playing a game. So when he used the Little Doctor—supposedly only a pretend weapon of mass destruction—he expected absolutely no one to be harmed. He saw the Bugger homeworld as just a new object in the game, something else they'd thrown at him to test him, and not a planet full of real living and thinking beings. And it wasn't his fault for not knowing better: the adults did an excellent job of hiding from a very bright eleven-year-old the true nature of the "game."

Ender does think of the game itself as training for the role of military commander, which he knows he's being groomed for and seems to accept. So he genuinely sees himself killing Buggers someday through his orders; he expects to kill eventually. But he also expects this to be morally permissible killing—killing in self-defense, since it was the Buggers who attacked humans the first two times (and Ender doesn't know that, for this third time, the adult commanders intend a pre-emptive assault on the Buggers and their homeworld full of non-combatants).

So in every respect, he has reasonable expectations that he will harm no one now, and is only training for self-defense in the future. Even the harm he expects to cause is limited—it will not in his mind end with the death of the species. If it's true that what matters morally is what we intend to do and our reasonable expectations about what will happen, then Ender has done nothing wrong. He certainly didn't *intend* to exterminate a species, and he had no reason to expect that he would by playing the training game.

Second, let's look at Ender's motives and character—the deeper psychology from which his intentions arise. Ender is sensitive, kind, and loyal. Others who observe him—Graff and the other military people, and Valentine, his sister—believe this. "He's clean. Right to the heart, he's good," one says. Ender sacrifices his family relationships and his childhood to preserve humanity. Ender will use violence, but only as a last resort, and when he does so, he thinks about what sort of violence will end future harm. When he does harm someone in self-defense—and he clearly has the ability to spot his opponents' weaknesses and exploit them—he nevertheless hates the dispositions in him that make self-defense harm possible.

If it's true that motives and character matter most, then again, Ender comes off fine. Ender can appear callous and hard-edged, but that's part of living in his environment: the roughness of male adolescence, with the Battle School and the military intentionally making the experience worse to 'toughen the kids up'. All through this toughening, Ender still doesn't lose his sensitivity and love for others.

There's a saying in moral philosophy: "Ought implies can." In other words, morality tells us that we *ought not* to do a certain action only if it's *possible for us to not* do that action. But Ender *cannot* have known better. So we can't say that he did the wrong thing; that he did what he morally ought not to have done. He didn't have the knowledge to do otherwise.

And the nature of morality itself says that expected outcomes matter most. Morality's job is to guide our choices, and it can only do that based on the (usually limited) information that we have; Ender can't have acted wrongly because he acted on the best information available to him. To put it another way, morality is basically about *decision guidance,* and it can't guide us in advance about actual outcomes—we don't know what those are yet, so morality can only tell us to consider expected outcomes. If morality were mostly about actual outcomes, it could only talk about right and wrong in hindsight. But the point and purpose of morality is instead to offer *prospective* advice as we make decisions. So morality is mostly about expected outcomes, the reasons we choose what we do.

There's also the problem of *luck*. Ender and the rest of us often don't know how our actions will turn out. We act based on what we think will happen, and sometimes through no fault of our own we're just wrong. Sometimes outcomes are just a matter of bad luck. It's messed up to think that the morality of our actions is hostage to chance. Ender did everything he could to protect what he valued—his family, broader humanity, and the Earth and its natural beauty. So we should judge the morality of his actions in terms of his reasonable expectations about protecting those things.

For these reasons, many people think that Ender hasn't acted morally wrongfully at the end of the book. He has not committed a "crime," just a mistake—though a gigantically tragic mistake.

Ender's Hand: Actual Outcomes

But there's a nagging sense that this isn't saying enough. Are actual outcomes going to satisfy that itch? If they matter most, then Ender does something deeply wrong.

It seems important that Ender's actions had real victims—billions of them. Whatever else morality is about, it's about real people and the harm that comes to them. It would be strange to say that Ender does nothing morally wrong when ten billion formerly living bodies are now dust because of him. Mazer Rackham thinks actual outcomes are crucial; he argues that even if the Buggers didn't know they were killing humans, they're still killers. A character in *Speaker for the Dead* says something similar about Ender: "Just because Ender didn't know they were ramen [that is, thinking beings] doesn't make them any less dead" (p. 26).

At one point, Ender and Mazer wonder whether killing non-queen Buggers even really counts as killing, since non-queens don't think for themselves. But non-queens do nurture their young; they seem to consider each other worthy of time and attention. Regardless, Ender kills the many queens who are centralized on the Bugger homeworld. It's more than just the high body count. With the exception of one single dormant queen, Ender wipes out an entire species. He commits near-*xenocide*. Bringing a unique and especially an intelligent species to extinction seems like itself a special wrong, above and beyond the huge mass deaths of species members.

Another reason to think actual outcomes matter most is that morality tracks what we *in fact do*, not what we *try* to do. In science, credit goes to those who actually discover things—Gregor Mendel, Marie Curie, Watson and Crick. The same goes for achievements in art and sports. "You are what your record says you are," NFL coach Bill Parcells says. Why isn't it that way with morality, too? Ender's record says he is the killer of billions.

What Ender himself thinks about what he did is telling. He thinks he has committed a giant violent crime. We feel *regret* for what we do, even if it's not what we meant to do, and that's why what actually happens matters more than what we only expect to happen. Ender definitely feels deep regret for his near-xenocide. And he doesn't just regret *that* lots of deaths happened; he also specifically regrets that *he* played a central role in causing those deaths. We regret not just what happens, but what happens at our own hand. And that regret is the mark of a morally healthy person. We wouldn't—and shouldn't—think well of Ender if, after hearing that the simulation training "game" was real, he had simply shrugged it off and thought, "Oh well—the xenocide is tragic, but it's not my fault, since I didn't know better." The 'meh' response is instead what we would expect of Peter, his callous older brother—definitely not a morally healthy person.

And the view that actual outcomes matter most avoids some weird implications of thinking that expected, not actual, outcomes matter morally. If expected outcomes are what matter most, too many actions, and some conflicting actions, would turn out to be morally right.

Suppose at the Battle School that Bonzo tricks Hot Soup into thinking that the figure at the end of a dark hallway is an enemy on his way to kill Ender, then Bonzo separately tricks Fly Molo in the same way. So Hot Soup mistakenly thinks Fly Molo is the assassin, and Fly Molo mistakenly thinks Hot Soup is the assassin. They see each other in the dark hallway, and each attacks, hoping to save Ender's life. If expected outcomes matter most, then both are morally justified in fighting each other—each would think he's defending a great friend and leader. But this is weird. It means saying that both aggressors do something morally right. The proponent of actual outcomes doesn't have to say that. Morality would be a mess of too many, sometimes directly conflicting, moral obligations if expected outcomes matter most.

There's another strange implication of an expected-outcomes-matter-most view. Suppose the hive-queen had figured out how to communicate with Graff before the final battle. She tells Graff what the dormant queen tells Ender later in the book: the Buggers only killed humans before they learned that humans are thinking beings, and now that they know better they resolve not to kill humans anymore. Graff could explain this to Ender and end the "game." And he should. But what's weird are the limitations on the *way* he can tell Ender. If expected outcomes matter most, Graff can't start by saying to Ender, specifically, "It would be morally wrong of you to use the Little Doctor." If expected outcomes matter most, Ender's use of the Little Doctor is not yet morally wrong (because its destructiveness would still be unexpected to Ender); and until Graff actually changes what Ender expects with the new information, Graff can't say otherwise! Graff would instead have to say, "Ender, what you're doing is morally right, unless I tell you some new information." That's messed up.

The point here is not that Graff shouldn't tell Ender the new information; the point is that if actual outcomes don't matter, it makes no sense to start by warning Ender that he's about to do something morally wrong—that particular warning doesn't change Ender's expectations. It's not even necessary, because the result of warning Ender and not warning him are the same: he does nothing wrong either way.

So looking to actual outcomes is the only way to honor the moral importance of billions of deaths—deaths that came at Ender's hand.

Speaker for the Dual

Both sides make some great points. What should we think?

We could just pick a side. That would mean biting the bullet about the ugly implications of one view. There's an intellectual price to pay for believing almost anything. Rarely are viewpoints clean and pretty and without blemish. And many people do exactly that here: pick a side and pay the price.

But maybe we can have our cake and eat it too. Maybe there's a way to preserve the wisdom in both views—a way somehow to think that both the actual and the expected matter morally, each in its own important way. Maybe morality speaks not with just once voice, but two. Here, then, is what we should say: Ender is a morally good person who does something morally wrong. Expected outcomes are about who we are, and actual outcomes are about what we do—and a full, fair evaluation of Ender or anyone else must include both, mind *and* hand.

We already mix these views when we say, "You did the right thing for the wrong reason." We would be saying the opposite about Ender: "You did the wrong thing for the right reason." And that seems perfectly apt. He acted for the right reasons, because he was and is trying to do the right thing, because he's kind and compassionate, and because moral goodness can't be hostage to bad luck. But he did something wrong, because he hurt real victims, because what we actually do in the world matters, and because his role in causing massive death gives him reason for regret. Ender does something morally wrong, but he is not morally blameworthy for it.

This dual perspective fits not only *Ender's Game*, but also— and especially—*Speaker for the Dead*, and Ender's decades-older view of himself there. Expected outcomes matter: Ender as the Speaker teaches that only motives, not actions, can be good or evil—he believes that he is not blameworthy for what he did (p. 26). He advises Human the pequenino to "tell your people not to grieve for what they did in ignorance" (p. 177). But actual outcomes also matter: Ender still regrets what *he* did in ignorance (p. 176). When he looks in the mirror, he sees guilt for the burden of a horrible act, and he's still thinking about it as a "terrible crime" that he must "atone for" (pp. 48, 51). And there's this conversation between the cocooned hive queen and Ender:

> <We know who killed us, and it wasn't you.>
>
> It was me.
>
> <You were a tool.>
>
> It was me.
>
> <We forgive you.>
>
> When you walk on the face of a world again, then I can be forgiven.
>   (p. 52)

Ender clearly takes both perspectives on himself: his motives were good, but he did something wrong, and so must work to repair and repay the damage in every way possible.

The good news is that sometimes the wrong and the blameworthy go together, as do the right and the praiseworthy. Sometimes—and hopefully often—it's possible to both be a good person and do the right thing.

The bad news, at least here, is that sometimes it isn't. The universe is a dangerous place for people trying to do good. Sometimes there's no way to be both morally admirable and morally right. Maybe then all we can do is try to prevent circumstances like this wherever possible.

And when we can't, we mourn and comfort the Enders we know.[1]

---

[1] We thank Shelly Kagan for a conversation about these arguments and their connection to *Ender's Game*.

25
Killing Children

ABRAHAM P. SCHWAB

A few hours before the final battle, Ender lay quietly sleeping in his room. He has yet to give the order to destroy the Bugger home world, but very soon he will. Now imagine that the Bugger response to the human's Third Invasion was quite different. Rather than waiting for the attack, they sent a surgical strike to assassinate the fleet commander.

And so, as Ender sleeps, a Bugger stands over him, watching him, and the queen who controls this Bugger wonders if she should follow through. She wonders if the Bugger should do what the Bugger was sent to do. Similar to questions we ask about using drone strikes to assassinate and military offensives to kill trainees, the Bugger queen asks herself: "I know I can kill this sleeping child, but should I?"

As a general rule, it's morally impermissible to kill anyone—including tweens who believe they're playing an elaborate video game. The quick and obvious answer to the would-be assassin is: "No, you should not kill Ender." But circumstances in this case may override this default view—Ender's continued existence as the battle commander for the human fleet threatens the Bugger home planet.

When Stilson and Bonzo threaten Ender with harm, Ender's defense of himself is justified. Whether or not killing Stilson and Bonzo is an over-reaction, he is entitled to defend himself from intended harm. Unlike Stilson and Bonzo, however, Ender, does not clearly *intend* harm to the Bugger queen or the home world. Ender believes he's only *training* to kill Buggers and not actually killing them. And even his commitment to killing

231

Buggers in the future is in some doubt. As he walks in to take the "final test" Ender doubts he still wants the role of fleet commander: "He saw Graff and remembered the lake in the woods outside Greensboro, and wanted to go home. Take me home, he said silently to Graff. In my dream you said you loved me. Take me home."

To answer the Bugger queen's question, it turns out we must first answer a few other questions: Does the intention of the harming individual matter in cases of self-defense? In the case of war, does the intention of the soldier matter? And what are you justified in doing to an individual who means you no harm, but nonetheless, will end up killing you if you don't stop them? To start answering the would-be assassin's questions, let's look at the distinction between combatants and non-combatants.

Combatants Versus Non-Combatants

Michael Walzer, in *Just and Unjust Wars*, hinges the distinction between combatant and non-combatant on the "essential" nature of a person's contributions to a war effort: a functionalist view of combatant versus non-combatant. This view provides a framework for arguing that some members of a society are not legitimate aims of military action during war.

As a matter of course, this combatant and non-combatant distinction falls largely along soldier and citizen lines. For example, on this view Ender's actions, as those of a commanding officer, are clearly those of a combatant. His role renders irrelevant his ignorance about what he does; it only matters that he is an essential part of the war effort and so a legitimate target of military assault. Peter and Valentine, in their roles as the writers Locke and Demosthenes, are non-essential to the war effort and so non-combatants. As public intellectuals, they may encourage the war, but they are not essential to its execution: they are but writers.

Drawing the distinction between combatants and non-combatants in this way prohibits targeting most civilians in military campaigns, including civilians who encourage violent behavior. According to Walzer's view, when an individual is not essential to the war effort, it's immoral to target them with military actions.

We could always reject this view of combatant and non-combatant. We could say that Ender should not be the appropriate target of a Bugger attack because he did not know that he was harming Buggers.

An Unknowing Enemy

We might say that the Bugger should not kill Ender despite his essential role in the attack on the Bugger home world because Ender believes he's still in training, and doesn't intend, for now, to kill Buggers. Implied by this view, the intentions of the individual mark the distinction between combatant and non-combatant: Ender's innocent intentions indicate that he should not be subject to violence.

This view only protects Ender to the degree that he's innocent. So we need to know: is Ender innocent? Specifically, when Ender orders the starships and fighters to aim the Little Doctors on the Bugger home planet, is he innocent?

In the strictest sense we'd have to say, yes, he is innocent. He appears unaware that he orders the destruction of the Bugger home planet, and there's a substantial difference between *hypothetically* wiping out a planet and *knowingly* wiping out a planet. Indeed, Ender's own thoughts suggest that he does not think anyone should ever destroy the Bugger home world: "if I break this rule [and fire the Little Doctor on the Bugger home planet] they'll never let me be a commander. It would be too dangerous."

And yet, if the Bugger killed Ender to protect itself in any context other than war, it would be justified by all but the most rigid of pacifists. When an individual's life is threatened, they are typically justified in taking the necessary steps to protect themselves. In killing Ender, the Bugger queen would be acting in self-defense. Ender may not intend harm to the Buggers and their home planet, but he poses a threat just the same.

Despite his innocence, violence against him seems justified, not as retribution, but as a matter of defense. If he were not such a proximal cause of the destruction of the Bugger home world, it might be harder to justify his execution. As it is, the Bugger queen, acting through her Bugger infiltrator, need only point to his imminent threat to justify their course of action.

Such justifications have significant implications for the use of drone strikes and other assassinations in the current war on terror. If we endorse the view that the threat Ender represents, innocence notwithstanding, justifies violence against him, we should also endorse the contemporary use of drone strikes and other military attacks on militants who pose a threat to us and others. So long as these militants represent a threat within some ongoing offensive, they are the legitimate targets of violent strikes. As acts of self-defense to eliminate a threat of imminent harm, these strikes and assassinations are justified.

The threat of harm may justify the use of violence against individuals involved in an ongoing military offensive, but what about individuals who have not yet begun to fight?

Lethal Training

Rather than the night before the final battle, let's imagine the Bugger standing over Ender as he sleeps some time during his days at battle school. Perhaps the week he became the battle commander for Dragon Army. Would the Bugger queen be justified in willing the Bugger to kill him then?

Earlier we concluded that Buggers could legitimately target Ender as a matter of defense because he was a threat of harm. While he trains Ender does not clearly threaten harm. At some point in the future he *may* be part of the war effort against the Buggers, but while training, he poses no direct threat. Given this fact, would a Bugger be justified in attacking him?

Answering this question hinges on distinguishing trainees from soldiers. Children at the Battle School are first referred to as "launchies" and later as "soldiers." For our concerns here, there are still trainees, despite the names that they may call themselves. A soldier, unlike a trainee, threatens harm within the war effort and, as such, is subject to the violent reprisal. Ender believes himself to be *training* to fight Buggers, and that is, in fact what he is doing. But because he plays no functional role in the war effort, should the Bugger queen stay the attempt to kill Ender?

This question matters to us because of changes in how we wage "war." No longer a nation-versus-nation affair, war often consists of militant groups attacking from the shadows. These covert operations make these militant groups most visible when training. As a result, their likely targets (the United States among others) have the best opportunities to attack during training exercises. Based on opportunity combined with a goal to keep down collateral damage, the Obama administration classifies all adult males in the area of a training exercise targeted by a US military strike as "enemy combatants."[1] This view of the Obama administration casts all trainees as justifiable targets of violence. Is this morally legitimate?

In certain cases, it must be. Imagine, for example, a soldier who has previously fought in a war and is now training for an additional, perhaps more specific skill set. Such individuals, who represent an ongoing threat in a war effort, must be legitimate targets of violent reprisal. Trainees who have never fought are a more difficult case. They occupy a uncertain space somewhere between a combatant and a civilian. A civilian in that they have yet to play a role in the war, and a combatant in that they have a predictable and likely future role in the war effort. We know that soldiers will die during conflict and trainees will replace them. As a result, much like the soldier who is not presently attacking, trainees represent future harms.

Does the threat of "future harm" justify violence against the trainee? It's tempting to say 'No, not until they have committed their first act of aggression'. Despite its intuitive appeal, this view does not stand up to scrutiny. For example, a person in a sleeper cell may have yet to act aggressively, but they are still legitimate subjects of violent confrontation. The person in the sleeper cell is no longer actively training—so perhaps, persons become the legitimate target of violence when they have completed their training. And yet, ambiguity persists. If they are a legitimate target of violence when they complete their training, why not the day before it's complete? It's easy to imagine that if they were one day short of completing the training, and the need arose, they would be sent into the field by their commanding officers. But there's no need to stop here. If the need arose, they would be sent into the field the day before the day before their last day of training. And it goes on like this. Following this line of reasoning, it seems trainees would be

---

[1] "Secret 'Kill List' Proves a Test of Obama's Principles and Will" (*New York Times*, 29th May 2012), www.nytimes.com/2012/05/29/world/obamas-leadership-in-war-on-al-qaeda.html.

legitimate targets of violence at any stage during training so long as they will take part in the war effort.

Advanced training camps of elite units make viable military targets because they represent a past and future threat of harm. It's less easy to see how trainees at boot camps represent the same threat of harm. Those who go to boot camp and don't make it—and there are always some who ice out—will never be a threat of harm. And the further back we go in the training process, the larger this number of individuals that will never be a threat.

And now we stand upon the edge of a slippery slope. Will there come a point where we can distinguish trainees who are legitimate targets of violence from those who are not, from those who represent threats of harm from those who do not? When we look at a particular trainee, we cannot know how their training will end. As Ender trains, what tells us that Ender is a legitimate target at some times, but an illegitimate target of violence at others? If he's a legitimate target when he's training, why not when he's getting ready to leave for training? Why not when he's being "monitored" (a sort of pre-training evaluation)? Why not before he was even born?

And now we see the dangers of a slippery slope argument. We start by recognizing trainees as legitimate targets of violence under at least some circumstances and ended up in the absurd position of asking if the unborn, who may at some point in the future be a threat of harm, are legitimate military targets. A rigid and neat conceptual distinction between trainees that threaten harm and those who do not may not be available. And yet, to avoid the genocidal implications of failing to draw this line—in which "removing future threats" becomes a name for "ethnic cleansing"—we should draw one as best we can. Perhaps a reasonable point to draw this line is when formalized training begins. Perhaps a little later.

The difficulty of drawing this line may explain, though not justify, the Obama administration's decision to count all adult males in an area of known terrorist activity as "combatants." How could you tell if they're part of the training program or not?

Minor Harms

Ender's maturity in action and thought constitutes one of the most enthralling aspects of *Ender's Game*. And yet, by the end of the Game he is an eleven-year-old boy. Should it matter to our hypothetical Bugger queen that Ender is a child? If the commander of the human fleet is only a tween, does that mean the Bugger queen shouldn't kill him? Because he's only nine years old when he's training, does that mean he should be spared?

One answer to this question follows neatly from our earlier analysis. Ender's innocence is independent of whether or not he is the legitimate subject of Bugger violence. The harm his actions will lead to, the threat he represents, legitimates violence against him. That his innocence emanates from his status as a child does not make him immune to violence as a matter of defense. And so, we're left to conclude that child soldiers are the legitimate targets of violence. Though they may be innocent, they represent the same threat of harm. They may not have chosen the soldier's life, but they are in it just the same.

But what of the treatment of children not by their enemies, but by their friends? Ender would not be in a position to be killed by this Bugger if not for the work of Colonel Graff, Major Anderson, and the others in fleet command. He would not be a legitimate target of the Buggers' deadly force if they had not chosen him for training, had not trained him, had not tricked him into leading fleet command. Was it justifiable for them to put Ender in this position, the legitimate target of deadly force?

Ideally, children should be left out of war altogether. Their innocence should be protected until they reach the age of maturity. The reality of war, though, may keep us from this goal. During wars, there are sometimes compelling reasons to involve children, rather than simply protect them. For starters, when the vicissitudes of war put children in harm's way, training may save their lives. Though costing them their innocence, it may save their future.

Additionally, when they have reached the age of maturity, these children are likely to be called upon to fight in ongoing wars. As such their training could be of substantial benefit to them. Finally, children, much like Ender, could play pivotal strategic roles in a war effort. Although most children would not be prized for their intellectual and social acuity, they could be used to achieve different strategic objectives. Given all these reasons to use children in war, we are left to ask, should they be used as tools in a war effort?

Throughout *Ender's Game*, Colonel Graff and Major Anderson often discuss their risky attempts to manipulate Ender for their strategic purposes, attempts that continually frustrate Ender. He knows he's being manipulated, isn't happy about it, but continues to play along. Dink gives the subsequent frustration its clearest articulation: "I was six years old when they brought me here. What the hell did I know? *They* decided I was right for the program, but nobody ever asked me if the program was right for me."

The most vivid justifications for using children as tools as Graff and Anderson do would be to ensure the survival of a group, culture, or population. To hear Graff tell it this's why they're using Ender: humans are the Third Invasion to ensure their survival. As Mazer puts it after Ender destroys the Buggers' home world: "*They* decided that [the destruction of the Buggers' home world] when they attacked us. It wasn't your fault. It's what had to happen."

Ender accepts this argument uncritically. This is not to say that Ender lets Graff and Mazer off the hook entirely after the battle. But his complaint is not about the fact that they were complicit in using children to destroy the Buggers' home world—it's that they used him to do it rather than Peter. Although Ender accepts Mazer's argument uncritically, we should not. Mazer and Graff's beliefs may be false. Their view of the Buggers may be skewed.

And this leaves us with an uncomfortable conclusion about the appropriate use of children in war. In the context of *Ender's Game*, the humans believe that they must use children to prepare for and execute an attack on the Buggers to maintain survival. But it's not at all clear that this belief is grounded in reality—it's simply a guess that the Buggers are going to come back—a guess that may very well be wrong. But, if we find the use of children acceptable within *Ender's Game*, wouldn't this mean that any militant's fervent (but potentially false) belief justifies the use of children to achieve their strategic objectives?

Battle School Officer Directory

STEPHEN AGUILAR is a graduate student in the Combined Program in Education and Psychology at the University of Michigan. He is also a "third," but luckily lives in a world that doesn't seem to mind. Rather than training to battle Buggers, he studies how game-inspired pedagogies can serve as a lever to increase student motivation, agency, and autonomy, and instill adaptive academic identities.

YOCHAI ATARIA is a doctoral candidate at the Hebrew University of Jerusalem. He writes mainly about the state of consciousness during traumatic experiences as well as cultural aspects of trauma. Most nights he can't get to sleep, wondering about the "hard problem" of consciousness. He likes to read classic novels and take long walks with his son and his dog (preferably not in zero-gravity conditions).

TIM BLACKMORE slaves away at a remote keyboard, writing about war, SF, and comics. The rest of the time he teaches non-virtual real-life classes at the University of Western Ontario, where he is a professor in Media Studies. He also reads for-real non-digital comics: how old fashioned is *that*?

JASON P. BLAHUTA is the pseudonym of a six-year-old boy who is consolidating his power and laying plans to take over the world by his sixteenth birthday. Or at least that's how his wife characterizes him. This ingenious avatar is of a harmless philosophy professor teaching social-political thought and applied ethics—the last person to be suspected of saving the world from its current cast of inane political actors.

Trapped in a law student's body, philosopher **DANIEL M. DRUVENGA** spends most of his time feverishly relaxing with digital interactions of other worlds and his indefatigable children of this world. Although often occupied with the law, he is usually thinking of other things. Quarter notes, carbohydrates, and the like.

DELIA DUMETRICA currently teaches about new media and communication theory at the University of Calgary. She writes about cool new technologies like videogames and social media and occasionally she gets it published! She recently put together a one-of-a-kind course looking at how new media is portrayed in science-fiction novels and movies, but in fairness, this is really just an excuse for reading more of the Ender saga.

DON FALLIS has written several philosophy articles on lying and deception, including "What is Lying?" in the *Journal of Philosophy* and "The Most Terrific Liar You Ever Saw in Your Life" in *The Catcher in the Rye and Philosophy: A Book for Bastards, Morons, and Madmen*. He is Professor of Information Resources and Adjunct Professor of Philosophy at the University of Arizona. He teaches most of his courses for the School of Information Resources over the Internet. Much like Ender, he was quite traumatized when he learned that these "students" that he was interacting with were actual living beings.

JOAN GRASSBAUGH FORRY is a visiting assistant professor of philosophy at Linfield College where she teaches sports ethics, environmental ethics, and feminism to launchies and football players. She writes on issues in sports ethics and serves on the executive council of the International Association for the Philosophy of Sport. In her spare time, she enjoys running with her two dogs and killing giants.

ALEXANDER HALAVAIS is an associate professor of sociology in the School of Social and Behavioral Sciences at Arizona State University, where he is also affiliated with the Learning Sciences Institute and the Consortium for Applied Space Ethics. In addition to training the next generation of leaders to apply creative tactics to solve complex problems, Halavais leads a jeesh dedicated to researching social and participatory technologies, and is working on a new book on participatory surveillance and its role in social change. He tweets as @halavais, as well as under a number of assumed identities.

JOSHUA M. HALL recently survived the battleroom known as "getting a PhD in Philosophy from Vanderbilt University." His (admittedly non-cosmic) accomplishments include eight peer-reviewed articles (in journals including *Asian Philosophy, Philosophy and Literature,* and *Dance Chronicle*), and managing not to commit xenocide (as far as he knows).

JEREMY HEUSLEIN was recruited into Philosophy by a gruff old man, claiming philosophical training was strategic for humanity's survival. Believing this, Jeremy is pursuing graduate studies at the University of Leuven in Belgium, specializing in Ancient Philosophy and Phenomenology.

JAMES D. HOLT is a Senior Lecturer in Religious Education at the University of Chester, England. He is a Latter-day Saint and holds a PhD in Mormon Theology from the University of Chester, and his research is now bringing together two of his passions: religion and scifi-fantasy. He's trying to work out how to incorporate his further passions for the Dallas Cowboys and Macclesfield Town FC into this somehow. The main focus of his life, however, is his gorgeous wife and four children who he is sure would have aced the tests for Battle School though he wouldn't have let them attend (not that there's a choice).

RANDALL M. JENSEN is Professor of Philosophy at Northwestern College in Orange City, Iowa. His philosophical interests include ethics, ancient Greek philosophy, and philosophy of religion. His favorite class to teach is Philosophy and Science Fiction. He has contributed chapters to many books like this one, including *Battlestar Galactica and Philosophy, Batman and Philosophy, The Hobbit and Philosophy,* and *Superman and Philosophy.* He's still trying to figure out how to convince his students that the survival of our species depends on their progress in his courses.

SHAWN MCKINNEY teaches philosophy, ethics, and logic at Hillsborough Community College in Ruskin, Florida. In an earlier profession he practiced law that focused on children or criminals (and sometimes both). His previous academic work was in philosophy of time and philosophy of education. When he was only a few years old, his parents gave him his first comic books and he never stopped reading them. Comics led to science-fiction and philosophy. No matter how much he reads, his wife is, and will always be, more cultured than he is. Now he has a daughter of his own and gives her comic books and hopes she will never stop reading them.

LOUIS MELANÇON, having studied masters of conflict such as Clausewitz and Mahan, is confident he could best Ender in a head-to-head game (of Candy Land). Louis is a US Army officer with a career spanning from tactical combat arms to strategic intelligence. He has been awarded the Bronze Star Medal, holds master's degrees from the National Intelligence University and King's College, London, and is working towards a PhD from the George Washington University. He has contributed to several of volumes in the Popular Culture and Philosophy series.

NICOLAS MICHAUD is an Assistant Professor of Philosophy at Florida State College Jacksonville. He edited *Frankenstein and Philosophy*. After long hours of rigorous practice (video gaming) he now believes that he is ready for Battle School. He is wrong.

PAUL G. NEIMAN is Associate Professor of Philosophy at St. Cloud State University. He hopes his time spent teaching international business ethics will one day land him a job teaching intergalactic business ethics for the IF.

JORDAN PASCOE is a philosopher, professor, and Hive Queen who teaches at Manhattan College in New York City. She writes about Kant, race, gender, and aliens. She's eternally grateful that her ability to communicate directly into the minds of others saves her from needing to prepare complex lecture notes, but she recognizes that her students sometimes find psychic explanations of the categorical imperative somewhat unsettling.

COLLIN POINTON is finishing graduate school Battle Room skirmishes in the philosophy department at Marquette University. He spends time being paranoid that it's all a big lie and he'll wake up to find a monitor attached to his neck—a possibility not helped by all the science fiction he reads and watches. He enjoys writing about intersections between literature, technological art mediums (like video games), and philosophical traditions like hermeneutics, aesthetics, skepticism, and phenomenology. Along with being a cyberpunk-Epicurean and struggling against the lies of society, he thinks becoming a "fictionalizing philosopher" is a great life goal; as is taking a torch to the "ivory tower" part of academics.

LUCINDA RUSH is the education reference librarian at Old Dominion University. In a previous life, she taught a battle school of adolescents how to sing and read music. She holds master's degrees in music education and library and information science.

ABRAHAM P. SCHWAB started battle school a bit late at the age of seventeen, when he spent four years in the Bulldog Army, Iowa Division, before graduating to the Rambler Army. After seven years in the Rambler Army, he was awarded a PhD in Philosophy with distinction. He has since gone on to train new launchies in the Bulldog Army, New York Division, and the Mastodon Army. He spends his training time on issues in applied ethics, and even has a Facebook page "The Applied Ethicist" to provide a safe space for past and future launchies to discuss difficult issues in applied ethics. His interest in military ethics, and so his chapter in this volume, was cultivated by the sheer numbers of veterans looking to retrain in the Mastodon Army.

Trained in philosophy of technology placed at Virginia Tech, Assistant Professor **ASHLEY SHEW** has received the requisite experience to oversee the education of students in Science and Technology Studies. She maneuvers, with the calmness of someone unaware of the full ramifications of their actions, around issues in emerging technology, applied ethics, technological knowledge, and animal studies.

KELLY SORENSEN is Associate Professor Of Philosophy at Ursinus College, where he teaches and writes about ethics. **THOMAS SORENSEN** is studying Comparative Literature at Brigham Young University, and has his parents to thank for a childhood not spent becoming a space general. Kelly and Thomas are twins separated by twenty-seven years, possibly due to interstellar travel time. Their writing skills complement each other, but not in a manipulative Locke-Demosthenes kind of way. During the academic year they communicate by ansible.

JENNIFER SWANSON is a graduate student and philosophy instructor at the University of Miami. As well as contributing to *The Good Wife and Philosophy: Temptations of Saint Alicia*, she has published on ethical issues involving nonhuman animals—her main research interest and the subject of her dissertation. She hopes that the combination of her published works as well as her completed dissertation will form the basis of a new religion on Earth, but is willing to settle for being Queen of a hive-mind of philosophy students.

JESSICA WATKINS teaches middle school Language Arts. She was raised to be an astronaut and a soldier, but has also always wanted to be a mother, so she blended all three into the perfect career. When she's not battling ignorance and apathy (not to mention worn-out books and broken hearts), she's watching the skies and waiting for our first female president.

With a resume suggestive of a witness protection program drop out, **DAVID M. WILMINGTON** has used the anti-aging benefits of near-light speed to work as a teacher (saxophone, English, and Spanish), network engineer, soccer coach, independent film poobah, and theologian. Since 2002, he has read and discussed *Ender's Game*—in classroom settings that only occasionally involved lethal violence and null gravity—with students ranging from seventh graders in Durham, North Carolina, to undergraduates in the Baylor University Honors College. Upon finishing a project on virtue ethics and contemporary apophaticism (and its inevitable TV movie adaptation), Wilmington plans to become Hegemon of something.

D.E. WITTKOWER teaches graduate and undergraduate courses in departments of Philosophy, International Studies, and Humanities at Old Dominion University, where he has the privilege to work with many military students and veterans, along with so-called "traditional" students. He suspects, though, that his classes develop some sort of hive-mind, susceptible to a certain German Little Doctor: every time he starts talking about Kant, they all seem to simultaneously go limp, and the light disappears from their eyes.

A Peek into the Hive Mind

9 780812 698343